KILLING CUSTER

The Battle of the Little Bighorn
and the Fate of the Plains Indians

by

JAMES WELCH

with

PAUL STEKLER

W · W · N̶O̶R̶T̶O̶N̶   *ndon*

For information about permission to reproduce selections from this
book, write to Permissions, W.W. Norton & Company, Inc., 500 Fifth
Avenue, New York, NY 10110

The text of this book is composed in ITC Modern No. 216 with the display type set in ITC Modern No. 216 and Monotype Old Style Bold
Outline No. 176.

Composition and manufacturing by R.R. Donnelley, Bloomsburg
Book design by Jacques Chazaud

Library of Congress Cataloging-in-Publication Data

Welch, James, 1940–2003
Killing Custer / by James Welch with Paul Stekler
p. cm.
Includes bibliographical references and index
1. Little Bighorn, Battle of the, Mont., 1876   2. Indians of
North America—Wars—1866–1895.   I. Stekler, Paul Jeffrey
II. Title.
E83.876W38 1994
973.8′2—dc20   94-5617

ISBN 978-0-393-32939-1 pbk.

W.W. Norton & Company, Inc.
500 Fifth Avenue, New York, N.Y. 10110
www.wwnorton.com

W.W. Norton & Company Ltd.
Castle House, 75/76 Wells Street, London W1T 3QT

2 3 4 5 6 7 8 9 0

Contents

Acknowledgments

I began this book in December of 1991 when my wife and a friend took off for India for the holidays. I wasn't invited along, so my dog, Bill, and I took long walks, I attended Christmas parties a little too faithfully, and I sat in a mild stupor in front of my computer screen every day, pecking away. I didn't get much done those four weeks, but I accomplished enough to hope I could finally do it.

But it wouldn't have occurred to me to write such a book without the inspiration of a filmmaker, Paul Stekler, who two years earlier had invited me to help him write a documentary filmscript which became *Last Stand at Little Bighorn*. I honestly never thought I would be interested in more than a general way in "Custer's Last Stand." But Paul's idea to get much of the history of the battle from the Indians' point of view not only inspired the film, but this book. Thank you, Paul, good friend. And thanks to associate producers Maia Harris and Anne Craig for helping me through those bewildering days of Rank Amateur meets Professional Filmmakers. Thanks also to Michal Goldman, the film editor, and her assistant, Laura Nix, for showing me how all elements of a film can be brought together into a tight, lovely package. Thanks to the film crew, cinematographer Jon Else, assistants Dan Hart and Roy Big Crane. Thanks to Fredericka Lefthand for introducing me and the film crew to some wonderful people on the Crow Reservation, like Kitty Deer Nose and Joe Medicine Crow, both of whom I also thank for their contributions.

And I would especially like to thank Bill Tall Bull and Ted Rising Sun for not only providing stories but displaying the pride of being Northern Cheyennes. Although I never met Johnson Holy Rock and Joe Flying By, they provided me, through film interviews, with a vast appreciation of the confidence and intelligence of the Lakota people. And thanks to the late Irene Fehliman for providing a look at the other side by talking with great energy about her father, trooper Charles Windolph, last living white survivor of the Battle of the Little Bighorn.

I would especially like to thank Barbara Booher, then superintendent of the Little Bighorn Battlefield National Monument, who helped immensely with the film and this book, and who also opened her heart to her fellow Native Americans when they said, "This is our monument too."

My wife, Lois, and our dear friend Ripley Hugo were my faithful readers every step of the way and caught me more than a couple of times when I was veering off the track. Special thanks and much love. And thanks too to the Missoula pros, Dee McNamer and Brian DeSalvatore, Beverly Lowry, Annick Smith and Bill Kittredge, and Connie Poten, who all encouraged me to attempt this nonfiction book—and provided valuable advice. Thanks also to Bill Bevis, who really did all the hard work of finding the Marias Massacre site and who shares my interest in Montana history and literature. And I owe a big debt of gratitude to a dear friend, Dana Boussard, who took time off from her very successful career to provide the cover art.

And, of course, very fond thanks to my editor, Gerry Howard, and my agent, Elaine Markson, who both said, "You've got the material—do it, then get on to your next novel." Easy enough for them to say.

And finally, a big thank-you and love to Juliette Crump, who, on a fine summer evening of rafting and fishing, said, "Why don't you just call it *Killing Custer*?"

Chronology

—◆—

1775   Teton Sioux, or Lakotas, reach the Black Hills from their original woodland territory around the headwaters of the Mississippi.

1804   Sioux meet Lewis and Clark expedition.

1851   Fort Laramie Treaty establishes various tribes' boundaries on the northern plains. Indians agree not to war on each other or on whites passing legally through their territories. Indians recognize "the right of the U. S. Government to establish roads, military and other posts" within their territories. In return, Indians will be protected against depredations by whites and will receive in total $50,000 a year for fifty years.

1864   Sand Creek Massacre, in which Black Kettle's Cheyenne band is attacked by Colonel Chivington and Colorado volunteers.

1865   U. S. government negotiates treaty with "friendly" Indians. "Hostile" Indians ignore it, thereby rendering it useless.

1866   U. S. government begins negotiations with hostile Sioux. Red Cloud and his warriors attack travelers along the Bozeman Trail to goldfields in Montana. Fetterman Massacre takes place, in which Colonel William Fetterman and his eighty troops are killed.

1868   Treaty of 1868. Army agrees to abandon forts on Bozeman Trail. The treaty creates Great Sioux Reservation and agrees that the Indians do not cede hunting grounds in Montana and Wyoming territories. Indians in turn agree to become "civilized." Massacre on the Washita River in Indian Territory, in which Black Kettle is killed. This act establishes George Armstrong Custer as great Indian fighter.

1873   Custer comes to northern plains. Guards Northern Pacific Railroad surveyors in Montana, has chance encounter with Sitting Bull and Crazy Horse. Panic of 1873; economy collapses, creating depression which will last until 1877.

1874   Custer expedition finds gold in Black Hills.

1875   U. S. government negotiates to buy Black Hills. Fails.

1876   U. S. government issues ultimatum that Indians have to be on Great Sioux Reservation by January 31 or be considered hostile. On March 17, General George Crook attacks Sioux/Cheyenne camp on Powder River. Sitting Bull organizes the greatest gathering of Indians on the northern plains. Battle of the Rosebud on June 17, in which Crook is forced to retire from "pincers" campaign. Battle of Little Bighorn, June 25, in which Custer and 210 men under his direct command are killed. In October, Colonel Nelson A. "Bear Coat" Miles arrives on the Yellowstone River to take control of campaign against Indians. Manypenny Commission demands that Indians surrender Black Hills or starve. Red Cloud, Spotted Tail, and other reservation chiefs, having no other choice, sign over Paha Sapa, their sacred Black Hills.

1877   Sitting Bull escapes to Canada in early May. On May 6, Crazy horse surrenders at Fort Robinson. On May 7, a small band of Minneconjou Sioux is defeated by Miles, thus ending the Great Sioux Wars. On September 6, Crazy Horse is killed at the hands of the soldiers and some of his own people. Manypenny Agreement is ratified by Congress, taking Black Hills and confining Indians to reservation.

1881   On July 19, Sitting Bull surrenders at Fort Buford in U. S. territory, is sent to Fort Randall for two years as prisoner of war.

1883   Sitting Bull is allowed to go to Standing Rock Agency, where he will live for the rest of his life across the Grand River from his birthplace.

1885   Sitting Bull tours with Buffalo Bill's Wild West show.

1887   Dawes Severalty Act, also known as the General Allotment Act, gives President power to reduce Indian landholdings nationally by allotting 160 acres to heads of Indian families and eighty acres to individuals, and opening up the rest of the reservations to whites.

1889   United States and Sioux sign agreement breaking up the Great Sioux Reservation. The Sioux will get six separate small reservations. The rest of the land will be thrown open to white settlers. A prophet out west named Wovoka introduces a new religion, based on the Ghost Dance, to Indian people.

1890   Ghost Dance religion sweeps Sioux reservations. Sitting Bull is killed on December 15 by Indian policemen, acting on behalf of U.S. government. Massacre at Wounded Knee on December 29, in which Big Foot and his band of Minneconjous are slaughtered by Custer's old outfit, the 7th Cavalry.

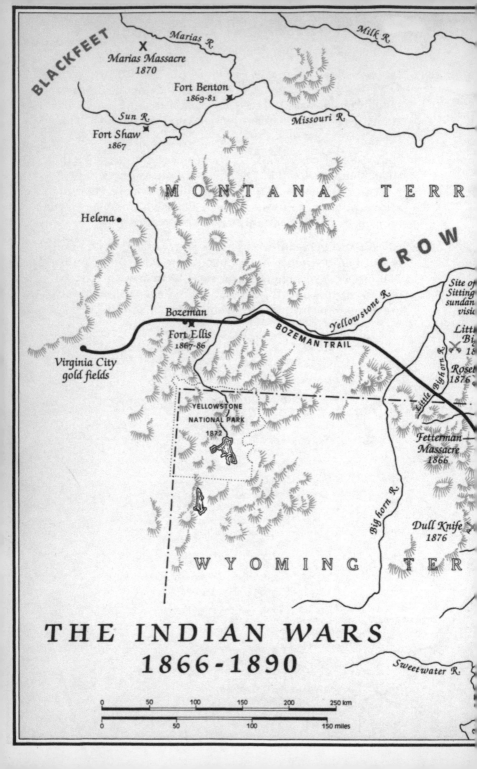

BLACKFEET

Marias R.

Milk R.

X
Marias Massacre
1870

Fort Benton
1869-81

Sun R.

Missouri R.

Fort Shaw
1867

M O N T A N A   T E R R

Helena

CROW

Yellowstone R.

Site of
Sitting
sundan
visi

Bozeman

Fort Ellis
1867-86

BOZEMAN TRAIL

Virginia City
gold fields

Littl
Big
18

Rose
1876

Little Bighorn R.

YELLOWSTONE
NATIONAL PARK
1872

Fetterman
Massacre
1866

Big horn R.

Dull Knife
1876

W Y O M I N G   T E R

THE INDIAN WARS
1866-1890

Sweetwater R.

0   50   100   150   200   250 km

0   50   100   150 miles

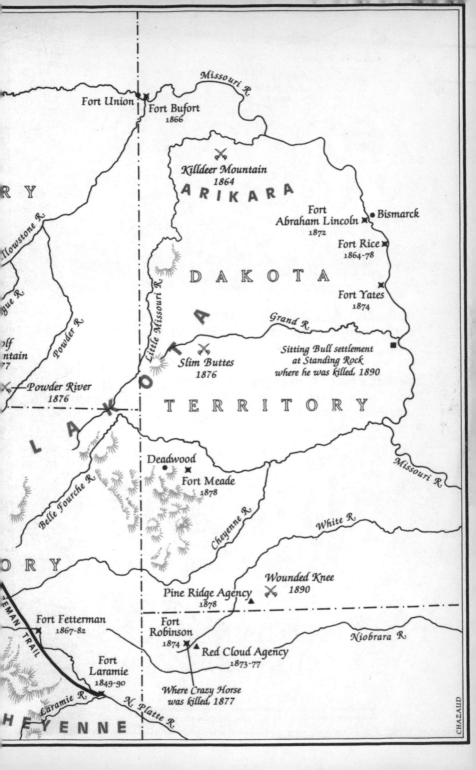

The Death Struggle of General Custer, printed in the *New York Graphic Newspaper,* July 1876. *Library of Congress*

The Battle of the Little Bighorn, ledger art drawn by Amos Bad Heart Bull, a Lakota, around 1890. His family was part of Crazy Horse's band at the Little Bighorn in 1876. *University of Nebraska Press*

Prologue

———◆———

One summer morning in 1990 I received a phone call from a filmmaker named Paul Stekler. He was calling from Cambridge, Massachusetts, where he has a film company called Midnight Productions. He sounded young, but his voice was calm and patient as he explained what the deal was. He had received a good sum of grant money to make a film about the Battle of the Little Bighorn, or Custer's Last Stand, whichever sounded most familiar to me. He went on to establish his credentials—he had produced and directed two of the Eyes on the Prize episodes, a series which encompassed the black civil rights experience in this country; he had made his own film on Louisiana politics; and he had worked as a writer on several other film projects. He had a Ph.D. from Harvard, had taught at Tulane for a few years, kicked around New Orleans for a while, hanging out in cafés, drinking strong coffee, then became involved in filmmaking. He wondered if I would be interested in helping him write the script for the Little Bighorn film. I had been mentioned favorably by two historians and writers, David McCullough and Alvin Josephy, both of whom I had met and liked very much.

I also liked the way Paul described the film—largely told from the Indians' point of view, with much historical background of both sides and interviews with descendants of both the Indians and whites who fought at Little Bighorn. He talked about using ledger art (Indians were given ledger books by agents to draw their perceptions of historical events), old footage of a Cheyenne warrior named Two Moons describing the battle ("It took about as long as it takes a hungry man to eat his dinner"), and Buffalo Bill's Wild West (which featured many of the Indian participants, including Sitting Bull and Black Elk). He talked of using old photographs of immigrants, city life back east, settlers, soldiers, and Indians—portraits of Indian chiefs, Indian camps, Indians on the move, Indians on reservations. He wanted a strong, simple narration to go along with these images.

As I listened to him talk about the project, I felt a small flicker of enthusiasm which surprised me. I had been approached by filmmakers before and I had always declined. Either I wasn't interested in the subject or I was involved in a novel or I didn't like the tone or point of view of the film. I am not a prolific writer, and to spend a lot of energy on a project I didn't fully believe in seemed wasteful. Besides, I am a fiction writer and sometimes poet who has worked in solitary for twenty-five years, and to get involved with such a communal activity as filmmaking goes against the grain.

But Paul's voice, now rising with enthusiasm, was starting to get to me, and I thought, maybe I could work with this guy. But I had one problem—I was absolutely inexperienced in film writing. It should be easy for you to learn, he said. I'll send you a bunch of documentaries, study them, see how other people do it. How much time does a writer normally spend on a project like this? You work in bursts, with time off to do your own writing in between, say three or four periods of two weeks each, initial script, rough cut, fine cut, locked cut, etc. These were foreign terms to me, but the whole thing sounded easy enough—a few intense writing sessions and time in between to pursue my own writing. I guess I felt at the time that documentary-script writing was not real writing. It was more like writing small bridges between images or to explain something we were seeing on the screen. Not difficult at all once I got the hang of it. I have since learned how complicated and sometimes convoluted a script can get. And I have also learned that filmmakers are notorious for underestimating the amount of time a writer will spend on a project.

Although Paul was beginning to convince me that this would be an important film, I didn't want to commit myself to such a large project without some time to think. I was due to teach a two-week summer writing workshop in Colorado the following week, so I gave him the phone number of the condominium where I would be staying and told him to call in midweek. During the drive down to Colorado, my wife and I discussed the pros and cons of getting involved. She knows how wishy-washy I can be and how I sometimes commit myself without thinking things through and then hate myself afterward. I have agreed to be on boards of advisers for various projects (having been told that the position was largely perfunctory) and have ended up working my rear end off. I served for ten years as a member of the Montana State Board of Pardons (parole board) and just plain burned out on the gut-wrenching sadness of human experience. I have read thousands of pages of manuscripts for the National Endowment for the Arts Literature Panel. I helped put together an anthology on Montana writing that ran 1,160 pages. Of course, there is a good feeling in being a part of such endeavors—you are doing something for others, you are putting back for once, instead of just taking. The fact that you are barely compensated for your time adds to this feeling of altruism. But the work itself is grinding, tense, and often depressing. Although there is no real comparison between this type of work and writing a script for a professional film company, the commitment of time away from one's own writing is similar. And that's what made me uneasy.

Paul, true to his sense of responsibility, called right at midweek, Wednesday morning. I was in the middle of a three-hour session with my group of writers in the living room of the condominium. I let the phone ring a couple of times while I excused myself and went into the kitchen to pick it up. But as I reached for the phone, I heard the cheery greeting of the condo owner on the answering machine, then Paul's voice. I said, "Paul, this is Jim," and he kept talking. I tried again, but it was clear that the answering machine had taken over and I didn't know how to stop it. Paul talked about the script possibilities, the people he had contacted, the research he had done, how if it was all right with me he'd fly out to Montana for a face-to-face talk, etc. I could only stand there and smile sheepishly at my writers as Paul's voice filled the room. When the one-sided phone call ended, the writers were looking at me with a kind of knowing expectancy (the real writer's life). Finally, a healthy young woman, a local who skiied (this was Aspen, after all, even if it was summer), said, "Go for it." And so I did.

Paul Stekler came to Missoula about a month later, around the middle of August. He stayed for four days, and mostly we talked and walked and watched documentaries that he had brought with him. Just as I'd expected, I liked him right away, and it was pretty clear that we could work together, if he had the patience—which it turned out he did. It was only toward the end of the project, when we were cutting out sentences, then phrases, then single words to get the film length down to fifty-two minutes, that our work got tense. But our battle was always with the script (and sometimes with the film editor, who had a sharp ear for language as well as an eye for images), never with each other.

At the end of that first visit we had put together an outline which would serve us for the rest of the project as a compass line, our deviations and meanderings always returning to true north. When I put Paul back on the plane, I had only a vague idea that this small bit of work would mushroom into an ongoing event that would consume my time and energy for the next year and a half. But it *was* an important film, not because we were going to debunk the Custer Myth—that has been done countless times even if not many have paid attention—but because we were going to explore the sometimes mundane reality of the events that led to the Battle of the Little Bighorn, and, more important to me, we were going to tell the Indians' side of the story. We were going to give the Sioux, the Cheyennes, and Custer's much-maligned Crow and Arikara scouts a voice.

The film turned out to be a great success. It was shown on November 25, 1992, the day before Thanksgiving, as part of the American Experience series on PBS. The ratings were high and the reviews were excellent. The project officially came to a close with that screening. As I watched it, my feelings included awe that filmmakers can create something so fine out of such a mountain of material, happiness that I had been a part of it, and relief that I was finished with it. No more research, no more scripts, no more Custer, Sitting Bull, and Crazy Horse. No more traveling back and forth to the battlefield and Cambridge.

But I wasn't really finished with the Battle of the Little Bighorn. In fact, the film was almost a dry run for a book I had contracted to do for Norton, which would tell the story in more detail than we had time for in the film. The book would be not only historical, but impressionistic—what were my thoughts on the battle, on the participants, on the period, on the "settling" of the northern plains? It was with more than a little trepidation that I began this book. Fortunately for me, Paul Stekler agreed to help out by providing his research, maps, photographs, reading skill, and moral support.

What can one say about the battle that hasn't been said before? Most Americans know (or *think* they know) the basic story. On June 25, 1876, Custer and his 7th Cavalry troopers attacked a large village of Sioux and Cheyenne people on the Little Bighorn River and were wiped out by a swarm of warriors. Custer made his Last Stand and died valiantly on a hilltop. Custer was an overweening fool who was more concerned with glory than good sense. Custer was a martyr at a time when this country, in the throes of a depression, desperately needed a martyr to take its mind off its larger problems. Custer was the flamboyant scamp of American military history. Custer embodied the ideals of a young nation. The Custer Myth.

Surprisingly, there is much to tell about the battle because of recent research which tells the story more exactly than has been done before. While no one will ever really *know* what happened on Calhoun Ridge and Custer Hill and in Deep Ravine, studies have been undertaken recently that make sense of the movements and actions of the 7th Cavalry. One historian uses topographic research and time/motion studies to track military maneuvers; an archaeologist, taking advantage of a fire that swept the battlefield in 1983, plots the entire area with a grid system to analyze artifacts, shot patterns, and groupings of troopers. Both approaches are convincing in their scientific results.

But both accounts are backed up by information supplied by Indian participants. And this is new in itself. For years, historians have tended to discount Indian testimony as unreliable and contradictory. For example, one of Custer's Crow scouts, a seventeen-year-old by the name of Curley, gave an account of Custer's Last Stand that met with ridicule from the beginning. Curley was the last man, on the army side, to see Custer and the 7th Cavalry alive. He was with them at the start of the battle, left under orders, and watched the beginning of the end from a distant hill. He was interviewed several times immediately afterward, then branded a liar and publicity-seeker. Why? Because the translators were incompetent and the interviewers led Curley to say what they wanted him to say. And he wanted to be agreeable. Now, many serious historians believe that he was correct in his original observations.

One of the common fallacies in regard to the Battle of the Little Bighorn is that there were no survivors. There were plenty of survivors—Sioux and Cheyennes. Many of the seeming contradictions in their accounts have been reconciled with the new research. The village was three miles long, and the various participants were at different parts of the battlefield, seeing what was in front of them. The wide-angle lens wasn't available to them at the time. That is why there is no comprehensive Indian view of the battle. But their individual accounts can be stitched together to provide a very plausible story of the fight.

The Battle of the Little Bighorn may be the most depicted event in our nation's history. Hundreds of books, from Custer biographies to as-told-to Indian accounts, have been written; thousands of illustrations, from the famous Anheuser-Busch lithograph of Custer's Last Fight (which hung in saloons and tobacco stores all across America) to Sioux and Cheyenne ledger drawings, have been displayed; and at least forty films, from *They Died with Their Boots On* to *Little Big Man,* have played in theaters around the world. Clearly, from the number of books still being published, there is a fascination with this tiny event that just won't die.

So what's special about this book? Maybe nothing. It certainly will not provide any startling revelations from a historical or military standpoint. But maybe it will offer the reader a comprehensive frontier environment which will provide an explanation for why this battle had to take place. And it did have to take place. It was as inexorable as any showdown in a clash of cultures which has been historically brought on by the whites. Only this time the wrong guys, the "red fiends," won—which is precisely why the battle has assumed such mythical significance in our history. It ranks right up there with such martyr myths as the Charge of the Light Brigade and the Battle of the Alamo. The thought of a large number of bloodthirsty savages slaughtering a small but noble band of white heroes becomes a powerful battle cry. The Sioux and Cheyenne victory at Little Bighorn in 1876 was a great achievement for Indians, but, with the exception of Sitting Bull's band, all of the participants surrendered within a year of the battle and were forced onto reservations. Thus, (white) justice won out and the forces of righteousness prevailed over the forces of darkness in the end.

I begin my account of the conflict between whites and Indians with an event that occurred on January 23, 1870, more than six years before Little Bighorn, in which 173 Blackfeet men, women, and children were slaughtered by U. S. soldiers. The Massacre on the Marias

River was more representative of what happened to Indian people who resisted the white invasion than Custer's Last Stand. I tell it not only because it happened to my own people, but because it needs to be told known if one is to understand this nation's treatment of the first Americans. And to understand the glory and sorrow of that hot day in June 1876 when the Indians killed Custer.

Lakota Sioux warriors gathered at the Laramie Peace Treaty negotiations at Fort Laramie, Wyoming Territory, 1868. *Smithsonian Institution*

Railroad crew working on the Santa Fe line near Atchison, Kansas, early 1870s. *Kansas State Historical Society*

1

On August 17, 1869, a young Pikuni warrior, Owl Child, led his small gang of dissidents under cover of darkness to the ranch of Malcolm Clarke, a man who had accumulated much wealth by trading with the Blackfeet for over thirty years. Clarke, known as Four Bears, was a respected man among the whites of Montana for having opened up trade with a tribe that possessed the reputation of being the most fearsome on the northern Great Plains. Unlike the Sioux, the Cheyennes, the Arapahos, the Crow, the Assiniboins, the Crees, and the Gros Ventres, the Pikunis, the southernmost tribe of the Blackfeet Nation, did not tolerate the earlier Americans who came west to trap, to trade, to settle among them.

Their territory in Montana had been invaded for the first time by Americans in the summer of 1806. Captain Meriwether Lewis, in an attempt to locate the headwaters of the Marias River (named by him for his fair cousin Maria Wood), ran into a small party of Pikuni warriors. He believed them to be Gros Ventres, and through his sign-talker, George Drouillard, beseeched them to live in peace with their neighbors and to trade with him in the future, an obvious ruse to save his hide, since he had no intention of returning to that barren, often hostile country. He gave a flag to one and a medal to another, men he perceived to be chiefs. That night the two parties camped together. Toward dawn a great commotion developed when a brave attempted to steal one of the white men's firesticks. Other attempts were made for guns; then the Indians tried to drive off Lewis's horses. By the time the dust settled, one of the Pikunis, the man to whom Lewis gave the medal, was killed, and another wounded. Lewis took back the flag but left the medal around the dead man's neck so the Pikunis would know who they were. Lewis then beat a hasty retreat down the river to join the other half of the expedition led by William Clark.

Much has been made of this incident by the whites, the only truly hostile encounter of the Lewis and Clark expedition, but more was made of it by the Blackfeet. From that time forward, they considered the Americans their enemies, although they still traded with the French, and then with the English across the Medicine Line in Canada. They considered the French the Real Old Man People, because they were the first to come from that place where Sun Chief rises to begin his journey across the sky.

But the Americans were not to be outdone by the Canadian traders. They returned to Blackfeet territory and in 1831 built a trading post, Fort Piegan, at the confluence of the Marias and the Missouri. The American Fur Company, a John Jacob Astor enterprise, wanted a special item from the Indians, and not only did the company have the goods to trade for that item, it had the means to transport it back to civilization—the keelboat. So began the trade in buffalo hides. Hides for goods—copper kettles, foodstuffs, beads, blankets, knives, mirrors, guns, ammunition, and eventually the white man's water, a potent brew of tobacco, capsicum, molasses, peppers, and alcohol mixed with river water and whatever else could produce a fire in the belly.

Although that first trading season went well, the Blackfeet burned the fort when the white men left. Subsequent trading posts were built. Fort McKenzie was built on very nearly the same site in time for the next trading season. Later, a few miles upriver at a very natural landing, Fort Benton, known as Many Houses to the Blackfeet, became the ultimate trading center on that part of the Missouri. The keelboats carried goods and people upriver, hides and pelts downriver. Eventually they were replaced by large steamboats, which could carry even greater quantities of trade items, as well as people and their supplies bound for the gold fields of Montana and to points west along the Mullan Trail, which culminated at Fort Walla Walla on the Columbia River. Here they could go down the river all the way to the Pacific Ocean.

In 1847, one of the traders for the American Fur Company, Malcolm Clarke, married a Pikuni, Cutting-off-head Woman, a member of the Many Chiefs band like her cousin, Owl Child. The Many Chiefs were led by Mountain Chief, a great leader who resisted the invasion of the white settlers and their soldiers, the seizers. Clarke, by marrying into Mountain Chief's band, secured his position as principal trader among the Blackfeet. He also gained the respect of the elders of all the bands by marrying one of their women. They brought their buffalo hides to Many Houses and returned to their camps with goods that were meant to make their lives easier, but in fact made them more complicated.

Owl Child, several years before, had ridden with a war party against the Assiniboins (Cutthroats) and had claimed a kill, although most in the party insisted that the kill belonged to Bear Head. During a heated argument, Owl Child leveled his rifle and killed Bear Head. Since that incident, Owl Child had become an outcast among the Blackfeet, although he did live off and on with Mountain Chief's band. But mostly Owl Child roamed, and his bitterness toward his own people increased. He considered the Pikunis weak for signing treaties with the *napikwans*—the whites—and allowing them to steal the land, to settle on the buffalo ranges. He did his part to make the *napikwans* suffer—stealing animals, destroying houses and property, occasionally killing a settler or miner. But in 1867, an incident occurred that would focus Owl Child's anger.

Malcolm Clarke had retired from his position as principal trader among the Blackfeet and began to ranch on a small tributary of the Missouri River called Prickly Pear Creek, north of Helena. He moved his family into a comfortable home, complete with attached smokehouse and several outbuildings for tack, grain, and equipment. It was a prosperous ranch by any standards, and those Blackfeet who saw it were impressed. In the spring of 1867, several of Cutting-off-head Woman's relatives came to visit and look over the large spread. Owl Child was among them. As fate would have it, Owl Child's horses were stolen during the visit. Naturally, he blamed Malcolm Clarke, and shortly afterward he stole some of Clarke's horses, driving them back to Mountain Chief's camp.

Clarke and his son, Horace, followed the trail and found both Owl Child and the horses in the encampment. Horace struck Owl Child with a whip and called him a dog. Clarke called him an old woman, and the men left with their horses. Now, it is not good to insult and beat a young Pikuni in front of his people. Such an action requires revenge, and although many of the chiefs were trying desperately to

Malcolm Clarke.
*Montana Historical
Society*

**Mountain Chief
(Big Bear).**
Smithsonian Institute

avoid trouble with the *napikwans*, they understood what Owl Child had to do.

So it came as no surprise that on the night of August 17, 1869, Owl Child and twenty-five young Pikuni warriors paid a visit to the ranch on Prickly Pear Creek. When they left, Clarke was dead and his son, Horace, was seriously wounded by gunfire.

More than any other of the many depredations against the white invaders, this single incident triggered the retaliation that would lead to the swift punishment of the Blackfeet, from which they would never recover. It was simply the last straw. Powerful men in the press and in the territorial capital of Helena roared loud and clear. They wanted nothing less than the total annihilation of these savages. They wanted the army to settle the Indian problem once and for all. United States Marshal William F. Wheeler produced a document listing fifty-six whites who had been murdered and more than a thousand horses stolen by the Blackfeet in 1869 alone. The *Helena Weekly Herald* stated that "the pleasant and innocent amusement of butchering and scalping the palefaces is believed by some likely soon to begin in good earnest."

Ironically, it was the United States Army that tried to mollify the outraged Montanans. General Philip H. Sheridan, originator of the famous maxim "The only good Indian is a dead Indian," Civil War hero and now commander of the Department of the Missouri, informed the citizens that he did not have enough men at present to attack "these Indian marauders." But he promised that as soon as recruits could be sent west he would propose a plan to punish the malfeasants. Actually, he already had a plan, a plan that he had used successfully against the Southern Cheyennes of the southern plains. He spelled out his plan in that earlier incident: "Let me find out exactly where these Indians are going to spend the winter, and about the time of a good heavy snow I will send out a party and try and strike them." That party, in 1868, had been led by General George Armstrong Custer, and that place of heavy snow was the Washita River in the Indian Territory of Oklahoma. Although Sheridan's superior, General of the Army William T. Sherman, approved an identical plan against the Pikunis, a few of Sheridan's experienced officers had misgivings. General Philippe de Trobriand, in command of Fort Shaw, reported, "I do not see so far an opportunity for striking a successful blow. The only Indians within reach are friendly, and nothing could be worse, I think, than to chastise them for offenses of which they are not guilty."

On New Year's Day, 1870, General Alfred H. Sully met with four peace chiefs of the Blackfeet Nation—Heavy Runner, Little Wolf, and Big Lake of the Pikunis, and Gray Eyes of the Bloods, or Kainahs. The one chief he wanted to speak with, Mountain Chief, head chief of the Pikunis, leader of the opposition to white encroachment, did not show up. Nevertheless, Sully outlined the conditions imposed by the United States Army to avoid war: capture, kill, and bring back the bodies of Owl Child and the others in his war party named in an indictment, and return all, or as many as possible, of the horses and other livestock stolen from the citizens of Montana Territory—and from the army itself. All to be done within two weeks.

Heavy Runner and the other peace chiefs agreed to these conditions, but they knew they were powerless to find, much less kill, the young warriors. They were rumored to be with Mountain Chief's band north of the Medicine Line in Canada. As for the livestock, many of the animals had been sold to traders and the others were hopelessly scattered among the bands.

Sully knew that the meeting had been futile, and when the two weeks were up, Sheridan's plan was put into effect. De Trobriand's scouts reported that Mountain Chief and his band had crossed back into Montana and were wintering on the Marias River, a good day's ride south of the Medicine Line. Colonel E. M. Baker was in charge of four companies of cavalry stationed at Fort Shaw on the Sun River. The army had finally mustered up enough troops to carry out Sheridan's command, which put simply in a telegraph on January 15 read: "If the lives and property of the citizens of Montana can best be protected by striking Mountain Chief's band, I want them struck. Tell Baker to strike them hard."

On January 19, Colonel Baker led his four cavalry companies, along with fifty-five mounted infantrymen and a company of foot soldiers, northward from Fort Shaw. The weather was almost as bad as it gets in that part of the country. Temperatures never rose above twenty below zero, and the winds swept off the Rocky Mountain slope in a constant fury. But Baker was determined to carry out Sheridan's command. He knew that the Pikuni band would be bundled up in their lodges, waiting out the storm. But one can only imagine what some of the green recruits, many of them from the east and south, thought as they hunkered down in their buffalo coats, riding across the godforsaken plains in treacherous weather toward an encounter with savages they had only read about in comic books and dime novels.

One of the men knew what he was getting into. Joe Kipp, a half-white, half-Pikuni scout also known as Raven Quiver, knew these people; he had married a Pikuni woman and had lived and traded with them for several years. And now he led the United States Army toward the Big Bend of the Marias River, where his own people were camped. He had to have known the likely results of such an expedition.

It has been stated by scouts and troops alike (and also by civilian Horace Clarke, who accompanied the expedition) that Colonel Baker was drunk when the attack began, that he had been drinking during the whole of the journey north. If he was drunk, it would not be an uncommon occurrence. Several of the officers out west had a similar problem. The same charge would be leveled against Major Marcus A. Reno six years later when he attacked, under Custer's orders, the large Indian encampment on the Little Bighorn River. The fact that Baker was drunk might not have mattered much in the overall scheme of things—life was hard and dreary and monotonous on the western plains—had it not been for a small but significant incident just prior to the attack.

In the dark hour just before dawn on January 23, 1870, the men were in position on a ridge above the Indian camp, waiting for light and the order from Baker to commence the attack. As the darkness turned to steel gray, Joe Kipp recognized some of the quiet lodges, recognized the painted designs on the buffalo-skin covers. It was the wrong camp. And he understood immediately what must have happened—Mountain Chief had gotten wind of the army's plan of attack and had moved his winter camp, and Heavy Runner, one of the peace chiefs, had moved his people to the site. Because the Big Bend of the Marias was well protected from the winter winds and because the game was fairly plentiful most winters, it was a popular camping area among the Pikunis. Kipp at once reported to Baker, "Colonel, that is not Mountain Chief's camp. It is the camp of Black Eagle and Heavy Runner. I know it by its differently painted lodges." To which Baker replied, "That makes no difference, one band or another of them; they are all Piegans [Pikunis] and we will attack them." Then he said to one of his men, "Sergeant, stand behind this scout, and if he yells or makes a move, shoot him."

Some in the camp said that the first volley of firing brought Heavy Runner from his lodge. He waved a piece of paper in his hand, an order of safe conduct signed by General Sully during that futile meeting on New Year's Day. Although Heavy Runner was at peace

Lieutenant Colonel Eugene Baker and his officers, 1871. Baker is in the center, holding onto the porch railing on the right side of the door. *Montana Historical Society*

Pikuni (Blackfeet) village beneath Backbone of the World (Rocky Mountains). *Thomas Magee Photo: Courtesy of Don Magee*

with the *napikwans*, he was among the first to fall. After thousands of rounds of ammunition had turned the air blue and thick with gunsmoke, 173 people lay dead, most still in their lodges. The soldiers approached the camp to quell what little resistance was left. They then cut the bindings of the lodges, collapsing them, and burned them with the people still inside. They gathered up all the food, weapons, and supplies they could carry and rode off toward Fort Shaw, driving the band's horse herds before them.

Although the numbers became a matter of controversy, it is clear that most of the dead were women and children and old people. Baker, in his report of the incident, claimed that all but fifty-three were able-bodied warriors, which even by army standards is an absurd body count. Most reports state that a great many of the able-bodied men were out hunting. The winter had already been cruel, many were hungry, and the hunters were out to get meat. Perhaps a more realistic breakdown of the dead was in a report submitted to his superiors by W.A. Pease, the Indian agent: Only fifteen of the dead Indians had been fighting men between the ages of twelve and thirty-seven, while ninety were women and fifty were children. One suspects that the rest of the dead were old people.

As if the massacre weren't bad enough, it came during a small-pox winter. The white scabs disease, as it was known to the Pikunis, was probably the most effective weapon the white people brought to the new world. More deadly than rifles, swords, artillery pieces, Gatling guns, and battle-tested horses, this disease killed many thousands of Indians, reducing tribal populations by a third, by a half, by three-quarters, often by even more. And it was deliberately used as a weapon on occasions.

As far back as 1763, Jeffrey Amherst, the English commander in chief during the latter part of the French and Indian War, called the Indians "more nearly allied to the Brute than to the Human Creation" and saw no reason to get along with this "execrable race." He further stated, "I am fully resolved whenever they give me an occasion to extirpate them root and branch." Amherst, after whom the college town in Massachusetts is named, made a suggestion to one of his subordinates: "Could it not be contrived to send the small pox among the disaffected tribes of Indians? . . . You will do well to try to inoculate the Indians by means of blankets. . . ." Smallpox became a routine weapon of war against the powerless immune systems of the savages.

Throughout the contact period with the whites, smallpox epidemics raged periodically, almost systematically. In 1837, three years after Prince Maximilian, the German naturalist and explorer, and the Swiss artist Karl Bodmer visited a Mandan village on the upper Missouri and remarked on the Indians' fine appearance, the tribe had been reduced from sixteen hundred to only one hundred. Villages along the Missouri were decimated, mothers, brothers, daughters, and fathers turned away from each other in desperation. Frozen bodies were stacked like firewood on the edge of camps.

So it was that the latest epidemic of the white scabs in 1869 and 1870 had laid low the camps of the Pikunis. The soldiers had massacred a village of helpless people. Ironically, the target of the United States Army, the "bad head" who had precipitated the action against the Pikunis, Owl Child, lay dying of the disease in Mountain Chief's camp, seventeen miles down the Marias River from the massacre site.

Baker's report of the incident, issued two months later, claimed that he did not know that the camp was that of the friendly chief Heavy Runner. Another report claimed that the Indians put up heavy resistance, firing from inside the tipis, which justified the heavy return fire that killed all within those lodges, women and children included. But word got out back east that the attack had involved friendly Indians and had been a cruel and indefensible act of savagry. It was especially the great numbers of women and children killed that outraged citizens and legislators alike. Vincent Collyer, secretary to the Board of Indian Commissioners, wrote: "At last the sickening details of Colonel Baker's attack have been received." His revelation of the casualty figures opened up a public debate that fiercely questioned the army's policy toward Indians.

Congressman Daniel Vorhees of Indiana stated: "I wash my hands of all responsibility for this system of warfare. It cannot be justified here or before the country; it cannot be justified before the civilization of the age, or in the sight of God or man." Another congressman also invoked the white man's God: "I say there is no warrant in the laws of God or of man for destroying women and children merely because their husbands and fathers may be marauders. I say that civilization shudders at horrors like this."

But there were military apologists in the halls of Congress. Job Stevenson of Ohio stood to "enter my protest against these sweeping condemnations of the Government and its officers. I for one, if I stand alone, avow my approval of the sentiment expressed in the orders of General Sheridan. They express the sentiments of war, and I have always believed . . . that in war the most vigorous policy is not only the best policy, but is the most merciful policy. General Sheridan says we must strike a blow with telling effect, and that is the only way to make war." He went on to state, "These savages who themselves never care for age or sex, these savages whose women and children make war on white women and children, these savages who dance for joy around the burning stake, these savages whose women and children are instruments and demons of torture to white women and children, are only to be warred upon, when you war at all, by a war of extermination."

Stevenson's speech was received by the majority of the membership as bellicose, even bloodthirsty. Many expressed amazement that one of their own could enter a plea supporting the army's "monstrous transaction," as Congressman Vorhees put it.

Much of the press around the country appeared to be equally incensed by the actions of Sheridan and Baker. The *Chicago Tribune* editorialized, "The account given by Vincent Collyer did not by any means present the worst features of the affair. There is nothing in the records of the Indian Office which surpasses the atrocities detailed in this paper. Several members of the House have been informed of its character, and steps are pretty sure to be taken in Congress looking to dismissing from the service those officers directly responsible for the atrocities committed." A couple of days later, the same paper wrote, "The affair is looked on at the Interior Department as the most disgraceful butchery in the annals of our dealings with the Indians." The *New York Tribune* was a little more circumspect: "This matter must be investigated and the facts obtained. It is shameful to have such statements [accounts of the atrocities] published by authority, if they are false; it is terrible to think of what happened, if they are true."

Closer to the frontier, the actions of Sheridan and Baker were received much differently. The *Helena Herald* of March 30, 1870, commented: "There is every reason to believe that the raid of Colonel Baker, in addition to ridding the Territory of the most murderous band of Indians in the country, has also had a very salutary effect on the other tribes of the Blackfeet Nation. There is a good prospect of future peace and security." The *Platte Journal* asked, "Shall we Williampennize or Sheridanize the Indians?" And the *New North-west of Montana* celebrated the victory but warned that "all the namby-pamby, sniffling old maid sentimentalists of both sexes who leave most of their brains on their handkerchiefs when under excitement, will join the jargon of discontent." In Congress, Montana's James T.

Cavanaugh led a group of army supporters by pointing out that it is necessary to chastise those responsible for "atrocities that shock humanity—atrocities that are nameless . . . nameless mutilations of both men and women . . . witnessed by my own eyes. . . . I endorse the order of General Phil Sheridan. I endorse the act of General Hancock. I endorse the conduct of Colonel Baker." In answer to a question involving his support of killing of defenseless women and children, he said, ". . . in the words of General Harney after the battle of Ash Hollow [in Nebraska], years ago . . . they are nits, and will become lice."

The national debate raged. Wendell Philips, a Boston abolitionist, stated in a speech to a Reform League meeting, "I only know the names of three savages upon the Plains—Colonel Baker, General Custer [for his part in leading the massacre on the sleeping village on the Washita in December 1868, little more than a year before the Massacre on the Marias], and at the head of all, General Sheridan. . . ." Other reformers condemned the action in equally vigorous terms.

But the military authorities, from Sherman and Sheridan on down the chain of command, supported Baker's attack, calling it justified and necessary. Sheridan wrote to Sherman, "Since 1862, at least eight hundred men, women and children have been murdered within the limits of my present command, in most fiendish manner, the men usually scalped and mutilated, their privates cut off and placed in their mouths; women ravished sometimes fifty and sixty times in succession, then killed and scalped, sticks stuck up their persons before and after death. I have myself conversed with one woman, who, while some months gone in pregnancy, was ravished over thirty times successively by different Indians, becoming insensible two or three times during this fearful ordeal; and each time on recovering consciousness, mutely appealing for mercy, if not for herself, for her unborn child. Also another woman ravished with more fearful brutality, over forty times, and the last sticking the point of his saber up the person of the woman. I could give the names of these women were it not for delicacy." Sheridan may have been obsessed with numbers, but his point that the Indians were savages was not lost on Sherman.

Sherman, a man of ingenuity, presented this line of defense in a letter to Sheridan: "The Piegans [Pikunis] were attacked on the application of General Sully and the Interior Department, and that these should now be shocked at the result of their requisitions and endeavor to cast blame on you and Colonel Baker is unfair."

Finally, the United States Army's internal investigation found

Sheridan and Baker innocent of any wrongdoing and considered the matter closed. The debate died down, then ended. Congress got on to other pressing matters, the newspapers had other news to report, and the reformers had other reforms to press. But two important decisions that would affect Indian policy forever came out of the Baker Massacre. One, although there had been a very strong movement in Congress to transfer control of Indian affairs from the Department of the Interior to the War Department, Congress now had no stomach for it. Most felt that it would be the old story of appointing the fox to guard the henhouse. And two, the military would henceforth have nothing to do with supervising the reservation Indians. Until the massacre, the Indian agents had been military men. Now, President Grant proposed to the Quakers, as part of his Quaker policy, that they select from among themselves capable individuals who could run the reservations in a more humane way. Although only a few Quakers answered the call, other church groups became involved. The bottom line of this new policy was that civilians, acting as agents of the government, would administer to the Indians. The military was out—at least, officially. As we shall see, the army maintained a strong presence in Indian country.

And so the matter ended on a national level. Despite the support of Sherman and Sheridan, "Piegan" Baker, as he came to be known, did not get promoted for his action at the Big Bend of the Marias River; in fact, he never got promoted at all. In August 1872, while escorting Northern Pacific Railroad surveyors, his command was attacked by a Sioux war party. Baker was so drunk that he refused to admit that a fight was going on around him. That was about the last anyone heard of the man whose actions prompted such sweeping change in Indian policy.

As for the Blackfeet, they never raised arms against the United States again.

The Big Bend of the Marias River was a favorite wintering spot among the Blackfeet. The black clay walls rise almost vertically from the river bottom to the top of the prairies. The river itself makes a large horseshoe bend, the apex of the bend striking the cliffs to the south. On the west side of the cliffs a series of ridges cut by deep ravines look down on the brushy flats which flank the river. It was onto these flats that Heavy Runner's people moved when Mountain Chief's band moved out. The dark, almost black ridges provided protection from the cold winds which blew above them. It was from these ridges that the soldiers waited for dawn to begin their killing.

One has to imagine what the camp looked like on that January day in 1870. The river has changed course several times in the ensuing years; the vegetation has changed from cottonwoods and willows to mostly greasewood and brush, in large part because of the presence of the backup from Tiber Dam, a few miles downstream. The trees have been cut down and the willows have disappeared from the yearly floods.

The massacre, as well as the site, has disappeared from public consciousness. It is dutifully noted in historical texts as a small paragraph or a footnote, then forgotten, while the writers get on to bigger and better things, such as the Battle of the Little Bighorn. Even the Blackfeet, while aware of the event, have not given it the attention it deserves in their tribal history. (Recently, educators George Heavy Runner and Darryl Kipp, descendants of the chief and the scout, have begun a series of field trips to the site, during which they tell Blackfeet children the history of the event and how it affects their people today). When I was writing my historical novel *Fools Crow,* I felt that I needed to visit the site in order to describe it truly, the way it must have been over a hundred years ago. Of course, I should have known that the spring runoff from the Rocky Mountains had altered the course of the river somewhat, but I didn't expect that the backup from Tiber Dam would reach this far upriver; nor that the woodcutters had cleared out the trees to accommodate a full reservoir in the spring.

It was in the late fall of 1985 that I decided to find the massacre site. I had talked it over with my wife, Lois, and a couple of friends— Bill Bevis, who teaches in the English Department with my wife at the University of Montana in Missoula, and Ripley Hugo, a poet and the widow of Richard Hugo, the celebrated poet and teacher, who died in 1982.

Ripley's family has always owned a cabin on the south fork of the Teton River, a river which, like the tributaries of the Marias (Badger Creek, Birch Creek, Cutbank Creek, and the Two Medicine River), runs directly east out of the Rocky Mountains onto the plains to eventually empty into the Missouri River.

I should note here that Montana is loosely but definitively divided into two parts—western Montana, which is the mountainous part; and eastern Montana, which is the plains part. They are separated by the Continental Divide. All the rivers on the west side flow into the Pacific Ocean; all the rivers on the east side flow into the Atlantic (via the Missouri, the Mississippi, the Gulf of Mexico). Very simple and neat. Eastern Montana comprises two-thirds of the state and is by far the more interesting part from a historical standpoint. It was here on the eastern plains that the great conflicts between the settlers from the east and the native peoples took place. It was here that the Massacre on the Marias in 1870 and the Battle of the Little Bighorn in 1876 took place. Since Montana is so enormous, the two conflicts took place many hundreds of miles apart and involved different Indian tribes' territories.

I live in western Montana but I come from eastern Montana. I was born on the Blackfeet Reservation, a figurative stone's throw from the Rocky Mountains. If I had been born with my eyes open I might have looked out the Indian Health Service hospital window and my first vision would have been the snow-capped Chief Mountain, the sacred mountain in the Rockies where many a youth went to have his vision. Nevertheless, the reservation was just off the foothills onto the plains, and that makes it eastern Montana.

But it was in Missoula, across the Continental Divide, official western Montana, that I decided with the help of my wife and friends to find the place where Heavy Runner, possibly an ancestor of mine, met his fate on that cold January dawn. I did have another motive, apart from the fact that I wanted to describe the site truly: My great-grandmother Red Paint Woman had been a member of Heavy Runner's band and, although shot in the leg by the soldiers, had managed to escape upriver, to the west, with a few other survivors. Red Paint Woman had told my father many stories of that time when he was a boy. Although an old woman, who refused to learn even grocery-store English, she remembered everything that had happened to her and her people. It was her stories, related to me by my father, that informed the many stories I told in *Fools Crow*, an account of the Blackfeet (Pikuni) people of that era that culminates in the Massacre on the Marias.

Bill Bevis had done some research in the Montana Historical Society library in Helena and in the University of Montana library, but nowhere could he find a reference to the exact site of the massacre. He asked several historians if they knew where it had taken place. I asked some Blackfeet friends if they could locate the site for me. Nobody knew where it was. Finally Bevis found a slim book written by a man named Ege and published by the the Old Army Press in 1970. It is a discussion of the tactics used by the military in that campaign. It does not concern itself with the morality of the act of such wholesale slaughter. Fair enough. It was a place to start. Ege makes a point of the fact that the exact site had been lost for several years prior to his own looking. There can be no doubt that after much sleuthing he found it. With a metal detector he found thousands of cartridge cases of the type used by the military during that period. On a black ridge just above the Big Bend of the Marias River.

In the center of the book, on two pages, is a grainy, poorly reproduced photograph of the site. It is taken from a ridge almost due west of the site. One can see the cliffs and the ridges, the bend of the river, the dark bottomlands, prominent features, but because it was taken from such a distance, the site looks like many other large river bends cut through the plains of eastern Montana. Try as I might, I could see nothing—not a pattern of trees or willows, not a flat that would look like a natural camping area, not a sign of man-made material—that would distinguish this particular landscape as a site of one of the most horrific massacres in western history.

We drove from Missoula to Ripley's cabin on the Teton River, a distance of four hours, late one cool, sunny September day. The drive was lovely, and we remarked on the first frosting of snow on the higher peaks, the gold of the turning aspen trees, the deer standing in thickets beside the road, and the ducks and geese in the marshes and potholes of the high valleys. We were happy to be on such a mission of high purpose, and when we crossed the Continental Divide at Rogers Pass, we were giddy with anticipation.

But it is when you break out of the mountains and suddenly you see the foothills, and beyond them the rolling golden plains that stretch east as far as the earth's curve will allow the eye to see, that you realize you live in a country uncommon in its sweep. This is the Big Sky, so named from the great novel by A. B. Guthrie, Jr. The sky is so big here that clouds, even the thunderheads that appeared south of us, seem as insignificant as the thousands of cars and motor homes each summer, filled with visitors who suddenly feel vulnerable and threatened by such vastness. Their predecessors, the settlers and homesteaders, felt this same vulnerability, modified somewhat by their faint hopes of "taming the land."

That night in Ripley's cabin we studied the photograph of the massacre site and several topographical maps that Bevis had gotten from the Bureau of Land Management. We read every word of Ege's description until we felt confident we could find the site in our sleep. I think we all may have been secretly wondering what we were going to do with the knowledge we would acquire the next day. After all, the site had been lost both before and after Ege's discovery. Would we tell the world? Would the world come and erect a visitor center, a blacktop parking lot for tour buses? Would it become another Little Bighorn Battlefield Monument, a shrine visited by thousands and thousands of curiosity seekers each year?

We made the two-hour drive the next morning across numberless county roads bordering sagebrush plains, wheat fields, abandoned homesteads and rusty machinery, new homesteads of house trailers and metal buildings, always heading north and east, until we stopped on a bridge that spanned the Marias River not far from present-day Shelby. By our calculations the site should have been about a quarter mile downriver from where we stood. We could see that far, and what we saw was a field of alfalfa and a line of cottonwoods along the river. That land was neatly farmed, and the alfalfa, ready for a third cutting, was bright green beneath a threatening gray sky. In fact, the weather had changed drastically from the day before. A biting north wind had driven the clouds down from Canada. As I stood on that bridge, my mood changed as surely as the weather. I knew that nothing significant had happened in that particular bend of the river. It just didn't have the look of the Big Bend of the Marias.

Back in the car we studied the maps again. We looked up and down the river, but there were no roads, not even any cow trails that we could see. Furthermore, both sides were fenced off, the fence posts spray-painted orange. An ominous warning in the west even without the NO TRESPASSING signs.

We had passed a farmstead at the top of the grade on the east side of the road. Now as we looked up and down the gray slow-moving river, we began to realize that the farm was our best, perhaps our only, prospect. But again, like the bright green alfalfa field, the trim buildings settled on an old landscape didn't offer much hope.

But we did try it. We pulled into the yard in front of a small but nicely kept double-wide trailer with several outbuildings behind it. But there was no one at home. After ringing the doorbell and waiting, Bevis and Ripley went around back to a large metal barn. They had a copy of Ege's book in hand. Lois and I waited in the car. After almost half an hour they came back, looking somber. Then with a sudden rush of wind they were in the car, laughing and yelling.

They had asked the farmer, an early-middle-aged man who was in his coveralls preparing his machinery for a long winter of idleness, if he had heard of the Massacre on the Marias. No, he hadn't. They said it had to have happened near there. Nope, doesn't ring a bell. Are you sure? Lived here all my life, never heard of it. Maybe your wife . . . ? Nope. Then they showed him the double-page photograph in Ege's book. Look familiar? Can't say that it does. Nothing around here looks like this? Everything around here looks like that. Well, thanks for your help. . . . Wait a minute, let me look at that picture again. After some studying he pointed to a slender object in the left forefront of the grainy photograph. I recognize that fencepost. The fencepost was on the promontory of a high bluff from which the photograph was taken looking down into the big bend. Yeah, I've been there. I know exactly where it is. He gave directions. You take the county road south about three miles, you come to a little dirt road on your left, it's easy to miss, it almost doubles back in this direction, but you stay on it, you go past the missile silo, you come to a gate, go through, and maybe a mile or so you're right here. He pounded the book for emphasis.

We did as we were told and we did pass a Cyclone-fenced missile site. It looked like nothing above ground—the only signs were the electronic presence detectors and a large slab of concrete—but deep beneath the earth a silo housed a Minuteman missile as tall as a six-story building. There are maybe a thousand such missiles in Montana. Montanans like to say they are the fourth-largest nuclear power in the world. (But this is no longer true. At the time of this writing, the Cold War has ended and the missiles are being deactivated.)

We passed through the barbed-wire gate and drove another half mile until the road ended. I turned off the motor and we stared straight ahead at the wooden fence post. Beyond it lay a vast space of sky, as gray as the day looked in the Ege photograph of 1970. I've often wondered if it was a clear day that January of 1870 when all hell broke loose and the spirits of 173 Blackfeet traveled to the Sand Hills, the resting place of departed souls. Nothing I have read indicates whether the sky was clear or cloudy, only that it was dawn and the temperature was around thirty below.

We got out of the car and walked up the rise to the promontory, and suddenly we could see a long way, all the way down the valley of the Marias to the backup of the Tiber Dam reservoir. We could see even farther than that, but we didn't need to. What we had come to see lay just below the promontory—the Big Bend of the Marias. And the landscape was black. The valley floor, the cliffs and ridges above it, the scrub brush upon it, even the river—all black beneath the gray sky. The only flashes of light were the windward sides of silvery sagebrush bending beneath the relentless north wind. We stood in silence for a few minutes, trying to take in that formidable landscape. Even without looking at the Ege photograph, we knew what we were seeing.

Lois found a game trail on the side of the promontory, a steep descent on the diagonal, tricky going. We slipped and skidded the hundred yards down until we were standing on the flat at the base of the promontory. The wind was not as strong as it had been on the top, but it still burned the cheeks and ears.

I remember wondering, as I wandered across the wasted flat, what the village must have looked like on January 22, 1870, the day before the massacre. It would have been a winter camp, bundled up against the cold, of less than forty lodges. Perhaps a few women

Site of the Marias Massacre. *Marc Gaede*

would have been walking back to their homes with water or a sheaf of sticks or buffalo chips to heat the lodge and cook what little winter stores they had. Normally, there would have been a few children outside playing with buffalo-rib sleds or small bows and spears. The men would have been visiting or perhaps gambling or making arrows. But it was a camp of death already. Smallpox, the white scabs disease, the white man's gift, had visited the Pikuni camps that winter. Medicine men, the many-faces men, the heavy-singers-for-the-sick, would have been singing, praying, administering their useless medicines to the dying. By the time that winter was over, a third to a half of all the people in all the bands would be dead. So it would have been a quiet camp on the surface, but within the lodges there would be much sickness, agony, terror, hunger, and exhaustion. And the Pikunis, the Blackfeet, would never fully recover from that winter. Even to this day.

I also remember noticing that as we walked across the flat we began to drift apart. By the time I got to where the heart of the camp must have been, beneath a low black ridge from which the soldiers fired their rounds into the lodges, I was standing by myself. As I looked up the gentle slope to the top of the ridge, I thought, This would be where the children played on their sleds. Perhaps Heavy Runner, or my great-grandmother Red Paint Woman, had stood on this very spot and watched them, heard their cries of delight. Perhaps Red Paint, who was not yet a teenager, was one of them. Some years later, as I stood on the bank of the Little Bighorn River, on the southern end of the immense camp of Lakotas, Cheyennes, and Arapahos, where Reno made his charge, I thought of the children playing in the river, riding their ponies, the girls picking flowers with which to make crowns or bracelets. In both instances I thought of children, perhaps because they are truly the innocents.

We stayed for two to three hours, climbing the ridge, looking at the slow dark river, leaving our always circling footprints in the crumbling dark gumbo, and then we left.

How does one compare this incident in western history with the one at the Little Bighorn, Custer's Last Stand? The difference could not be in the numbers alone. Here, 173 Indians were killed. There, 263 white men, 210 under Custer's command, not to mention sixty to one hundred Indians, died. Both were large numbers of fatalities by western standards of that time. Why, then, is Custer's Last Stand such an important part of this nation's history, and why is the Massacre on the Marias known to so few people? In both cases, the United

States Army and Plains Indians were involved. The Indians would say they were defending their territory, or exercising their right to be free upon it, to follow the buffalo as they had for centuries; the white authorities would say that they were punishing the Indians for depredations against the white settlers, traders, rivermen, wood gatherers, and miners, or for leaving the reservations without permission. In any case, contrary to some opinion, these actions resulted from a clash of cultures. What caused this clash is evident. The Indians lived on territories that the whites wanted. Most such collisions occur when one culture wants something from the other. It is always astonishing when the invading culture feels it has the divine right (call it Manifest Destiny or whatever) to take that something in this case, land—from the other.

It is important to point out, with the quincentennial year of Columbus's "discovery" of America just past, that initially the Indian tribes of the North American continent, for the most part, welcomed the pale-skinned men who came to these shores and eventually began to move west. They were not the bloodthirsty savages that later yellow journalists and dime novelists made them out to be. In the beginning the Indians wanted something from the whites—commerce. They wanted coffee, and sugar to put into that coffee; they wanted pans to cook their meat in; they wanted guns to kill that meat; and they wanted horses to give them the mobility to find that meat more readily. They were willing to give up some of their territories to get these commodities. To be sure, there were incidents begun by Indians that resulted in localized hostilities; but there were more incidents begun by the whites' desire to dispossess these "savages," who did not know how to use the land "properly." By the time the whites invaded the northern plains in force in the 1850s and 1860s, the general consensus of opinion in America was that the Indians should be driven off these lands permanently. Some in the Congress, in the government, and in the army echoed the cries of those on the frontier that if the Indians did not relinquish their land peacefully and move to ever-shrinking reservations, then genocide should be considered a reasonable option. So when Sheridan's order came down that "if the lives and property of the citizens of Montana can best be protected by striking Mountain Chief's band, I want them struck," it didn't matter a whit to the army and to the citizens of Montana that the wrong band, a band led by a peace chief, had been struck. "Annihilation" was a word used frequently by the whites of that period. "Nits make lice" was a common phrase. For those who think "annihilation" is too strong a word, consider that it has been estimated that there were 75 million Indians in the Americas, perhaps six million in the contiguous United States area, when Columbus arrived. By 1900, only 237,000 Indians in the United States remained.

Perhaps the largest difference (and the most ignored) between the Massacre on the Marias and the Battle of the Little Bighorn six years later was that Baker was successful in carrying out the army's orders and Custer wasn't. In one incident a large number of Indians were killed; in the other, a popular western hero's entire command was wiped out. Was Custer a fool who rode to his death, as Sitting Bull, the great Sioux leader, stated, or was he a martyr who died in the cause of righteousness, as both the frontier and eastern press contended? Did it matter that some perceived Custer as a fool, others as a hero? Not much. The fact that Custer *died* mattered. His death was proof that the Indians were savages and should be dealt with just as the whites dealt with all the savages they encountered around the world. Ironically, Baker, who was successful in killing a lot of Indians, never became a hero and died an obscure drunk. Custer, in being killed, was elevated to mythical status by the press and the poets. The Custer Myth was born.

And that myth of the martyr making a heroic Last Stand against a red horde versus the mundane fact of an unruly drunk successfully killing the wrong Indians was probably the big difference between the two events. In spite of the outcry from Quakers, abolitionists, preachers, civil rights groups, and a few prominent congressmen and government officials, not many Americans lost sleep over the Massacre on the Marias. Most felt the Indians deserved it for standing in the way of progress. Tough. But the Custer "massacre" (in spite of the fact that he attacked a peaceful camp) touched a wellspring of hysteria. It became the rallying cry for the final push westward ("Get the first scalp for Custer!") and the subjugation or annihilation of the "red fiends," as they became known in the press. And thus began the long determined effort by the whites to destroy Indian cultures, which goes on today in a more subtle form in government, schools, and churches.

One more thing—whites wrote the history of these and all the other conflicts that resulted from the coming together of the two races. Needless to say, this history has been carefully distorted throughout the years to justify the invasion and subjugation of the indigenous people. While there is some "lo, the poor Indian" rhetoric in these historical accounts, the writers were as much a part of the invading culture's establishment as the politicians and military men. In 1859, Horace Greeley wrote, "To the prosaic observer, the average Indian of the woods and prairies is a being who does little credit to human nature—a slave of appetite and sloth, never emancipated from the tyranny of one animal passion save by the more ravenous demands of another. . . . I could not help saying, 'These people must die out—there is no help for them. God has given this earth to those who will subdue and cultivate it, and it is vain to struggle against His righteous decree.' " Custer himself wrote a similar description of the Native Americans in his *My Life on the Plains.*

It has been only recently that historians have begun to incorporate Indian accounts of events like the Battle of the Little Bighorn into "official" accounts. Perhaps the first book to do this in a popular way was *Bury My Heart at Wounded Knee,* by Dee Brown. Because it was deemed subjective and too slanted in favor of the Indians by the Custer Battlefield Historical and Museum Association, it is not, as of this writing, sold in the bookshop at the visitor center.

The Indian wars on the plains are a tragic part of this country's history. The Battle of the Little Bighorn is but one of many battles fought as the hostile forces sought to sweep away the Indians and the Indians fought to stay alive. The Massacre on the Marias is far more emblematic of the Indians' fate, as they were defeated tribe by tribe by the whites who pushed into their territories in violation of treaty after treaty. The outcome of the Indian wars was never in doubt. It is a tribute to the Indians' spirit that they resisted as long as they did. Custer's Last Stand has gone down in history as an example of what savagery the Indians were capable of; the Massacre on the Marias is a better example of what man is capable of doing to man.

2

In early June of 1876, on a hot dry plains day, several bands of Teton Sioux, or, as they called themselves, Lakotas, held a sacred ceremony at the Deer Medicine Rocks, a grouping of tall standing boulders etched with prehistoric carvings along the Rosebud River in Montana. Present were the Hunkpapas, Oglalas, Minneconjous, Blackfeet Sioux, and Sans Arcs, and a few families of the Brulés. A holy man, experienced and honored by the people, selected the right rustling-leaf tree for the lodgepole, the centerpiece of the ceremony. Several warriors counted coup on the trunk before a group of chosen virgins set upon the tree with axes. As the tree began to fall, several men caught it, for it must not touch the ground. Six chiefs then carried it to the Deer Medicine Rocks, a site sacred to the Lakotas and Cheyennes. (The Cheyennes, although they were present, were invited to participate only as onlookers.)

At the Sun Dance site, the warriors stripped the holy tree of its lower limbs and painted it blue, green, yellow, and red, each color symbolizing one of the four horizontal directions. They built an arbor of willows and cottonwoods to provide shade against the burning sun. Then several men purified themselves with a sweat and a smoke before entering a large lodge near the center of the great hoop. Here they made prayers to Wakan Tanka, the Grandfather, the Father, the Great Mystery. A holy man then filled a sacred pipe with grains of tobacco representing six directions, including sky and Grandmother Earth, the Spotted Eagle, all the fliers and four-leggeds, each time invoking their help to make the ceremony correct and to take pity on the people. They gathered objects together which would be used in the ceremony—buffalo skulls, robes, a small drying rack, special paints and grasses and herbs.

When the holy men had finished their preparations, the people began to erect the medicine lodge. First they raised the rustling-leaf (cottonwood) tree amid much rejoicing, both men and women giving the tremolo when the tree stood straight, leaves and branches pointing up at the sky. Then they built a circle around it of twenty-eight forked posts, and from each post they placed a long pole which was bound high up in the medicine tree. They left a sacred opening to the east, for that is where the light comes from. At last the structure was a lodge and the lodge was built to honor the sun.

This ceremony, common to all Plains tribes, took place during the Moon of Making Fat (June) or the Moon of Blackening Cherries (July), always during the full moon, for it lit up the ignorance of the black sky. The Lakotas called the ceremony *wiwanyag wachipi*, or dance looking at the sun. Today it is called the Sun Dance.

During the preceding year many men and women would have taken vows, usually at times of adversity or near-death, to sacrifice before the holy tree. At the same time, youths were preparing to be initiated into manhood. Most of the sacrifices included slashing, or cutting pieces of flesh from arms or chest, or cutting off a finger, but some of the men vowed to undergo the piercing ceremony, to dance before the pole, to endure terrible pain to expiate sins, to control passions, to enter the spiritual realm of Wakan Tanka.

The most common form of piercing was through the breast. Two sticks pierced the breast, one on each side, then were fastened to rawhide strings that hung from the medicine tree. The warrior danced, sage tied around wrists and ankles, sage wreath around his head, blowing an eagle-bone whistle, leaning back away from the tree until the strings were taut. Then he danced some more to the fast drumming, and more still, until at last, mercifully, the skin ripped and the sticks broke free and he fell to the ground, released from his past transgressions or in fulfillment of his vow to the Grandfather, Wakan Tanka. Some piercing involved hanging buffalo skulls from sticks and rawhide strings. It was more difficult to break the skin this way, and often, after much suffering, a holy man would cut the skin with a knife, releasing the twig, string, and skull. Some danced with two skulls, some with four. Another piercing placed a man in the center of four poles dug into the ground. Rawhide lines were attached to the poles and to four sticks piercing the man. He danced and whirled and blew his eagle-bone whistle, but it was almost impossible to break free this way. Again a holy man could come to his assistance. There was no dishonor in this if the dancer showed courage and humility.

After a succession of complex rituals, a medicine woman, who had handled the sacred pipe during the proceedings, gave it to the pipe keeper, who offered up more prayers and gave thanks to Wakan Tanka, thus ending the four-day ceremony.

But this Sun Dance on the Rosebud in early June of 1876 was a special one, if only because it had been called for by the head chief, Sitting Bull. He had prepared for this dance a few days before by loosening his long braids, removing the feathers from his hair, washing off his red paint, and filling his long pipe with tobacco. He climbed a high butte along with his nephew White Bull and his adopted brother Jumping Bull and vowed before these witnesses that he would sacrifice for the good of his people. He looked into the sun, held his pipestem up, and sang and prayed to the Great Spirit. He asked for an abundance of buffalo and other animals; he asked that his people be allowed to live good lives and be of good heart. Then he promised to perform the sun-gazing dance for two days and two nights. He also promised the Great Spirit a fat buffalo. He and the witnesses smoked the pipe to seal the bargain.

A few days later, the Sun Dance began. It must have been one of the largest in history, for there were many thousands of Sioux and Cheyennes present. The camp spread all across the valley floor and was probably a couple of miles in length. At the gathering's final camping place, several days later on the Little Bighorn, the village was said to be eight thousand strong and three miles long.

Sitting Bull had prepared himself physically and spiritually for the sacrifice, one he had made many times before as a Lakota youth, then as a holy man. Now, naked to the waist, he walked to the medicine pole and sat down, his back leaning against it, his legs straight out. Jumping Bull approached with a finely ground knife and a steel awl. He knelt before the leader and with the steel awl lifted the skin of his arm away from the flesh beneath it. He cut off a piece of skin the size of a match head. He worked his way up the arm until he had cut fifty pieces of skin from it. Then he started up the other arm, cutting fifty more. Sitting Bull did not flinch as the blood poured from his wounds. He sang to Wakan Tanka, asking for mercy for himself and his people. The cutting of a hundred pieces of flesh from his arms took half an hour.

Sitting Bull danced all day and all night and half the next day. The people gazed in awe at the stocky figure of their leader, his long hair loose and his arms covered with blood. At last he could no longer dance and appeared ready to faint. His good friend and fellow chief Black Moon caught him and laid him gently on the trampled earth. After a time, his head came back and he said something in a low voice to Black Moon.

Black Moon stood and turned to the people. "Sitting Bull wishes to announce that he just heard a voice from above saying, 'I give you these because they have no ears.' He looked up and saw soldiers and some Indians on horseback coming down like grasshoppers, with their heads down and their hats falling off. They were falling right into our camp."

The people were happy with this vision, for they knew what the words meant. The soldiers had no ears to listen to the truth that the Sioux and Cheyennes wanted to be left in peace to hunt and to be together on the ground of many gifts. The soldiers who wanted war were coming to their camp and would be killed there. The announcement was clear enough. The people rejoiced. Wakan Tanka would protect them.

The Sun Dance ended quickly after Sitting Bull's vision. The people were filled with resolve and fighting spirit. The dance itself lasted only two days, but it was never forgotten by the people who were there and those who came after them. Long after the sacred pole had rotted and fallen down, its remains later paved over in the construction of Route 39, the site of the medicine lodge remained burned in the imagination of the Sioux and Cheyenne people, for it was there that the last great vision of victory and hope would be proved true. Even the Ghost Dance vision, thirteen years later, in which all the white people were swallowed up by the earth and all the buffalo returned, did not fulfill itself. By that time, the Lakotas had no physical means to implement the vision. They were harassed by Indian agents, Indian policemen, and soldiers because the whites had declared the holy dancing illegal. The *wasichus* were afraid of the vision. As for the Lakotas and their allies, they could not make the magic work. Even their Ghost Dance shirts proved powerless in the face of such persistent opposition.

But here on the Rosebud, the Lakotas, the Cheyennes, and the few Arapahos were strong, well fed, and moderately well armed, with thousands of horses, with space and time (although both would prove to be fleeting), and with a vision from a leader who had led them to this spot and would lead them when the soldiers and their

Lakota Sun Dance, ledger drawing by Short Bull. *American Museum of Natural History*

Sitting Bull, Tatanka-Iyotanka. *Smithsonian Institution*

Indian allies—the Crows, the Arikaras, and the Shoshones—came calling.

At the time of Sitting Bull's vision, the assembled people knew that the soldiers were close by, looking to capture them, disarm them, and drive them to the Great Sioux Reservation. On December 3, 1875, the Secretary of the Interior, Zachariah Chandler, after meeting with the President, Ulysses S. Grant, and the Secretary of War, William W. Belknap, sent a communiqué to the Commissioner of Indian Affairs: "Referring to our communication of the 27th ultimo, relative to the status of certain Sioux Indians residing without the bounds of their reservation and their continued hostile attitude towards the whites, I have to request that you direct the Indian agents at all Sioux agencies in Dakota and at Fort Peck, Montana, to notify said Indians that unless they shall remove within the bounds of their reservation (and remain there), before the 31st of January next, they shall be deemed hostile and treated accordingly by the military force." It was now four and a half months past the deadline, and instead of the "hostiles" surrendering their arms to the authorities, many Indians who *were* on the reservations had made their way west to join Sitting Bull's growing village. These reservation Indians had dealt with the whites before and had found that they were not to be trusted. They were afraid the same thing would happen to them that happened at the Marias River and Sand Creek and Ash Hollow. When the soldiers could not find the "hostiles" they simply punished the available "friendlies" by massacring them.

The winter of 1875–76 was an especially cruel one. The weather was so severe that the army in Dakota was forced to suspend operations in the field. The runners sent out by the army had great difficulty in reaching the "hostile" camps to deliver the ultimatum. Blizzards swept the Dakota and Montana plains all winter, and the temperatures were commonly far below zero. In fact, by the time the runners reached the several camps, it would have been impossible for the Indians to comply with the January 31 deadline; the runners themselves did not make it back by then. There has been speculation that the authorities did not want the roaming Indians to meet the deadline. This would give the army an excuse to rid the great hunting grounds of Montana of Indians once and for all, thus opening the territory for white settlement. But the Indians could not have known this. They were too busy trying to survive the blowing snows and harsh temperatures. Game was scarce. The horses around the camps were starving. And the people could do nothing but wait out the weather. Much suffering and death would have resulted had the Indians attempted to come in.

Virtually all the bands of Lakotas and Northern Cheyennes who were not on the reservation were camped along the Powder River in Montana that winter. They felt safe this far from the military posts in the Dakotas and Nebraska. What they hadn't anticipated was a winter expedition from the south. But on March 1, General George A. Crook, along with Custer perhaps the army's most experienced Indian fighter, led seven hundred fighting men, thirty-one scouts, sixty-two civilian packers with their pack animals, eighty wagons with eighty-four teamsters, and five light ambulances out of Fort Fetterman north along the old Bozeman Trail. They were supplied for forty days with food and camp items, including a beef herd, which would supply two-thirds of the men's meat, the other third coming from a supply of bacon. On the second night out, a band of Indians drove off the beef herd, thus immediately reducing the meat rations by two-thirds. Things didn't get much better, with Indian sharpshooters keeping the camp awake and tense much of the time. The expedition was to be commanded by General Joseph J. Reynolds, a Civil War hero who was getting along in years and was completely inexperienced in fighting Indians. Crook had originally intended to come along as an observer, but after the beef incident and the sharpshooting, he took command, relegating Reynolds to overseeing camptending duties.

Although the weather remained bitterly cold, the expedition progressed north toward the Sioux and Cheyenne winter camps in Montana. But the scouts noticed that the Indians were tracking them all the way. By smoke signals the Indian kept one another informed of the troop's movements. Finally Crook devised a plan whereby the ten companies of cavalry would leave the main expedition under cover of darkness and continue rapidly north. Meanwhile the infantry and supply trains would retire to old Fort Reno, back in the other direction. At 7:00 P.M. on March 7, the cavalry left camp. They rode thirty-five miles that night. They had stripped themselves down to bare necessities—one buffalo robe or two blankets, no spare clothes, no tents, full rations of hardtack, sugar, and coffee, half rations of bacon, and enough grain for the horses for fifteen days. This proved to be a questionable decision, for the weather steadily worsened and the cavalrymen found themselves fighting through snowdrifts and blizzards in subzero temperatures. For the next few days they traveled in a northerly direction, the scouts always on the lookout for signs of a village or the tracks of a large party. The soldiers moved from one drainage to the next, always without success. Finally one of the scouts, Frank Grouard, who insisted that he was born in the Sandwich Islands in the South Pacific to a Mormon missionary and his Polynesian wife and who would shortly gain fame with the Custer expedition to the Little Bighorn, predicted that the Indians would be on the Powder River. Crook had had every intention of sending the scouts all the way down the Tongue River to its confluence with the Yellowstone, which would have effectively negated his chances of finding any Indians at all.

Crook was getting nervous, for he had left Fort Fetterman with high expectations that his winter campaign would break the backs of the "hostiles," and he had convinced his superiors that if the Indians weren't found and soundly beaten this winter, by spring they would have scattered all over the buffalo country. It would be useless to pursue them. But if he could surprise them in their winter camps, bundled up against the cold, the Indian campaigns on the northern plains would be over—and Crook, a moody man not given to sharing his thoughts or plans with subordinates, would go down in history as the greatest Indian fighter of them all.

In desperation he listened to Frank Grouard, who was the only scout who thought that the Indians would be off toward the east, along the Powder River and not on the Little Bighorn River as most of the others thought. Grouard, in a moment of rashness perhaps, told Crook he could find the Indians within three days. Crook took him up on the offer.

On March 16, Grouard reported that he had backtracked a small group of Indian hunters to a village on the Powder River. Crook and his officers were delighted with the news. They turned in that direction and that evening made a cold camp. Crook put General Reynolds in charge of three battalions that would ride that night to the Powder River and attack the village at dawn. Crook would lead the other two battalions and the pack animals farther up the Powder River to await the victors.

Because of a snowstorm and pitch blackness, during which Grouard often had to get down on his hands and knees to find the trail, the troops did not attack the village until nine o'clock the next morning. The terrain was steep and broken by gullies and washes full of brush, but the troops divided into battalions and made their charge.

One battalion under Captain Henry E. Noyes attacked the village from the north, one of its companies charging right into camp, pistols blazing, surprising the still-sleeping Indians. Another company headed for the horse herds and was successful in driving them off. But one company which was supposed to provide rifle fire from nearby bluffs did not reach them in time to help the soldiers in among the lodges. A reserve battalion did not show up at all.

Although the attack was a surprise, the Indians, many naked in the subzero morning, reached cover on the edge of the village and began to return fire. The soldiers became confused and apprehensive and soon found themselves under siege in the village. But before retiring from the battlefield they managed to burn the lodges and everything in them, leaving the Indians with no shelter, no clothing, no food, and no horses.

The attack had been only a partial success. They had not killed or captured the Indians, who escaped almost unscathed, while the cavalry lost four men, and six others were seriously wounded. Moreover, they had been ordered to burn up robes and food that they themselves could have used. The men had nothing but a day's ration of hardtack and the clothes on their backs. As they made their way to the rendevous with Crook, the officers and men were openly bitter and demoralized. To add insult to injury, that night as they slept, the Indians from the village stole almost all of their horses back. Crook was not happy with the results of his long, arduous journey and later would court-martial Reynolds for botching the only opportunity to catch the Indians napping in their winter lodges. As for Crook, he would not take the field against the Indians again until June. And that expedition would result in the Battle of the Rosebud on June 17, in which Crazy Horse's warriors would force Crook to retire again—a result that quite likely contributed to Custer's death on the Little Bighorn eight days later.

The camp the soldiers had attacked on March 17 was that of He Dog's Sioux and Old Bear's Northern Cheyennes. He Dog's small group had just left Crazy Horse's camp to give themselves up to the soldiers at Red Cloud Agency and had stopped to camp with Old Bear's people for a couple of days. Because He Dog was a friend of Crazy Horse, Frank Grouard would later say that Crazy Horse himself was there, which was not true.

Kate Bighead was in the camp. A Southern Cheyenne, she had also been in Black Kettle's camp on the Washita River in Oklahoma in November 1868 when Custer made his famous surprise attack at dawn. She described the Washita attack: "Our chief, Black Kettle, and other Cheyennes, many of them women and children, were killed that day. It was early in the morning when the soldiers began the shooting. There had been a big storm and there was snow on the ground. All of us jumped from our beds, and all of us started running to get away. I was barefooted as were almost all the others."

Custer's innovative winter dawn attack on the Southern Cheyenne village eight years before the Battle of the Little Bighorn established him as the most popular Indian fighter on the frontier. Before this victory, Custer had been chasing Indians all over the central plains of Kansas without success. He complained that the Indians never stood and fought, that they committed a raid, then vanished into the hills. He wanted them to stand and fight, as men had fought in the Civil War, where he received a battlefield commission as brevet major general at the age of twenty-three.

Custer had come a long way in a very short time from his days at West Point, where he amassed hundreds of demerits and graduated last in his class. During the Civil War, he had led several saber charges into Confederate lines, virtually all of them successful in putting the rebels on the run. He lost a great number of men in these all-out charges. According to historian Stephen E. Ambrose, Custer had the highest casualty figures of all the Union division commanders in the war. He had a dozen horses shot out from under him, but he attracted the attention of his senior officers, who began to look at him as a great morale-booster for the whole Union Army. The press was equally enchanted with him. He became "the boy general" with the "golden locks." He wore outlandish costumes—a sombrero, tight-fitting black hussar jacket, Mexican spurs, and oversize knee-high boots, among others. One of his fellow officers said, "He looked like a circus rider gone mad." Custer thrived on the publicity. He became a great favorite of General McClellan, commander of the Army of the Potomac, and his staff. Custer was fun to have around. He played practical jokes. He was insouciant but always obedient. And he was totally without fear. He especially enjoyed fighting against his old classmates from West Point, who had left the academy early to accept commissions in the Confederate Army. He fought them with high spirits, and when one of them was captured Custer visited him in prison, bringing money and tobacco and decent food. He sent letters to his opponents, although it is not clear how these letters got to the other side. In one battle, he overran the position of a close friend from West Point days, Tom Rosser, captured Rosser's supply train, and the next day appeared in Rosser's confederate uniform. He sent a note to the taller Rosser complaining about the size of the uniform.

The Civil War was Custer's greatest moment of glory. He had emerged unharmed and a true hero. At Appomattox he had personally accepted General Robert E. Lee's white flag of surrender. He had been given the table, as a present for his wife, Elizabeth, on which the terms of surrender were written. But ironically such glory came to an end with the surrender.

After the war, Custer lost his battlefield commission and became a captain in the regular army. He spent his first postwar year in Texas, restoring order and keeping the defeated rebels in line, a boring and inconsequential assignment for a war hero. Then, in 1867, he was promoted to lieutenant colonel, second in command of the 7th Cavalry, one of four new regiments formed to fight Indians on the plains. Custer wasn't thrilled. He had expected more, but for the time being it was enough. At least he would be fighting Indians. And since the commander of the 7th Cavalry was on detached duty, Custer became the de facto commander. And thus began his career as Indian fighter and his aimless soldiering over the central plains in search of Indians. That his wanderings in Kansas in the summer of 1867 were virtually pointless is backed up by the number of Indian casualties: two. All summer. Meanwhile, the Indians had killed over two hundred whites during that period.

If Custer could not find Indians, he could at least find trouble. The 7th Cavalry, like almost all of the post–Civil War units, was stricken by dissension. Older officers had been passed over for promotions and found themselves serving under younger, more ambitious officers like Custer.

Enlisted men, mostly Civil War veterans who were afraid of civilian life, immigrants who could not find other work, adventurers, lawbreakers on the run, and farm boys, grew to hate army life on the plains—the boredom, the sudden terror, the bad food, the loneliness—and consequently blamed their officers. The officers blamed each other and their commander—in this case, George Armstrong Custer. Strong factions developed. Thus the morale, almost from the inception of the 7th, was bad.

Custer deserved a lot of the blame. He drove his men and their horses hard, sometimes beyond endurance; he was unsympathetic to their situations; he expected his sometimes unreasonable orders to be carried out without question; he left his column frequently to go hunting. On one such hunting trip, he was chasing a buffalo alone

**General George Armstrong Custer,
Civil War hero and media star.**
National Archives

and shot his horse in the head when the buffalo swerved. He was all by himself, lost, slightly injured, on foot in hostile territory. Fortunately, the column caught up with him a couple of hours later. Presumably, he found another horse and resumed command. But the "Boy General" had become an object of ridicule and hatred among officers and men alike. His men began to refer to him as "Iron Butt," "Hard Ass," and "Ringlets." Captain Frederick Benteen, who later disobeyed an order to come to Custer's defense at the Little Bighorn, was a confirmed Custer-hater from the very beginning. To be fair, Custer did have his supporters—Tom Custer, his brother, among others.

The discord came to a head in September 1867, when complaints

Custer and his wife, Elizabeth, dining in a field tent in Kansas during the army's largely fruitless campaign against the Cheyennes in 1867. *Little Bighorn Battlefield National Monument*

against Custer were sworn out by a Captain West, a subordinate, and General A. J. Smith, commander of the military district, and he was ordered to stand charges for a court-martial. The more serious accusations included abandoning his command at Fort Wallace in western Kansas to visit his wife, Elizabeth, who was in eastern Kansas (Custer was afraid she would try to cross Indian country to visit him or be stricken with cholera), and having deserters shot on the spot without hearings. That he was a deserter himself did not seem to occur to him. He was convicted of both counts, as well as six others, and sentenced to a year's suspension from rank and command and forfeiture of his pay for that period.

Custer retired to his home in Michigan to "enjoy the cool breezes of [Lake] Erie," but ten months later, in September 1868, he was reinstated by General Philip Sheridan, commander of the Department of the Missouri, to lead a campaign against the Southern Cheyennes in Oklahoma.

That Custer had proved to be the best field commander on the frontier speaks volumes about the competency and enthusiasm of his fellow officers. Very few officers had experience in fighting Indians. General Winfield Scott Hancock, a true Civil War hero, led a troop of mounted soldiers and infantrymen, complete with artillery pieces and pontoon bridges, across the endless plains in search of horseback Indians. At least he tried. Many officers were more than a little reluctant to push their commands out onto the Kansas plains where they would be surrounded by Cheyennes, Arapahos, Kiowas, and southern Oglalas determined to defend their territories.

"Little Phil" Sheridan had chosen Custer specifically for a new battle strategy—a winter campaign. In the past, the army had mounted its campaigns in the spring, summer, and fall, during the good weather. Of course, during those seasons the Indians were most mobile, almost impossible to catch. In a burst of insight, Sheridan came up with the idea that in the winter the Indians were in their permanent camps, less likely to be on guard, more likely to be bundled up in their lodges against the cold. The Indians could be found, and they would be vulnerable to attack. The only drawback was that the men would be exposed to some of the harshest weather they would ever encounter. Many experienced scouts thought the troopers would not be up to the task.

Custer, for all his shortcomings, was more than enthusiastic. He had spirit and the ability to drive men hard in any weather and on any terrain, and he loved to fight. That he was unloved by most of the

7th Cavalry did not matter. His job was to kill Indians.

He got that chance on November 27, 1868. The previous day, his scouts had picked up the tracks of ponies, indicating a party of Indians heading from Kansas to Oklahoma. Custer had no idea where the tracks would lead, but he followed them all day and into the night. A winter storm had passed over the area a while before, dumping fresh snow, which made the tracking, even by night, fairly easy. But the winter winds had crusted the surface of the fresh snow, and the 720 cavalry horses made a very loud approach. Custer, fearing an early discovery, had the main body of troops trail several hundred yards behind while he and two Osage scouts continued on the tracks.

Just before midnight, they crawled to the edge of a bluff which overlooked a river valley. One of the scouts announced he could smell smoke. The other heard a dog bark. Custer could not see anything, and he did not smell smoke or hear the dog. But in the quiet moments of listening, he heard a baby cry. He had found his Indians.

Custer divided his command into four detachments, which would surround the village, north, south, east, and west, and wait for dawn. On his command, they would charge from the four directions.

At first light, Custer turned to the band leader and directed him "to give us 'Garry Owen' [his favorite song]. At once the rollicking notes of that familiar marching and fighting air sounded forth through the valley, and in a moment were re-echoed back from the opposite sides by the loud and continued cheers of the men of the other detachments, who, true to their orders, were there and in readiness to pounce upon the Indians the moment the attack began. In this manner the battle of the Washita commenced."

The "battle" in the village was short, barely fifteen minutes. The soldiers drove the people from their lodges barefoot and half naked, shooting them in the open. Many of the warriors managed to reach the trees, where they began to return fire; a few of them escaped, but after a couple of hours, the firing ceased and 103 Cheyennes lay dead in the snow and mud. Custer reported that they were fighting men, but others said that ninety-two of them were women, children, and old people. Black Kettle, the sixty-seven-year-old leader of the band, and his wife, Medicine Woman Later, who had survived nine gunshot wounds at the Massacre of Sand Creek four years before, had been shot in the back as they attempted to cross the Lodge Pole or Washita River. Their bodies, trampled and covered with mud, were found in the shallow water by the survivors.

The soldiers seized everything in the village—guns, bows and arrows, decorated clothing, sacred shields, tobacco, dried meat, dried berries, robes, and fifty-one lodges—and burned it. In addition, they captured 875 horses and mules. Custer gave the order to slaughter these animals by cutting their throats, but the horses feared white-man smell and shied away, and after several attempts, the men grew tired. Custer gave the order to shoot the animals instead. Custer himself slaughtered camp dogs. Then the 7th Cavalry took its captives, mostly women and children and old ones, and headed north to its base of operations, Camp Supply.

Custer's attack on the village of Southern Cheyennes was hailed as a great victory in the Indian wars. For the first time, a substantial number of Indians had been killed and captured. Sheridan was be-side himself with delight—his plan to attack at dawn on a cold win-ter day had worked perfectly. He even rode down from his field head-quarters at Fort Hays to Camp Supply to welcome Custer as a conquering hero. General William Tecumseh Sherman, Commander

Illustration of Custer's surprise attack on Black Kettle's Cheyenne camp at the Washita River. *Library of Congress*

of the Army, was equally pleased, as were numerous politicians and newspaper editorial writers.

But there were a couple of flies in the ointment. The most immediate was, what had happened to Major Joel Elliott and his eighteen-man detachment, who had ridden off downstream from Black Kettle's village in pursuit of fleeing Indians? They were missing. And why had Custer not stayed to search for Elliott? These questions led to the other uncomfortable one—Custer had done absolutely no reconnaissance before he attacked. He didn't know what was upstream or downstream. For all he knew, there could have been six thousand Indians camped nearby on the Washita. And there were. Villages of other Southern Cheyennes, Arapahos, Kiowas, Comanches, and Prairie Apaches either heard the shooting or were contacted by runners. They mounted large war parties, but it was a small party of Arapahos who first came upon Elliott and his soldiers, who were chasing a group of women and children attempting to escape downstream. Soon other parties came to the scene and forced the soldiers into a defensive position in a ravine, where the soldiers formed a cartwheel, their feet toward the center, shooting in all directions, including straight up, according to some warriors. It didn't take long to finish off Elliot's detachment.

It wasn't until two weeks later, when Custer, Sheridan, and several companies of soldiers returned to the Washita, that the mutilated and decomposed bodies of Elliott's men were found.

Custer explained that they had spent all day fighting, then destroying the village and horse herd, and there wasn't time to conduct a proper search for Elliott, as "it was now lacking but an hour of night [and] we had to make an effort to get rid of the Indians, who still loitered in strong force on the hills...."

But the more serious question—why had Custer not scouted the area before attacking?—went unanswered. Apparently Custer had not learned this aspect of strategy at West Point. During the Civil War, he often charged blindly into the rebels, not knowing about nearby forces and not even caring.

Much has been made by scholars and contemporary observers alike of Custer's reckless arrogance. Perhaps this arrogance was born of the fact that Custer had not paid a high price for his lack of proper preparation. Both in the Civil War and on the Washita, he had claimed victories in spite of the lack of reconnaisance. Civil War journalists coined a phrase to cover the young general's success: Custer's Luck. Perhaps Custer came to believe that this luck led to invincibility.

Kate Bighead had no such sense of invincibility. She had been in both Black Kettle's Southern Cheyenne camp on the Washita in 1868 and the Northern Cheyenne camp on the Powder River in 1876 when they were surprised by a dawn attack. (To further complicate the coincidence, Black Kettle's band had been attacked by the Colorado militia at Sand Creek in 1864, another famous massacre.) And like the survivors of that band of Southern Cheyennes who trekked through the cold to safety, these Northern Cheyennes, almost naked and certainly hungry and exhausted, began to move north down the Powder River, away from their burned camp. Kate Bighead: "Three days later, all of us walking, we arrived at Crazy Horse's camp of Oglala Sioux. The Oglalas gave us food and shelter. After a few days the two bands together went northward and found the Uncpapa [Hunkpapa] Sioux, where Sitting Bull was the chief. The chiefs of the three bands decided that all of us would travel together for the spring and summer hunting, as it was said that many soldiers would be coming to try to make us go back to the reservations."

When spring came and the grass grew long and green enough to nourish the horses, other bands joined them—the Minniconjous and Sans Arcs in force; some Yanktonais, Two Kettles, and Blackfeet Sioux; a few Arapahos—and the three camp circles became five, with some of the smaller groups camping with relatives and friends in the larger groups. Many of the Indians had left the reservation in Dakota after surviving a harsh winter of starvation and constant threat from the soldiers to join the great gathering. When the large camp of Indians moved, they moved in orderly procession, with the Cheyennes in the lead (this honor was bestowed on them because they had exhibited great courage in the attack on their village) and Sitting Bull's Hunkpapas, the largest group, protecting the rear. Crazy Horse's Oglalas camped behind the Cheyennes, partly to offer protection, partly because many of the Cheyennes and Oglalas were related by marriage.

Earlier, when the three bands of Hunkpapas, Oglalas, and Cheyennes had decided to come together as one village, Sitting Bull became the de facto big chief because his band, the Hunkpapas, was the largest, and because he was the most forceful leader. But with the arrival of the many other bands, it became clear that a hierarchy was needed. Without such a structure, conflict would become inevitable, and so Sitting Bull summoned all of the leaders to council. The first order of business was to choose a head chief of all the bands, all the people, a man they would all listen to and obey, if he spoke wisely and truly.

To appoint a head chief over all the Lakota bands was a radical departure from past practice. Each band had its own chiefs, sub-chiefs, war chiefs, society leaders, clan leaders. No matter how many bands got together, they retained this parallel structure of leadership. A chief of the Oglalas had no say in the affairs of the Hunkpapas, for instance. And certainly no Lakota chief would dare tell a Cheyenne tribesman what to do. But the Indians who had gathered for this momentous occasion knew that they needed a particular leader, one who could keep the bands and tribes organized and unified, especially when war came.

Two Moons, an ambitious minor Northern Cheyenne war leader who would later be appointed chief of his people by the white authorities, stood in council and said: "I can see that it will not take you long to choose your leader for this war. You already have the right man—Sitting Bull. He has called us all together. He is your war chief, and you always listen to him. I can see no reason for another choice."

The response of the chiefs was positive. By popular (although not unanimous) acclamation, Sitting Bull became the head chief of all the bands. Perhaps more than one chief at the council breathed a sigh of relief, for the head chief of such a large war machine would surely be held most responsible for hostilities against the whites.

Sitting Bull had already been declared a "hostile" by the United States government, and all the people with him were now officially enemies of the state. It is quite certain that even had Sitting Bull been able to comply with the military edict that he surrender by January 31, he would not have done so. He was not a "reservation Indian." He had avoided contact with the whites since they had come into his territory. He, like Crazy Horse, had not been present at the Fort Laramie Treaty of 1868 and so did not consider himself and his people beholden to its conditions or benefits. He had spurned all offerings of rations and the safety of the reservation (from the soldiers, ironically enough). He had urged his Hunkpapa followers not to take the white man's gifts, especially their liquor, because then they would become dependent on and want to live around the *wasichus*. And he later would scorn the reservation Indians when they made a deal to sell the sacred Black Hills to the whites. He would propose that the Indians get a scale and sell the earth "by the pound." He said, "We have plenty of game. We want no white men here. The Black Hills belong to me. If the whites try to take them, I will fight." But he did not fight then and continued to avoid the white men and their reservation, preferring to remain out on the hunting grounds. He would have nothing to do with Red Cloud and Spotted Tail, two Sioux chiefs who had long ago led their people into the agencies that later bore their names. Red Cloud, an Oglala war leader, had led his warriors in forcing the army to close its forts along the Bozeman Trail, the overland route through Wyoming and Montana to the Virginia City goldfields, thereby rendering the trail useless. Actually a stalemate had existed for some time before the closing. The Indians could not get the soldiers out of the forts, and the soldiers could not get out to protect travelers on the trail. It was reported that when the demoralized soldiers left they could see smoke behind them as the Indians torched the forts.

Red Cloud and his fellows, in spite of Sitting Bull's contempt, had gained concessions for their people in the Treaty of 1868. The treaty had been called for by a United States peace commission in an effort to end the war on the northern plains, which was tying up valuable troops who were needed elsewhere, including the central and southern plains. General Sherman himself led the peace commission, much to his dislike. He thought the United States should deal with the Indian problem forcefully, make the Indians surrender unconditionally rather than sign a treaty with them, thereby allowing them concessions. He was convinced that the white buffalo hunters would eventually eliminate the Indians' main source of subsistence and force them onto the reservation. Sheridan believed this too: "Let [the buffalo hunters] kill, skin, and sell until the buffalo is exterminated, as it is the only way to bring lasting peace and allow civilization to advance." Sherman and Sheridan were right—before the coming of the white men an estimated fifty million buffalo roamed the North American continent; by 1888, there were less than a thousand left in the United States. As historian Ambrose points out, "The buffalo hunters, not the army, cleared the Indians off the plains."

Nevertheless, Sherman bowed to pressure from Congress to do something about the Indian problem quickly. They were sick of pouring money down a rathole. The war was costing the government $150,000 a day, an enormous sum back then. The railroads also put the pressure on, refusing to build any more track in the hostile country until assured that the workers would not be attacked.

Red Cloud, the chief that the peace commissioners wanted most to sign the treaty, was in no hurry to do so. First, he wanted to make meat for the winter. Then he wanted to war on the Snakes (Shoshones) who had killed his son. This would not be the first or last time Red Cloud thwarted government efforts to make a final peace.

In 1875, he displayed a similar reluctance to get together with the whites over the sale of the Black Hills. One of Red Cloud's favorite ploys was to make more demands when he finally sat down with white negotiators. Even his tribesmen grew impatient with him at times. After several months of dawdling, Red Cloud and Man Afraid of His Horses, another Lakota chief, finally came in.

The two sides got together at Fort Laramie on November 4, 1868, and after much haggling over details and irrelevancies, Red Cloud put his mark on the treaty (Spotted Tail, the Brulé chief, had already signed it) on the 6th, just twenty-one days before the massacre on the Washita. Supposedly, the war on the northern plains was over.

Under the articles of agreement, the Indians received all of South Dakota west of the Missouri River, including the Black Hills.

General William Tecumseh Sherman (third from left) and other peace commissioners meeting Indians in a tent at the Fort Laramie peace treaty negotiations, Wyoming Territory, 1868. *Smithsonian Institution*

This territory was to be called the Great Sioux Reservation. In addition, a vast hunting area which lay between the Black Hills and the Bighorn Mountains in Wyoming and Montana (the Powder River country) was unceded to the whites. No whites could enter it. It would remain a hunting ground until the buffalo were gone. And finally, the peace commissioners agreed to close the forts for good along the Bozeman Trail. This latter concession was moot, since the forts had been abandoned several months earlier.

In return, the Indians agreed to go to the Great Sioux Reservation, to take up farming, to live in houses, and to send their children to the white man's school. They promised not to war with the whites, not to disturb the Union Pacific railroad builders, not to attack the settlers who would move into their former territory. The Indians agreed to give up their buffalo ways for "civilization."

Peace at last. Civilization at last. The treaty set well with all of the whites save the military, which still thought the Indians could and should be whipped into submission. Reformers were happy that the Indians would adopt the Christian way and join the rest of civilized America. Politicians and railroad magnates and newspaper publishers were happy that the Indians were out of the path of progress. Frontier settlers were happy with proof that their lives *were* worth a plugged nickel—if still wary.

Most of the Indian people were happy that they would have a large reservation, that they would receive rations, that their children would be safe, and that they would still possess their sacred Paha Sapa, the Black Hills, from which legend said they originated.

Like all treaties negotiated between the United States government and the tribes, this one was broken almost immediately and repeatedly (and is still being broken today by the government in its refusal to return the Black Hills to the Indians, or at least offer an acceptable settlement). It is clear that neither side intended to honor the agreement. Indians left the reservation to hunt elsewhere. Many refused to farm, and those who tried found the land mostly inarable. Many did not send their children to the white man's schools, especially the boarding schools, which were, in some cases, a thousand miles or more away. And, of course, Sitting Bull and Crazy Horse, who were supposedly bound by the treaty they never signed, remained free, far from the white man's jurisdiction.

As for Red Cloud, he used the treaty signing as an excuse to obtain ammunition so he could go out and make war on the Crows. He later said he didn't think the treaty covered war with other tribes.

Furthermore, he wanted to return to the unceded territory as quickly as possible to resume the hunt.

One of the major problems with the treaty, from the Indian standpoint, was that the government set up the agencies along the Missouri River, the eastern edge of the reservation, far from the buffalo herds. This was a deliberate effort to get the Indians away from their "wild" lifestyle. It was reasoned that the Indians would make permanent settlements along the Missouri and live like the whites. With each Indian family on its own farm, looking out only for itself, the dreaded tribalism would eventually just wither away. And from the white point of view, that was the whole point of the treaty—destroy the tribal cohesiveness that allowed the Indians to resist the taking of their country. One of the popular sayings of the time was "Kill the Indian, save the man."

Red Cloud and the other signers felt that they had been tricked. They were simply not ready to give up their traditional ways. If they had been more sophisticated (which they soon became), they might have likened this move to telling the people in the industrial cities in the east to abandon their factory jobs and take up farming. Only Spotted Tail led his people to an agency along the Missouri.

The U. S. government violated the treaty in numerous ways. The most immediate violation involved the issuing of rations to those who had settled at agencies. The meat rations were slow in coming and often were of such poor quality that they were unfit to eat. Blankets and clothing did not arrive before winter set in. Farm implements were in short supply. To be sure, much of the problem was directly attributable to graft and corruption among Indian agents and their suppliers. But the government did next to nothing to correct the problem.

And as we shall see, perhaps the biggest violation occurred over the Black Hills, which were protected under the articles of the treaty. This blatant shattering of the 1868 treaty, which was precipitated by Custer himself, led directly to the Battle of the Little Bighorn.

Spotted Tail, a Brulé Sioux, had for a time been declared the chief of all the Sioux by the U. S. government, because he was the most compliant of the leaders. The whites would deal only with him—and with Red Cloud, whom the whites feared and to whom they gave more authority than he possessed among his tribesmen. These two men, who were not considered big chiefs by their people, would gain great power by their dealings with the whites. And they would eventually give the whites almost everything they asked for. Small wonder that Sitting Bull spurned these chiefs' entreaties to surrender his arms and horses to the army.

Sitting Bull was the greatest chief ever on the northern plains, perhaps the greatest chief ever anywhere, but even he was not capable of fighting the white soldiers on their terms. Although a few of his followers had modern repeating rifles, the vast majority possessed old muzzle-loading smoothbores, and very little ammunition for these—no match for the soldiers' modern rifles, sidearms, artillery, and gatling guns in a pitched battle.

But pitched battle was not the Indian way of fighting. Quick skirmishes, in and out, sometimes daylong fights with few casualties, then home to recount the dangers and honors—that was the Indian style. It was better to count coup upon an enemy than to kill him. One could use a coup stick or the butt or barrel of a rifle or musket, a bow or quirt, or simply the hand. The point was to touch the enemy, preferably a well-armed enemy, to put one's life in jeopardy, to steal his honor, his manhood, then ride away in disdain. Anybody could kill a man, but to count coup, to put oneself at great risk, required the courage and cunning of a mountain lion. Of course, this approach to personal honor often led to capture, injury, or death. Mourning a loved one who had tempted fate and lost was a way of life in Indian society. Women slashed their legs, cut their hair ragged, smeared their bodies with ash. Men mourned in a less ritualistic way. More often, they swore revenge, joining the next war party or horse-stealing raid against the offending tribe.

Sitting Bull had counted coup on the enemy when he was fourteen winters. He had followed a war party out of camp to a rendevous point and managed to convince the party, which included his father, Jumping Bull, that he was ready to make war. Although his name at the time was Slow—for his deliberate, almost awkward manner—and he had only bird arrows in his quiver, he had killed his first buffalo four winters before. His father, overcome with pride at his son's courage, gave him a skinned, feathered coup stick. Good-Voiced Elk, the war leader, allowed the young man to tag along but admonished him to stay out of the way. Eventually, the party discovered a similar party of Crows coming their way and planned an ambush. But Slow, like any foolish youth, was determined to make a name for himself. Half-naked, on his small pony, bird arrows in his quiver, he rode out at full gallop right at the startled Crows. Then all the Hunkpapa warriors, seeing an opportunity slipping away, charged after Slow. The Crows turned and fled, most of them outdistancing their enemies, because they were a long way off when Slow began his one-boy attack. But one unlucky Crow was riding a slow horse and Slow was gaining ground. Thinking it better to stand and make a fight than to be killed running away, the Crow dismounted and notched an arrow, but before he could let fly, Slow was upon him and cracked him across the arm with his new coup stick. As he rode away, he yelled, *"On-Hey!* I, Slow, have conquered him." The men then killed the Crow. Because of his great courage in counting first coup on the enemy, his father named him Tatanka-Iyotanka, Sitting Bull.

Although he is remembered as a holy man, a wise man, a chief, Sitting Bull had to earn his reputation first through many such courageous acts. He proved himself time and time again in his young manhood, leading raids and war parties against other tribes. Later, when Sitting Bull had become an emblem of savagery, even evil, the

Drawing by Sitting Bull (seen on horseback) depicting his bravery in battle as a younger warrior. *Smithsonian Institution*

white authorities and their "reservation Indians" tried to discredit him by calling him a coward because he had not fought at Little Bighorn. The fact that Sitting Bull was forty-two years old, past fighting prime, and the principal chief of all the assembled Lakotas and Cheyennes, and had just undergone the fasting and self-torture during the Sun Dance on the Rosebud, did not matter to these detractors. The real reason he was branded a coward was that the whites still feared him as a leader and were apprehensive about his role on the reservation when and if he came in. It was clear to them that he was a troublemaker and would prove disruptive to the process of taming the Indians.

But in the late spring and early summer of 1876, Sitting Bull was at the height of his power. He led a gathering of Indians estimated at eight thousand or more—almost by accident. Neither he nor the white authorities could have guessed that the relatively simple but botched attack by Crook's forces on the Cheyenne village on March 17 would lead to the largest gathering of "free" Indians on the northern plains. But once he realized his power, Sitting Bull sent word back to the reservation for the Indians there to come join him. The runners rode hard and fast to all the agencies on the Great Sioux Reservation to deliver Sitting Bull's message: "It is war. Come to my camp at the Big Bend of the Rosebud. Let's all get together and have one big fight with the soldiers!" And they came.

Later, when Custer and his 7th Cavalry came upon the Sun Dance site on the Rosebud, the Arikara scouts studied a drawing in sand they had discovered in a sweat lodge. Hoofprints on both sides of a ridge, indicating U.S. troops on one side and Sioux warriors on the other. In the middle, many soldiers with their heads down, pointing toward the Sioux. Also they found three red stones, a sign that the Sioux expected a great victory. The Arikaras knew that the Sioux medicine was too strong, that Custer and all his troops would be killed. None of the whites, least of all Custer, believed them. By this time Custer smelled blood and was worried only that the Indians would escape.

3

Even before the Sun Dance on Rosebud Creek in June of 1876, many agency Indians, responding to Sitting Bull's invitation earlier that spring to join him for good times and good hunting as well as a good fight, had left the Great Sioux Reservation in western South Dakota for one last fling at the old-time style. Many of them had been on the reservation for eight years, since the Laramie Treaty of 1868. Supposedly, they had given up their weapons and most of their horses when they first came in to the agencies. The government, for its part, was to provide them with commodities for subsistence—beef cattle, pork, flour, coffee, sugar, tobacco, blankets, and clothing—but the corruption among the agents, the suppliers, and the freight contractors was so gross that the Indians had been reduced to a chronic starving condition. The cattle were scrawny things, the pork was usually spoiled, and the other items were either tainted in some way or of such inferior quality as to be almost worthless. And of course there was never enough of any of these annuity goods, spoiled or not. Even if the Indians had been able to keep their weapons in large number, they wouldn't have done much good. The buffalo had virtually disappeared from the Dakotas.

It is small wonder that the reservation Indians were eager to join Sitting Bull and Crazy Horse. Even Red Cloud's son, Jack, left Red Cloud Agency to head west to the hunting grounds of Montana. Others left Spotted Tail Agency, named for the other important peace chief among the Lakotas.

Not all of the young men left the agencies for the pleasures of the hunt and the good times promised them by Sitting Bull. Most of them had spent the most important years of young manhood on the reservation. Now they saw an opportunity to make war, particularly on the Crows, and to steal horses—things they should have been doing all these years they had wasted at the agencies. Although they knew that the government had issued an edict that the "free" Indians were to report to the reservation by January 31 of that year, and had ignored it, none of them could have known they were about to participate in one of the most notorious events in white American history.

To explain the appeal of joining the "free" Indians in Montana it is necessary to contrast their lifestyle with that of the reservation Indians. And to do this, one must speak of the leaders of the two factions.

Red Cloud, after he closed the army forts along the Bozeman Trail prior to 1868, had with many misgivings accepted the major terms of the Laramie Treaty. He saw the handwriting on the wall, which spelled out this: Although he and his warriors had won a significant victory over the whites, such victories in the future would be only temporary—the *wasichus* were coming in great numbers and their firepower would overwhelm anything or anybody who stood in the way. Red Cloud saw this happen, and he was sophisticated enough to attempt to negotiate deals with the whites that would provide a kind of pension policy for his reservation people. Spotted Tail saw things the same way, but he was less effective than Red Cloud and consequently resented the other chief's importance in reservation affairs. After all, Spotted Tail had been made peace chief of all the Lakotas by the whites, but the negotiators paid more attention to Red Cloud's speeches.

Both chiefs had been to Washington and had met the Great Father and other leaders of the white man's government and had been presented with gifts, such as horses and medals and white man's clothing—and money. Both understood the importance of the green paper in the world of their adversaries, but both wanted more and better of the goods promised them by treaty—as well as more money for their people.

Sitting Bull and Crazy Horse, by contrast, wanted nothing from the white government but to be left alone. Sitting Bull had never had anything to do with the whites and their agencies. He and his Hunkpapas were roamers, followers of the hunt, and spent their time in northwestern Dakota Territory, along the Little Missouri River, and in Montana Territory, along the Yellowstone, Powder, Tongue, and Bighorn rivers. Crazy Horse had spent much of his youth among the whites in Nebraska and Wyoming Territory, and he had developed no affection for them. He had even less affection for the "hang around the fort" or "loafer" Indians, a new breed that had been created by the reservation system.

Both chiefs knew that once their Indian people were sucked into the white man's world, they would never be free or self-sufficient again. They also knew that the reservation Indians who were coming to join them for one last fight, one last touch of the old ways, would

A mountain of buffalo skulls. By the late nineteenth century, impoverished Indians collected buffalo bones and sold them for use as fertilizer at 6 cents a ton. *Detroit Public Library*

return to the reservations for the next handout from the government. Nevertheless, they welcomed these families and bands with graciousness. They were also thinking to build up their numbers before the inevitable confrontation with the soldiers.

Although they were expected to stay on the Great Sioux Reservation in South Dakota and leave it only by permission, many Indians came and went as they pleased. This practice was tolerated by the agents only because they knew that the Indians would become more and more dependent on the government now that the buffalo were disappearing. White hide hunters, such as Buffalo Bill Cody, were wiping out the vast herds to supply Northern Pacific railroad builders and restaurants with buffalo meat, as well as to satisfy the market for robes for winter coats, and even bones for fertilizer. The Indians would eventually have to stay on the reservation waiting for the annuities, which were becoming less frequent, less abundant, and of lesser quality. Sitting Bull would have none of this. He chastised the reservation people: "You are fools to make yourselves slaves to a piece of fat bacon."

Eventually it was the white man's greed that led directly to the last Indian wars on the northern plains. The government of President Ulysses S. Grant had been looking for an excuse to put *all* Indians on the reservation once and for all, and they found it in the Black Hills.

The Black Hills, from a distance, look as black as their name—and almost furry. They are surrounded by hundreds of miles of rolling plains, which from a distance seem to be a never-changing tan color. Of course, when you drive through these plains, you become aware of drainages, wet or dry, of higher ridges with stunted pines, of hills and coulees, of small settlements with a convenience store/gas station, post office, grain elevator, a couple of bars, and a few houses sprinkled behind the businesses. From a long way off, from any direction, you see the low irregular black lines of the Black Hills against the horizon, and they offer possibility, even excitement, after such a day's drive. It is not hard to imagine that the Sioux and Cheyennes, coming back from a war party against the Crows, felt the same excitement.

My wife and I made such a drive in 1974 from Missoula to Sturgis, South Dakota, to attend my college roommate's wedding. It was on the return trip several days later that I made my first visit to the Little Bighorn battlefield. In those days, I didn't know the full history of the Black Hills. I knew they were considered sacred to the Lakotas and Cheyennes, I knew that Black Hills gold (which was made into a unique kind of pastel gold jewelry) came from there, and I knew that Mount Rushmore was one of the great tourist attractions of America.

What I didn't know and soon found out was that the Black Hills harbored all kinds of silliness—Flintstone's Bedrock City, Panhandling Jackasses, Shrine to Democracy, The Cosmos, Reptile Gardens, Holy Shrine Wax Museum, Bear Country, and Timber of Ages Petrified Forest, just to name a few. An hour's drive to the north lies the town of Spearfish, famous for killing Christ every summer night in its passion play. Nearby Sturgis has become even more famous as the annual rendezvous point for all the bad bikers in America. For several days in the heat of summer, there are more Harley-Davidsons in Sturgis than in the rest of the free world—all within the shadow of Bear Butte, the birthplace of Crazy Horse.

Not far to the southwest of Sturgis, just inside the Black Hills, are the towns of Deadwood, where Wild Bill Hickok was shot in the back while holding a full house and Calamity Jane made a nuisance of herself, and Lead, home of the Homestake Mine, one of the largest gold mines in the world (which incidentally made William Randolph Hearst a rich man). Farther south you come upon Harney Peak, at 7,242 feet the highest point in South Dakota, named for General William S. Harney, famed old Indian fighter. South of this landmark lies the town of Custer, named for guess who. Custer was, as it happened, the location of one of the last battles between Indians and whites.

On January 21, 1973, Wesley Bad Heart Bull, a Lakota whose ancestor Amos Bad Heart Bull provided much information about the Battle of the Little Bighorn through his ledger art, was stabbed to death by a white service station attendant in a bar in Buffalo Gap, a crossroads midway between Custer and the Pine Ridge Reservation. The attendant was charged with second-degree manslaughter and bailed out of the Custer jail on $5,000 bond. This incident was almost identical to one which occurred in January of 1972, a year earlier. In that case, Raymond Yellow Thunder, a middle-aged Oglala, was beaten to death by a gang of drunken whites in the American Legion parking lot in Gordon, Nebraska. They, like the service station attendant, were charged with second-degree manslaughter, but they were released without paying any bail. It seemed that the Nebraska murderers would go unpunished. But this 1972 killing did not go undetected by Indian people, and in the process, brought the American Indian Movement (AIM) to national prominence. Dennis Banks and Russell Means, the leaders of the movement, organized a caravan of Indians that drove down to Gordon and marched in the streets and demonstrated until local officials were forced to promise that the trial would take place—and that the local police chief would be fired. Two of the killers, brothers by the name of Hare, were subsequently convicted of manslaughter.

This triumph was one of the last in a series of events which catapulted AIM into the public eye. In 1964, a group of Indians landed on and claimed the abandoned Alcatraz Island in San Francisco Bay under a provision of the 1868 treaty; in 1971, AIM members occupied Mount Rushmore in the Black Hills, demanding that the government honor the 1868 treaty, which would mean the return of the Black Hills and all of western South Dakota; in 1972, Aim organized the Trail of Broken Treaties, in which Indians from all parts of the country, in cars, vans, and buses, converged on Washington to occupy the Bureau of Indian Affairs building to call attention to the plight of Indians in America.

But it was the Bad Heart Bull incident which directly touched off the most violent confrontation between Indians and whites in the 1970s. The location was a small creek, Wounded Knee, on the Pine Ridge Reservation in South Dakota, and it occurred almost one hundred years after the Little Bighorn and almost eighty years after the original incident on that creek, the Wounded Knee Massacre, in which Big Foot's band of Ghost Dancers were slaughtered by the United States Army.

To protest the Bad Heart Bull murder, AIM led a caravan to Custer, a town Indians consider one of the most redneck of all in Sioux country, to protest the light manslaughter charge against the gas station attendant, Darold Schmidt, and the low bail. They demanded that the state's attorney charge Schmidt with murder. The state's attorney refused. There was much angry shouting, jostling, threatening. Police and Indians went at each other with fists, clubs, tear gas, and firebombs. By the time it was all over, the Indians had set fire to a couple of police cars and an abandoned building, and several of them, including Russell Means, were arrested.

Shortly thereafter, Means and Dennis Banks led a large group of AIM members to the Pine Ridge Reservation and took over the hamlet of Wounded Knee. They chose that particular reservation because the chairman of the Tribal Council, Dick Wilson, ran a brutal administration, characterized by beatings, even killings, of traditional Indians who protested the corruption of his regime. Wilson's "goon squads" were hated and feared by all but Wilson's supporters. AIM also chose Wounded Knee because that's where in January 1890 the 7th Cavalry, Custer's old troop, which included five officers who had survived the Little Bighorn, murdered three hundred Sioux men, women, and children with little provocation in perhaps the most senseless and heinous crime ever against Indian people. They then threw the frozen corpses into a mass grave. With the last shovelful of dirt, Indian resistance to the white man in America effectively came to an end.

But not quite. AIM had reawakened the consciousness of Indian people, and now, in 1973, at this remote site remembered by Indians as a symbol of the white man's inhumanity, a new battle had been joined.

As the militants proclaimed a new Independent Oglala Nation, President Nixon ordered in heavily armed federal marshals and FBI agents to help the Bureau of Indian Affairs police. They set up roadblocks and laid siege to the new nation, a siege which would last for seventy-one days throughout the cold winter of 1973 and claim gunfire casualties on both sides.

It is said that the militants went too far in their demands—such as the ouster of Dick Wilson, a declaration that all reservations are independent nations, the recognition that western South Dakota as well as five other western states were still Indian territory by treaty. And it is true, if only because the past cannot be undone without the admission that the United States repeatedly, knowingly, violated the 1868 treaty. But it is also true that the Wounded Knee militants were successful in bringing the nation's, and the world's, attention to problems in Indian country. The occupation was covered by all major newspapers and television networks, and the sophisticated AIM leaders controlled them masterfully. They got their message out, and for most Americans the news was not good. Liberals, and even moderates, experienced old-fashioned guilt over what their people did to the Indians of this country—and were still doing. The images of Wilson's cowboy-hatted goon squads, the marshals, and the FBI agents in their jumpsuits, with aviator glasses and automatic weapons, confronting Indian men, women, and children in blue jeans, light jackets, and braids, was not something anybody would soon forget. And the fact that things haven't changed appreciably on the Pine Ridge Reservation, or on any other reservation for that matter, should be a source of continued concern. But it won't be. After the occupation, most of the AIM members drifted off and the government got back to business as usual, which didn't include Indian problems—poverty, substandard housing, unemployment, poor medical care, and social diseases, such as alcoholism and drug addiction. The nation turned its back.

Fifty miles away from Wounded Knee lies the heart of Paha Sapa, the sacred Black Hills, deemed inviolable by treaty, a happy hunting ground that fed a nation's greedy gut a hundred years before.

In the summer of 1874, George Custer led a highly publicized military and scientific expedition into the Black Hills. General Phil Sheridan, commander of the Department of the Missouri, had to think of an excuse to direct such a blatant violation of the 1868 treaty. He was not at a loss. After the fact of planning the operation, he said that the Indians had violated the treaty, first by murdering settlers in Nebraska and then by interfering with the railroads. To make the incursion legal, Sheridan said the purpose of the journey was to establish a fort in the vicinity of the Black Hills, which was permitted under the terms of the treaty. President Grant was thoroughly and enthusiastically behind the expedition.

According to Private Charles Windolph, a German immigrant who not only became the last white survivor of the Little Bighorn to die (he died in 1950) but won a Medal of Honor there as one of Captain Benteen's troopers, it was a major excursion that included ten companies of the 7th Cavalry, two companies of infantrymen, a three-inch artillery piece, two Gatling guns, a detachment of Indian scouts, numerous white guides, interpreters, civilian teamsters, packers and herders, and a sixteen-piece all-German band which every morning played Custer's favorite tunes. In all, around a thousand men, 110 six-mule-team Studebaker wagons, and three hundred beef cattle moved out of Fort Abraham Lincoln in North Dakota. Accompanying the group was a handful of scientists, including the young George Bird Grinnell, son of a wealthy banker, who would later become renowned for his studies of Plains Indians and for his part in establishing Glacier National Park, and at least two practical miners, Horatio Nelson Ross and a man named McKay. Colonel Fred Dent Grant, the President's son, was also present but had no official position and reportedly got "tipsy" on numerous occasions. Custer, a teetotaler, placed him under arrest on one occasion for drunkenness.

The Black Hills were considered sacred by both the Cheyenne and the Sioux. The Lakotas say a man followed the buffalo from Paha Sapa onto the plains and that was the beginning of their tribe. Johnson Holy Rock, an elder in the Lakota tribe, quotes Red Cloud as saying, "A man can be skin and bones when he enters the Hills, and when he comes out the next spring he is fat and slick like the buffalo. He says, that is my food source, that is where my people come from." The Lakotas and Cheyennes traveled many miles from wherever they were on the plains to cut lodgepoles for their tipis and travois and Sun Dance lodges. It is difficult to emphasize too strongly how important, how spiritual, was Paha Sapa to the tribes around them. The Black Hills were the center of their universe, a source of strength and reassurance, especially since the whites came onto the northern plains. And they were off-limits to the whites by treaty. They belonged to the Indians.

And so for the *wasichus* to invade the Black Hills under the guise of a scientific expedition was the ultimate slap in the face to the Indians. According to Windolph, the expedition was like a long picnic: "We'd make great campfires and almost every evening there'd be a band concert. General Custer was mighty proud of our Seventh Regiment band. They were all mounted on white horses and he had them along on all his expeditions and campaigns. They'd never fail to play the regiment's own song 'Garry Owen.' That was an old Irish battle song that Custer adopted for the Seventh's own. . . . We had a mighty fine band, and on the nights when the moon was out and the stars cracking in the sky, and the air was crisp and cool, it was something to stretch out before a big open log fire and listen to the music. Soldiering wasn't half bad those times."

To the Indians, the expedition was by far the biggest instance of the government's string of broken promises. Although they were fighting mad, they weren't mad enough to fight such a large, well-armed force. And so they could only watch helplessly as the whites put the first wagon ruts in their sacred hills. They called the trail the "thieves trail" and Custer the "chief of the thieves."

Although none of the northern Indians claimed to have seen Custer before, most had heard of him. The Southern Cheyennes knew of him, and a few had actually seen him, because of his campaign in Kansas and Oklahoma against them which culminated with the massacre on the Washita. But there were only a handful of Southern Cheyennes on the northern plains. The Lakotas had had a couple of run-ins with him before his expedition through Paha Sapa. Sitting

Members of Custer's 1874 Black Hills expedition, including President Grant's son Fred (at extreme right) and Captain Frederick Benteen (older man in the middle, with his hat at a sharp angle), relaxing. *South Dakota Historical Society*

Custer and his scout Bloody Knife pose next to a grizzly bear that each claimed to have shot during the 1874 Black Hills expedition. *South Dakota Historical Society*

Bull and Crazy Horse had fought him one year earlier, in 1873, on the Yellowstone, although they did not know their opponent was Custer. Both groups called this somewhat mythical figure "Long Hair" and had grudgingly respected him as a fighting man. Not anymore. Now he was merely a thief, like all of the white men who wanted something from the Indians and would get it by thievery or force.

The real purpose of the Custer expedition was to check out rumors, which had been circulating on the frontier for some years, that gold lay in great abundance in the Black Hills. One rumor told of gold nuggets as big as fists caught in the roots of a downed tree. Another rumor had it that when it rained the streams glittered with color. Perhaps the rumors were exaggerated, but the two miners with the expedition did find gold. Virtually every stream they panned showed color, some more than others but all well worth the miners' trouble. Even the soldiers caught the gold fever and were elbow to elbow with the miners at stream's edge.

A group of four reporters, one of them from the *New York Tribune,* whom Custer had brought along for publicity purposes, wrote fervidly of the discovery, some under the simple bold headline "Gold!" A scout by the name of Lonesome Charley Reynolds, who later would die at the Little Bighorn, took the dispatches and rode by night and hid by day through Indian country all the way to Fort Laramie in Wyoming, a distance of over one hundred miles. There the telegraph broadcast the astounding news to the world.

Within a year of the discovery there were fifteen thousand miners in the Black Hills, eleven thousand in Custer alone. By the following year the number jumped to twenty-five thousand, and more were coming; for a time, Deadwood had one of the largest Chinese populations in the United States. Although the miners were there illegally, it was decided that they needed protection, and this was the excuse that the Grant administration needed to make war on the Indians who would not come in to the reservation.

But first the whites tried to buy the Black Hills. Almost all of 1875 was given over to negotiations. Red Cloud, Spotted Tail, and the other reservation chiefs made a trip to Washington, supposedly to discuss the sale of the Black Hills. The negotiations became a circus of offers, demands, counteroffers, counterdemands. It was unclear who was in charge of either side of the negotiations. The Indians thought they were dealing with the Great Father, but Grant very reluctantly spoke with them for only a few minutes—and not about the Black Hills. Many of the whites thought Red Cloud and Spotted

Tail spoke for all Indians. Apparently the white negotiators had not read the 1868 treaty very carefully.

Often the negotiations took strange turns. In one instance, the commission offered the Indians $25,000 if they would give up their hunting rights in Nebraska. In another, the whites agreed to look into matters of fraud at the agencies before the Indians would begin to seriously negotiate the sale of the Black Hills. At one point both President Grant and Secretary of the Interior Columbus Delano suggested that the Indians give up not only the Black Hills and the unceded hunting territory in Montana, but the reservation as well. They thought it would be in the Indians' best interest to move south to the Indian Territory in Oklahoma.

Red Cloud did not distinguish himself with either the whites or the Indians in these negotiations. He was recalcitrant and deliberately obtuse and often demanded things the whites would not give. The other chiefs became impatient with him, puzzled by his behavior, and angry as they saw their opportunity slipping away. The Washington visit ended with virtually nothing resolved, except for the sale of the Nebraska hunting rights. Meanwhile, Red Cloud's standing with both the reservation and the "free" Indians had been seriously compromised.

On September 20, 1875, the Sioux Commission came to the reservation to continue negotiations for the Black Hills. This time the commissioners were serious. And so were the Indians—up to a point. The Indians by this time had been factionalized into three groups: those older reservation Indians, led by Red Cloud and Spotted Tail, who wanted to sell the Hills for a fair price; other more militant reservation Indians, led by Young Man Afraid, who feared that giving up the Black Hills would lead to the inevitable relinquishment of the hunting grounds in Montana, which would leave them with nothing but a reservation governed by corrupt agents; and finally the "free" Indians, called "hostiles" by the government, led by Sitting Bull and Crazy Horse, who simply wanted the whites out of their lives and territory for good.

After much folderol, which included continuing jealousy and rivalry between Red Cloud and Spotted Tail, a spot was picked for the meeting—eight miles from Red Cloud Agency (neither chief would go to the other's agency). The commissioners, along with their interpreters and 120 cavalry soldiers, set up a large fly to shelter themselves from the sun and waited. Gradually a few Indian leaders began to show up. Red Cloud, true to form, stayed out for another day.

The Treaty of 1868 stated that three-fourths of all adult male Indians had to vote on any changes in the treaty. At first the commissioners were afraid that not enough Lakota men would attend the negotiations, but they eventually found themselves surrounded by fifteen thousand Indians, which made them more than a little nervous.

Around noon another incident occurred which made them fear for their lives. Two hundred mounted armed warriors swept down from the hills to the council site, whipped their horses into a gallop, and circled the astounded white men. Dust hung in the air so thick they could barely see beyond the fly. No sooner had these warriors formed themselves in a line facing the commissioners than another group, then another and another, repeated the performance. By the time the display ended, there were seven thousand of these mounted warriors, whooping, waving their weapons, and shaking their fists.

Suddenly the lines parted and Little Big Man, a member of Crazy Horse's camp, rode up to the commissioners, stark naked except for a flowing warbonnet. He had a rifle in one hand and shells in the other. He said he had come to kill the white men.

Young Man Afraid and a small detail of Indian policemen managed to disarm Little Big Man and hustle him away, but his performance had excited the other young men. They became more threatening, feinting charges at the white men, running their horses away and racing back, shouting threats, brushing up against the cavalry troopers. Except for their war paint and a few items of finery, they were stripped for war, and it looked like the parley would be over before it got started for lack of commissioners.

But again Young Man Afraid (who was dead set against selling the Black Hills) rode forward. He reminded the warriors that such an action as they were proposing would bring the army down on them with deadly force. Their wives and children would pay a heavy price for wiping out this small band of whites. He told them to go away and think about this. Although the young warriors still made threatening gestures, they respected Young Man Afraid as a chief, a brave warrior who came from a long line of chiefs. They grumbled among themselves but they left.

What these young men did turned out to be invaluable to the Lakotas. They caused a few days' delay in the negotiations, which allowed the rank-and-file Indians to discuss and rethink their positions on the sale of the Black Hills. Even the leaders of the negotiations became less inclined to give the commissioners what they asked.

But the talks resumed on September 27, 28, and 29, led by Red Cloud and Spotted Tail. If the commissioners thought they were dealing with ignorant savages, the two chiefs disabused them of this notion in a hurry. Spotted Tail, who upon returning from Washington earlier in the year had gone into the Black Hills with his Indian agent and had set a price of $7 million on them, spoke with the air of a business tycoon: "As long as we live on this earth we will expect pay. We want to leave the amount with the President at interest forever. I want to live on the interest of my money. The amount must be so large that the interest will support us."

Red Cloud left nothing to chance:

. There have been six nations raised, and I am the seventh, and I want seven generations ahead to be fed. . . . These hills out here to the northwest we look upon as the head chief of the land. My intention was that my children should depend on these hills for the future. I hoped that we should live that way always hereafter. That was my intention. I sit here under the treaty [of 1868] which was to extend for thirty years. I want to put the money that we get for the Black Hills at interest among the whites, to buy with the interest wagons and cattle. We have much small game yet that we can depend on for the future, only I want the Great Father to buy guns and ammunition with the interest so we can shoot the game. For seven generations to come I want our Great Father to give us Texan steers for our meat. I want the Government to issue for me hereafter, flour and coffee, and sugar and tea, and bacon, the very best kind, and cracked corn and beans, and rice and dried apples, and saleratus and tobacco, and soap and salt, and pepper, for the old people. I want a wagon with a span of horses, and six yoke of working cattle for my people. I want a sow and a boar, and cow and bull, and a sheep and a ram, and a hen and a cock, for each family. I am an Indian, but you try to make a white man out of me. I want some white men's houses at this agency to be built for the Indians. I have been into white people's houses, and I have seen nice black bedsteads and chairs, and I want that kind of furniture given to my people. . . . I want the Great Father to furnish me a saw-mill which I may call my own. I want a mower and a scythe for my people. Maybe you white people think that I ask too much from the Government, but I think those hills extend

Red Cloud, war leader of the Oglala Sioux, during the Bozeman Trail war.
Smithsonian Institution

Red Cloud on a trip to the east, after he had settled on the reservation.
Cumberland County Historical Society

clear to the sky—maybe they go above the sky, and that is the reason I ask for so much. . . ."

Red Cloud may have had the direction wrong, but his notion of the value of the Black Hills to the whites was right on. By 1975, according to historian Stephen Ambrose, the Homestake Mining Company had taken approximately $1.5 billion worth of gold out of the bowels of the Black Hills.

Of course, the Sioux Commission, which had a fair degree of leeway in the negotiations, thought $7 million plus Red Cloud's perks was far too high a price to pay for a piece of land that the whites would eventually get anyway. And so the talks petered out with the matter unresolved.

An interesting sidelight to these negotiations involves a custom that had prevailed in white-Indian relations in the west since the time of Lewis and Clark—the giving of presents. Many students of this period of history insist that had the commissioners brought along presents, they would have had a better chance to negotiate the sale of the Black Hills. There can be no doubt that Indians liked presents. G. P. Beauvais, a longtime Sioux trader and onetime negotiator, said that "if a great feast had been made for all the chiefs and an immense pile of blankets and other presents had been placed in the middle of the council circle, they would have come to terms long ago." This sounds a bit too simple, but it was a clear display of disrespect on the commissioners' part to omit such an important part of the ceremony. On the other hand, it may have been a sign of the Grant administration's growing impatience with and contempt for these savages who stood directly in the path of an expanding frontier.

Why did the United States of America place such importance on the acquisition of the Black Hills? Why was its government willing to stop at nothing to get them? As one might suspect, the answers lay far to the east of Paha Sapa.

Prior to the Civil War, the American economy was primarily based on rural, agricultural areas of production—cotton and tobacco in the south, dairy farms, produce farms, and timber in the north, and wheat, an important crop in the west as well as the north. Many of the people in these areas were nearly self-sufficient. The things they could not grow they traded for, or bought with dollars that they earned on their crops. Some got rich, some comfortable, some lived a subsistence type of life. But all were less dependent on, less vulnerable to, the ups and down of a national economy.

After the Civil War, a different type of economy began to evolve. Industries directly and indirectly related to the war effort gathered steam in the cities, and rural people, many of whose farms had been consumed by the war, began to flock to these urban areas to provide the necessary labor. Immigrants saw new opportunities in America and began to sail off to New York, Boston, and the other industrializing cities. Soon America had been transformed from a nation driven by agricultural products to one powered by large factories and service industries. A national economy had been born.

And it grew. Farsighted men saw a long way down the road, and they saw expansion, growth, prosperity. They saw land-grant railroads spanning the nation all the way to the West Coast, they saw the development of large steam engines which could run whole assembly lines, they saw the proliferation of banking empires, newspapers, and mercantilism. All they needed to do was expand west, to bring the whole country under one economic roof. The entrepreneurs of the Gilded Age, robber barons like Jay Cooke, saw unprecedented money-making opportunities not only in the industrialized east but in the untapped resources of the west.

Government, anxious to establish economic prosperity after the disastrous war, allowed these captains of industry to run roughshod over existing restraints. Graft and corruption became an integral part of the system. Grant's administration was so riddled with under-the-table dealings that it scarcely functioned for the good of the people, much less efficiently. As social historian Richard Slotkin puts it, "Hardly a week passed that did not see some new scandal revealed, implicating cabinet officers, senators, members of the president's family in acts of bribery, influence peddling, and profiteering."

The Northern Pacific Railroad became the symbol for the age. Pushing across the plains from Duluth to the mouth of the Columbia River, it was to establish an agrarian economy, claimed Cooke, which would feed the hungry industrial cities. Although the Southern Pacific and Union Pacific railroads had already been completed and trains were running on a regular schedule, it was the northern plains that appeared to have the greatest potential for establishing a paradise on earth. Or so went the rhapsodic line of Cooke. (Custer, after his expedition into the Black Hills, became just as effusive as Cooke, writing about the "Garden of the West" where flowers grew so luxuriantly that the soldiers could pluck them without dismounting from the saddle.)

In actuality, Cooke had borrowed heavily from American and

European investors to build his railroad, and he needed settlers to take his train west, buy land from his railroad, establish communities and farms, and ship their produce back by railroad. He needed a land rush, and he needed it immediately. He turned to his friends in government—and to the newspapers. Publishers such as August Belmont of the *World* and James Gordon Bennett of the *Herald* moved in the same elite social circles in New York as Cooke. They took up his cause, providing editorials promoting the west and the railroads. In return, Cooke took out large advertisements and prospectuses in their papers to create the impression that hordes of settlers were streaming west from the eastern United States and Europe. But first he had to lay track through hostile country.

It was this desperate push to finish the railroad that provided an opportunity for Custer to meet his future adversaries on the Little Bighorn for the first time in 1873. The 7th Cavalry under Custer helped to provide protection to the Northern Pacific surveyors along the Yellowstone River in Montana. Although it was mostly a lark for Custer, who spent most of his time shooting buffalo, antelope, elk, wolves, foxes, deer, geese, ducks, prairie chickens, and sage hens, it was serious business for his commander, Colonel David S. Stanley, and the surveyors. Stanley once placed Custer under arrest for riding far from the surveyors and their infantry escort, leaving them open and vulnerable to an Indian attack. A high-placed friend interceded and Custer was released to continue his romping.

On August 4, 1873, Custer was once again far ahead of the rest of the military escort when he was attacked by a large force of Indians led by Crazy Horse and Sitting Bull. It was only the impetuousness of the young warriors and their lack of firearms that enabled the 7th Cavalry to come out of the skirmish relatively unharmed. But the fighting was close enough for Crazy Horse and Custer to look each other over, if they had known who the other was. Crazy Horse was not particularly noticeable—he was slight and light-skinned, and he did not adorn himself with finery. Neither he nor the other Indians recognized "Long Hair," just as they didn't later at the Little Bighorn. It has become part of the Custer myth that all the Indians on the northern and southern plains knew him on sight and called him "Son of the Morning Star." It was only the Arikaras, and possibly the Crows, both allies, who called him that. Interestingly, Crazy Horse's first look at Custer was of a white man in his underwear and socks. Custer had been napping in the warm afternoon when the surprise attack occurred.

In the early fall of 1873, the European investors had had enough

Custer with Indian scouts, including Bloody Knife (pointing at map), during an 1873 expedition to the Yellowstone River in Montana Territory. *Burlington Northern Railroad*

of Cooke's chicanery and demanded their investments back. On September 18, Cooke's bank collapsed. His railroad immediately went bankrupt. Then the stock market crashed—and the Panic of 1873 was on. George Bird Grinnell, whose father's firm had been devastated, said the crash "came on out of a clear sky." Farm prices fell drastically, industries went bankrupt, workers were thrown out of work, and a long, hard depression followed. It was to last for four years.

With the economy in ruins, and the country reeling from unemployment that reached 20 percent in the cities, and farmers having to give up their farms and move to the cities, and crime on the rise as desperation grew, the nation's leaders searched for solutions. Many of the industrialists, as well as farmers' groups and labor leaders, wanted more paper money printed to rejuvenate the economy. Grant's conservative administration rejected that idea, preferring to keep to the gold standard. But there was not enough gold to allow the economy to maintain the status quo, much less grow.

And that desperate need led to the Custer expedition into the Black Hills. It is difficult to imagine in this age of trillions of dollars' worth of debt that such a move would cure this nation's economic woes. And in truth, the gold in the Black Hills did not provide an absolute panacea; but the acquisition of this land would lead to the subjugation of the northern plains tribes and lead to the final opening of the west.

So, after the negotiations with Red Cloud and the other leaders in 1875 failed, the way was free to use force—which led to one of the most shameful episodes in American history.

General Phil Sheridan had used the excuse of Indian troubles to order the military expedition into the Black Hills. His official reason was to establish a fort in the vicinity to control the Indians; unofficially, it was to find out if the rumors of gold were true.

Now that the negotiations were over and the miners were still coming, it was decided that they needed protection. The Indians who were to blame for all the lawlessness were those "free" Indians in the unceded territory in Montana. And the solution to this problem was relatively simple on the face of it: to capture the "hostiles" by force and drive them to the reservation. That the occupation of the Black Hills by the miners was a clear violation of the 1868 treaty mattered only slightly. The government only needed the lame excuse of the miners' *being there* to take action against the Indians.

And so, on December 6, President Grant issued the order that all the Sioux and Cheyennes were to be on the reservation by January 31, 1876, or be declared at war with the United States. The final justification for the declaration was that the Sioux were harassing the Crows in Montana. That the government felt the need to protect the Crows too at this late date was opportunistic, at best.

And Sitting Bull and Crazy Horse, instead of coming in from the cold, issued their invitation to the reservation Indians. "We will have good times!" said Sitting Bull.

4

O n a late June day of 1974, less than a hundred years after the gathering of the tribes, my wife and I were eating lunch in the back of our Volkswagen bus at the Custer Battlefield National Monument. The sky was a cloudless pale blue, and the wind which buffeted the bus from time to time was hot and dry. We had parked in the shade of a medium-sized evergreen tree, one of a grove of medium-sized evergreens planted on a strip between the parking lot and the national cemetery with its orderly rows of gray grave markers. These stones mark the graves of veterans of many wars—including the First and Second World Wars, the Korean War, and the Vietnam War—since the Battle of the Little Bighorn. But other stones, bone-white, are scattered all over the battlefield, marking the original burial sites of the Custer dead, about fifty of them closely grouped on Last Stand Hill. Each of the simple white stones reads, U.S. SOLDIER, 7TH CAVALRY, FELL HERE, JUNE 25, 1876, with the exception of the officers' stones, which are inscribed with their names. The remains of the enlisted soldiers were later collected from these locations and moved to Custer Hill, where they were buried in a large trench at the base of the obelisk. (Recently, the bones of an unknown 7th Cavalry soldier were found buried in the bank of the Little Bighorn River. On June 23, 1991, 115 years later, he was reburied in the national cemetery with military honors, including a rifle volley from his old enemies, the Northern Cheyennes.) Interestingly, the remains of the officers were disinterred in 1877 and shipped east for reburial. Only one officer, a Lieutenant John J. Crittenden, remains buried where he fell—at the request of his parents.

As we ate our sandwiches and drank our pop, trying to digest all that we had just seen and heard at the visitor center, we were interrupted by a large voice outside the open sliding door: "Do you know this is a national monument?" We looked up and saw an older wellfed man in the green-and-gray uniform of the National Park Service. He had one hand on top of his Smokey hat and the other extended as though he wanted to point at us but thought better of it. "Do you know this is a national monument?" he repeated. I said yes. "Then you know you're not allowed to eat here." Why not, I asked. He looked at me, and I could tell he thought I must be crazy. There could be no other explanation for my question. "Because," he said, "this is a national monument." My wife and I understood immediately and put down our sandwiches and pop and stared shamefacedly at the floor of the bus. This caused him to soften a little. "Look around, enjoy yourselves, but after this pay a little attention to the rules." We thanked him for pointing out our sacrilege, and when he turned away to attend to other duties I gave him the finger. I was young then.

That was my first visit to the Little Bighorn battleground, and, in truth, it didn't do very much for me. Like any kid in America I had grown up with the legend of Custer's Last Stand. I had seen the movies, notably *They Died with Their Boots On,* starring Errol Flynn as Custer and Anthony Quinn as Crazy Horse. I had read about Custer's Last Stand in history books and comic books. I can't think of a hero who has taught kids more about dying in mock battles than General George Armstrong Custer. I had even been Custer myself once, standing on a small sandy hill in the backyard when I was six or seven, suddenly clutching my chest when one of the "Indians" shot me, falling and tumbling down the hill to lie motionless while the battle raged on about me. Of course, we didn't really know who Custer was—he was just one of those mythical figures like Robin Hood and Davy Crockett that get passed from generation to generation.

What made this particular reenactment different was that it was played out in the town of Browning on the Blackfeet Reservation in Montana and the "Indians" *were* Indians. I, Custer, was an Indian too, a member of the Blackfeet tribe. We also played cowboys and Indians, no particular cowboys and no particular Indians, just a lot of galloping around on make-believe horses, dodging from house to tree, shooting our cap pistols from behind garbage cans. The fact that I was a "breed," part Indian and part white, did not determine which role I would play. Or maybe it did. I suppose I could play either role with validity. But nobody seemed to find it strange that a little "full-blood" kid could play a cowboy emptying his cap gun at an advancing wave of Indians.

We were influenced by the movies we saw in those days. This was in the late forties and early fifties, and the Browning theater showed more than its share of cowboy-and-Indian movies, cowboy-without-Indian movies, and settler-and-cavalry-and-Indian movies. It was this last formula that interests me now, because it elicited the strangest response from the audience. It should be kept in mind that virtually the entire audience for these movies was made up of Blackfeet Indians, ranging through all ages, but mostly teenagers and little kids like me. The theater would be dark and fairly quiet throughout most of the movie, as the settlers arrived in Indian country, put up their cabin and barn, turned their cattle out onto the far-as-you-could-see grasslands, hugged each other, fought off a few curious but menacing Indians, and continued to work the land in a responsible fashion. But as the Indian problem worsened, maybe a few cattle, or even a neighbor, killed, the audience began to grow restless and tense. And eventually in the big showdown, the settler (or maybe a group of settlers) had to fight a gigantic mob of Indians. As their wives reloaded and the children attempted to put out fires caused by flaming arrows, the men emptied their guns out windows, doors, through the roof where a menacing savage had crawled, apparently to attempt a descent down the chimney. But soon it became clear that they were fighting a lost cause. One or two of them had been killed or wounded, the ammunition was running out, the cabin was burning out of control, the wives and children were praying or singing "Nearer My God to Thee." Suddenly one of the men, in that eerie silence that always occurred when the Indians were regrouping for the final onslaught, would say, "Did you hear that?" and the audience would tune up their ears. And sure enough, it was the faint notes of a bugle blowing "Charge," and the camera would pick up a cloud of dust, a glint of steel, an American flag, and then it would be on the face of a furiously riding Errol Flynn, John Wayne, Randolph Scott, or Joel McCrea, grim and sweaty under a sweat-stained white hat with its crossed sabers, and the next shot would be of a large number of cavalry troopers, the thunder of hoofs growing deafening—and the audience would cheer! Just like thousands of audiences all across America, the audience would cheer this lovely spectacle of these men in blue atop their sweat-streaked but beautiful horses, stretched flat out, bugle blaring, guidon whipping straight behind them. And why not? These guys were going to rescue the poor beleaguered families, and in the process, give the savage miscreants the beating of their lives. And that's exactly what they did.

It was only after the cheering stopped and the lights came up that one saw that all these faces smiling in relief were Indian faces. In those days not many Indians cared that they were rooting against themselves. The Indians in the film had been portrayed as the very embodiment of evil, and Hollywood had staked its existence on the notion that whipping the forces of evil (Indians) made people feel good, even Indians, who would pay their money and eat their popcorn in anticipation of the happy ending, and when it came it was like the satisfaction of whipping the boys in the next town in basketball.

It took the consciousness-raising in the 1970s and 1980s by activists and traditionalists for many Indians to really notice the perversion of Indians rooting against Indians. And it was only during this time that Hollywood made a couple of blockbuster efforts to portray Indians sympathetically, as people. I remember watching *Little Big Man* (1970) with awe, for not only was Custer portrayed as a vainglorious fool (which he was not), but the Indians, the Sioux and Cheyennes, were human beings—they made love, had babies, had strong family and tribal ties; they worked for a living and lived well within their environment. The point of the interaction between whites and Indians was not how tragic it was that Custer and his troops rode to their deaths but how tragically the Indians, whose tribal names were invariably a version of "the human beings" or "the people," were treated during that period. It is a well-known propaganda tactic to reduce your enemy to "animals," rats, mangy dogs, snakes. And the United States government, the army, and the media were not above using such a tactic against the Indians. And they were very successful. "Nits make lice," and therefore it was perfectly okay to kill not only adults but their children as well. They were all less than human.

Little Big Man accomplished the feat of humanizing Indians by depicting individuals living in a society, with its own special structure, mores, and values. It succeeded by showing the variousness of the individuals within that society. The other major film about Indians, from a more recent period, was *Dances with Wolves,* which on the surface seemed much like Little Big Man in that it portrayed a plains society of American Indians, its day-to-day life, its ceremonies, its concerns. But the main group of Indians in the film, the Sioux, were too homogenized, too nice. One would think that the Sioux were a peace-loving group of people who only fought when their enemies, in this case the Pawnees and the whites, pushed them to the brink. The fact is that the Sioux were the most numerous and powerful tribe on the northern plains, and they thought nothing of removing other Indians from their traditional territories by force. Black Hawk, a Lakota warrior, explained it: "These lands once belonged to the Kiowas and the Crows, but we whipped those nations out of them, and in this we did what the white men do when they want the lands of Indians." He might have mentioned many other tribes—Pawnees, Arikaras, Mandans, Hidatsas, Iowas, Omahas, and others—who were whipped out of their lands by the Sioux. The Sioux did not forge alliances with other tribes, with the exception of the Cheyennes and the Arapahos, with whom they intermarried.

But the main problem of *Dances with Wolves* is the homogeneity, the interchangeability, of the Indian characters. Graham Green is fine as Kicking Bird and Rodney Grant does a good job as the rebellious Wind in His Hair, but the other Indians were so much background in their buckskins and robes, in their clean camp, even in dramatic scenes such as the feast after the buffalo hunt. Too much camera time is spent loving Kevin Costner's face. It is also worth pointing out that Costner's character, Lieutenant Dunbar, falls in love with the only other white—a captive woman with wildly teased hair and a thick tongue—in Indian country. It almost seems that Costner kept a shrewd eye out for what America would want (and wouldn't want) in an Indian movie. That Costner did create a few temporary jobs for a few Sioux Indians should be recognized. That *Dances with Wolves* created a lot of false hopes that more movies would be made in Indian country should also be recognized. In the flush of the Academy Awards triumph, in which *Dances with Wolves* won every important Oscar available, Costner and screenwriter Michael Blake professed their immense love for Indians and virtually predicted a steady stream of feature films about Indians, and involving Indians in the production, because of their success. With very few exceptions, it hasn't happened.

In truth, I didn't know much about the participants in the Battle of the Little Bighorn that day in 1974 when my wife and I were caught red-handed eating lunch at the battlefield site. I had certainly heard of Sitting Bull, Crazy Horse, and Custer, and names like Rain in the Face, Gall, Reno, and Benteen seemed familiar, probably from my moviegoing youth, but I didn't really know much about the Sioux, the Cheyennes, the Crows, and the soldiers of the 7th Cavalry. Furthermore, I didn't know *why* the battle occurred. I knew that it had to do with whites moving west—the infamous Manifest Destiny—to claim the lands that the Indians occupied. I knew that the soldiers had been sent to the frontier to protect the whites, to tame the Indians. But I didn't know about the financial collapse of America in 1873, the desperation of the railroad tycoons to move settlers and material west on their new trains, the discovery of gold in the Black Hills in 1874. I didn't know that the Indian "problem" on the plains began in the 1860s and that Red Cloud, the Sioux chief, had successfully (for the moment in historical time) closed the Bozeman Trail and negotiated a decent treaty with the whites in 1868.

All I really knew in 1974 was that a large number of Indians had come together at this spot and had whipped the United States Army.

So why was a white man in a military-style uniform telling me I couldn't eat lunch here? Shouldn't this have been an Indian monument dedicated to all those brave souls who fought off an enemy attack and in the process protected their wives and children and old ones from great harm? Shouldn't an Indian be able to feast in peace and savor one of the few victories by Indians over whites?

Custer Battlefield National Monument. Some say it is the only national monument in America named for the loser. But where is the monument recognizing the bravery of the Indians who fought and died there?

Things have changed. In June 1991, Congress voted to rename the battlefield the Little Bighorn Battlefield National Monument. And as soon as the political bickering in Congress ends and a design is picked, there will be a permanent monument recognizing the Indians. One hundred fifteen years later, almost to the day, there was an official recognition that the Indians were human beings, not simply "hostiles," not simply obstacles to be overcome. It goes without saying that the name change and the erection of the Indian monument met with fierce opposition. One of Montana's two congressmen (now reduced to one because of population readjustment), Ron Marlenee, fought tooth and nail to prevent such heresies. The Custer Battlefield Association was strongly opposed. Custer buffs all over the country weighed in on the side of bigotry.

Happily, Marlenee was defeated in a runoff with Montana's other congressman, Pat Williams, in the recent general election, the Battlefield Association was not successful in influencing the congressional vote, and the Custer buffs will have to learn to live with the changes.

On my first visit, the official monument, a blocky obelisk bearing the names of the fallen soldiers, and the visitor center were the most significant features on the landscape. A road led past the center, past the obelisk, and on for another mile or two. Now the road has been extended the five miles or so to Reno Hill, where Major Marcus A. Reno and Captain Frederick W. Benteen and their troops were held under siege for a day and a half after Custer's soldiers were killed. From here one can look to the east to the Wolf Mountains, to the Crow's Nest, where Custer's scouts, Crows and Arikaras, first saw the immense encampment along the Little Bighorn. Custer couldn't see it—even with a spyglass offered by one of the scouts. Another scout told Lieutenant Varnum, Custer's chief of scouts, to "look for worms." That would be the immense horse herd grazing on the west hills above the valley. The scouts could also see smoke rising from where the lodges would have been. But the lodges themselves were hidden by stands of trees and a tall embankment. Finally they convinced Custer that there was a camp there and it was the very encampment of Sioux and Cheyennes they had ridden hundreds of miles to attack. Custer trusted these scouts and agreed that the 7th Cavalry had finally reached their destination.

What the scouts saw from the Crow's Nest was a wide green valley marking the course of a meandering river called the Little Bighorn by the *wasichus*. Many Indian tribes, including the Crows, Lakotas, and Cheyennes, knew this river as the Greasy Grass. The river course was flanked by cottonwoods, and the valley was, or probably had been, covered with many types of native grasses and bushes. The thousands of horses had probably grazed it down to virtually nothing in the earlier days of the encampment. On either side of the river valley, green-hued hills rose up and rolled away to the skyline. Even in late June the hills in that part of the country maintain a spring color. It is only in July and August that the hills turn the golden tan that one associates with eastern Montana. So it must have been a very peaceful, lovely valley that Custer gazed down on.

Now only the hills and the cottonwoods along the river look much the same as they did to Custer and his scouts. The valley has been leveled, seeded into alfalfa, bluejoint grass, some grain, all irrigated. Ranch buildings in various states of repair are scattered throughout the valley, sheltered by cottonwoods, Russian olives, poplars, and willows along the nearby irrigation ditches. Many of the ranches have small dome-shaped structures made with willow frames covered by blankets and quilts out behind the buildings. Sweat lodges. This is now the Crow Reservation, a reward bestowed on the Crows for their service to the government during that period of conquest. To be fair, this *was* Crow country until the Sioux and Cheyennes beat them out of it. The Treaty of 1851 had given the Crows all of the land west of the Powder River to the headwaters of the Yellowstone River. The Crows knew that the only way they could get their country back was by throwing in with the whites. And it has worked out for them. The Crow Reservation is one of the more prosperous reservations in Montana, while the adjoining Northern Cheyenne Reservation is one of the poorest. (By most standards, both reservations—all reservations except those that offer gambling—are doing poorly in spite of government paternalism.) It has been a tender point with the Cheyennes and Sioux that the battlefield site, a popular attraction visited by hundreds of thousands of American and foreign tourists each year, is located on the Crow Reservation. But the Crows themselves have not found a way to take advantage of this serendipitous arrangement. There are two trading posts across Highway 212 from the entrance to the battlefield. Although both do a nice business during the tourist season, it is unclear how much of this profit goes into the Crow coffers. A very large motel complex, built not too many years ago by the Crow tribe, sprawls on the edge of Interstate 90, abandoned, vandalized, and falling down.

Interstate 90, which runs the length of the Little Bighorn valley, is the most intrusive element on this historical landscape. There is a railroad track alongside it, but the track has been there for years and years and has managed to blend in by circumstance of longevity. A visitor hardly notices it, and the periodic freight trains remind one that the railroads became a part of the wild west early on. But Interstate 90 is a long double strip of bleak concrete that parallels the battlefield less than a mile away at any given point. In one place it is built over the skirmish line set up by Major Reno after his famous charge into ignominy. In other places it cuts through the outer edges of the Indians' enormous village. In one sense it makes travelers and tourists on their way from Chicago to Seattle a part of history for a few seconds.

At the time of my first visit in 1974, visitors were few and far between, but many of today's tourists turn off at the suggestion of large green freeway signs, drive the half mile east on 212 to the entrance to the monument, and park either in the parking lot or along the access road, wherever they can find room. Today, motor homes as long as battleships crowd the parking areas. Tourists in blue jeans and cowboy boots, brightly colored and lettered shorts and T-shirts, mill around the parking lot, some going to the visitor center, others leaving, still others bypassing the visitor center to walk up to the top of Last Stand Hill, where Custer and the troopers under his direct command perished under a rain of arrows. The moods of the visitors vary. Some are resolutely upbeat, caught up in the carnival atmosphere of large numbers of people, making jokes about arrow shirts and Sitting Bull's tonsorial parlor (haircuts, two bits); others are solemnly awestruck, as though this were a sacred place, sort of a Notre Dame under the Big Sky; others still are downright grim, and these are the hardest to figure out. Are they grim because of what happened to Custer, or because of what happened to the Indians before and after this minor victory?

Languages you might hear around the visitor center include French, Dutch, German, Japanese, Spanish, Danish, Lakota, Salish, Navajo. Tourists come in large numbers from Europe and Japan, sometimes traveling hundreds of miles on tour buses from the nearest large cities. Indians come from all over America—many on the powwow circuit, a series of summer celebrations on reservations all over the west—because this site represents a moment of glory for Indian people and they can stand on hallowed ground walked on and ridden over by some of the most noble "hostiles" ever assembled in Indian country. It makes Indian people proud to point out to their sons and daughters and grandchildren that here something good happened. It suspends for an hour or two all the bad things.

Interpretive lectures are conducted every half hour or so by park rangers on the veranda of the visitor center. Often these rangers will dress up in the long johns and blue wool pants that the troopers wore on that hot, one-hundred-degree day. Often they will display one of the .45 caliber Springfield single-shot carbines that the troopers used—very ineffectually in the close combat. They will point out the markers where Custer and his troops fell on Last Stand Hill. They will talk about Calhoun Ridge, where the soldiers panicked (although they will not use the word "panic"); Medicine Tail Coulee, where Custer did or did not try to ford the river to get at the village; Weir's Point, four to five miles to the southeast, where Benteen and other officers looked this way and saw what they thought was a cloud of dust but weren't sure; the Reno/Benteen Hill beyond Weir Point, where the defeated Reno and the fresh but tardy Benteen managed to outlast the Indian sharpshooters who were picking them off one by one. And finally they will point down to the cottonwood-lined Little Bighorn, where the village was said to have stretched for three miles. Unfortunately, from the visitor center's vantage point, it is difficult to imagine the village or the people in it. Tourists will interrupt occasionally to ask questions that they hope are intelligent. "Was Sitting Bull really a chief, or just a medicine man?" "Is that really Custer's jockstrap in there? Was he wearing it that fateful day?" "Was Reno really a coward? Didn't he get court-martialed later for window-peeking?" Yes, he did. And the canned rap goes on until finally the tourists are left to go into the visitor center, into the bookshop where *Bury My Heart at Wounded Knee* is not sold. They can buy approved "as told to" accounts by Indians who were there. And they can find any number of books on Custer, on military strategy, on the Indian "problem." They can buy posters, reproductions of the famous Anheuser-Busch painting of the Last Stand, maps. They can go downstairs and watch a twenty-minute movie which essentially reiterates what the park ranger told them on the veranda. And finally they can wander into the museum wing, where they will see buckskin outfits worn by Plains Indians (as well as a white buckskin suit similar to one worn by General Custer), military uniforms, weapons from both sides, old photographs of the period, some of the battlefield, and finally, Custer's jockstrap.

The road that winds from the squat cinder-block visitor center to the Reno-Benteen siege site is interesting in that you are driving slowly over plains country that would normally be missed by the tourist in a hurry. Here you see the tough grasses, the sagebrush, and the almost startling clumps of yucca along the roadside. From Custer Ridge you see the ravines that look almost gentle from the valley floor, but here are as deep and ominous as they were on that June day in 1876. If it weren't for the other cars and motor homes crawling along the paved road, you could almost imagine yourself riding a horse, along with the other troopers, and wishing you were back home in North Dakota, or New York, or Ireland, or Germany, where many of the soldiers came from. All around, scattered in clumps, are the white stones where the soldiers fell. One marker, different from the others, is right along the roadside between Custer and Calhoun ridges. It is easy to miss, because it is so near and your eyes are accustomed to looking into the distance. But it is the only marker that shows the location where an Indian was killed, a Southern Cheyenne leader named Lame White Man. Lame White Man was killed by his

Sioux allies, who mistook him for a Crow scout. Another marker is so far in the distance that you might miss it too. But if you look far to the east from Calhoun Ridge you will see it, all by itself, near a barbed-wire boundary fence. There is a story attached to it, a story not too old, maybe apocryphal. It concerns a park ranger, an Indian man, who pointed out the marker to a group of tourists. "See that stone way over there? They say that one of the soldiers almost got away. He was running hell bent for leather when an Indian rode him down and killed him. If he'd have just got over that barbed-wire fence, he'd have made it." According to the story, the ranger was fired for making fun.

As you wind down from Calhoun Ridge, you see off to your right Greasy Grass Ridge. Here the Indians pinned the soldiers down with long-range shooting, while hundreds of other Indians were crawling through the long grasses, sage, and yucca near Deep Ravine to get near enough to the soldiers on Last Stand Hill to leap up and surprise them, a tactic that worked perfectly. It is worth mentioning because the Plains Indians do not get enough credit for such strategic moves on the battlefield.

Eventually the road descends to a point near the river where Medicine Tail Coulee, a dry coulee except during spring runoff and violent rainstorms, empties into the Little Bighorn. Some historians hypothesize that Custer and his troops attempted to ford the river here to get into the encampment. Others say that only two out of the five companies came down to look for a ford—or to draw fire to divert the Indians from Reno's troops, who were engaged in a deadly struggle at the other end of the camp. Indian accounts mention soldiers here. Lame White Man had been taking a sweat bath and only had time to wrap a blanket around himself and gather his rifle and moccasins. It is clear enough that no whites crossed the river. They were driven back by a rapidly organizing force of Cheyennes and Sioux.

In June of 1992, a group of Indians, led by Russell Means and other activists, held a Sun Dance at Medicine Tail Coulee, a kind of counter-demonstration to the anniversary of the battle. Because it was also the five hundredth anniversary of Columbus's journey to the New World, the Sun Dance took on added significance to the Indians. To add even more significance, or controversy, the Indians blocked the road to the Reno-Benteen siege site for four days, the time it takes to complete the traditional Sun Dance. The road at Medicine Tail Coulee is on Crow Reservation land and is privately owned.

At any other time of year this activity would not have created such a stir with the monument personnel, but the anniversary of the battle brings in hordes of tourists, especially Custer buffs, who use the occasion to pay homage to their fallen hero. (A short time later, the buffs held their own demonstration of a sort. They set up a card table near the obelisk, just outside an iron picket fence that holds the stone markers of those killed on Custer Hill, and placed a white table-cloth and a pitcher of water and plastic glasses on it. A large bearded man in brown slacks, white shirt near to bursting, and suspenders, presided over the ceremony. Then the buffs, one at a time, took a glass of water and poured it over the fence, to give the parched spirits of the soldiers one last drink.) To block the road to the other important sites renders a trip incomplete, and therefore unsatisfactory, for serious visitors. The blocking of the road was especially troubling to Barbara Booher, an Indian woman of Cherokee/Ute descent who was then superintendent of the Little Bighorn National Battlefield. Her appointment to the position had created a firestorm of protest from politicians and others who believed the monument was to whites and only for whites. Her appointment had been praised by as many people, both Indian and white, as a long-overdue recognition that Indian people had as much to do with that piece of ground as the soldiers—in fact, her presence might help to balance the equation. She weathered that controversy by determination and diplomacy, and she has weathered many controversies since, none of her own making. She has described the superintendency of the monument, her first position at that level of responsibility, as "boot camp." (Barbara Booher has since been promoted to a new position as Indian affairs director at the Park Service's regional office in Denver. The job involves working with fifty-one Indian reservations in Montana, Wyoming, Colorado, Utah, and North and South Dakota. Her replacement as superintendent of the Little Bighorn National Monument is Gerard Baker, a Mandan-Hidatsa Indian.)

The closing of the road by the Sun Dancers was only the latest in a series of confrontations. The year before, again during the anniversary, a group of Indians marched to the beat of a drum from the visitor center to Custer Hill. There they made speeches, feasted, and round-danced very peacefully. Barbara Booher joined the dancing. She must have felt greatly relieved, because the rumor was going around that Russell Means was determined to show up with two hundred mounted warriors to "take over" the battlefield. (The ever-controversial Means, incidentally, has stated that only two hundred warriors were involved in the Custer fight. The numbers were inflated because whites at the time could not believe that Indians could win a fair fight.) Perhaps it was the presence of several patrol cars from the Crow Reservation, the county sheriff's department, the Park Service, and the highway patrol and a bunch of cops walking around with walkie-talkies that deterred the present-day warriors. Whatever the cause, a crisis was averted.

The closing of the road by the activists was certain to create a pressure-cooker situation again, and again Barbara Booher stepped up to deal with it. She talked to Means and the other leaders and made the determination (undoubtedly with the aid of her superiors in the National Park Service) that the Indians could close the road to hold their four-day Sun Dance, since both the road at Medicine Tail Coulee and the place of the ceremony were on Crow land. The visitors could learn about the Reno-Benteen site from exhibits and literature and interpretive programs at the visitor center. This decision could not have pleased all of the tourists, but it was the fair one and was accepted as such.

In her three years as superintendent, Booher had to walk the fine line on several occasions, but she is a strong, calm woman not given to caving in to pressure. In many ways, in these changing times when many of the old western myths are being reassessed, she was the perfect person for the job.

From the low point where the mouth of Medicine Tail Coulee empties into the Little Bighorn, you begin an ascent up a ridge southeast of the coulee. This ridge reaches its apex at a notched hill called Weir Point. It was at this high point that Captain Thomas B. Weir, and later Captain Frederick Benteen, and others looked across to the Custer fight. Weir and his company determined that a fight was in progress, but they didn't know it was just about finished until the Indians looked back and saw the soldiers and began to gallop toward them. Benteen, declaring that "this is a hell of a place to fight Indians," and his troops took off, riding at a fast clip back to Reno Hill. And that's where Reno and Benteen and their companies underwent a day-and-a-half siege. Had not Generals Terry and Gibbon and their troops arrived from the west it is quite probable that the soldiers on Reno Hill would have been wiped out too.

Reno Hill is the last stop on the road across the battlefield. It is a little more than a mile southeast of Weir Point. One can still see evidence of breastworks, small semicircular depressions in the earth that make an arc from north to east to south (that is how fragile the plains are). To the west is the steep descent down to the Little Bighorn River. It is up this bluff that the remainder of Reno's 140-man battalion climbed in their flight from the Indians in the valley after their ill-fated charge on the village of over seven thousand people, almost two thousand warriors.

Toward the end of the second day of besiegement, the Indians got word from scouts that other "longknives" were coming from the west. That late afternoon they set fire to the brush along the river, packed up their village, and fled south to the Bighorn Mountains. The Battle of the Little Bighorn was over.

From Reno Hill you have a clear view, to the east, of the Wolf Mountains, over which both the Indians and later the cavalry crossed to get to the fatal site. If you look through a small hole bored into a pole you see the exact location of the Crow's Nest, where Custer's scouts first saw the signs of a large village. You can also see, halfway between the Crow's Nest and Reno Hill, the location of the famous "lone tipi" on Reno Creek where one of Crazy Horse's warriors died from his wounds and was buried with his possessions after the Indians' attack on General Crook's southern column on the Rosebud, effectively putting Crook out of the Indian wars for an extremely crucial period of time—most important, out of the Battle of the Little Bighorn. Had he triumphed and continued north, and the timing had come out right, which it could have, the battle might have had a very different outcome.

To the south from Reno Hill you see the valley of the Little Bighorn River and farther on the snowy Bighorn Mountains, where the Sioux and Cheyennes split up into separate bands. Most of the reservation Indians went back to the Great Sioux Reservation in the Dakotas; the other "free" Indians scattered to pursue the buffalo—and to get as far away from the Little Bighorn as possible. The Indians all knew that the battle had been a great triumph; they also knew that it would bring many more soldiers determined to make them pay for their victory.

So this is the battlefield, which is described in most literature on the subject as "bleak" or "barren," as in the "bleak hillside," the "barren landscape." Having grown up in country similar to this in northern Montana, I find it anything but bleak or barren. In fact, the Little Bighorn valley reminds me a lot of the Milk River valley on the Fort

Belknap Reservation, where my family had our ranch And we considered that valley a beautiful place to raise families, to run cattle, to grow alfalfa and bluejoint, to ride double on a big white horse.

Perhaps it's a matter of perspective. The whole tour is designed to show the battle from the white point of view. In describing the battlefield, I have placed the reader in Custer's shoes, in Reno's and Benteen's shoes. This is the perspective that the tourist gets. The road follows the various positions of the 7th Calvary. The manifold literature tells the story from these positions. The tourist is encouraged to look down from these rolling hills, these ridges, and imagine what it must have been like for the soldiers to be completely overwhelmed by half-naked, yipping savages.

If by chance you cross the river and drive a road paralleling the river on the reservation side, you get a much different perspective of the battlefield. In fact, you might even forget that you're here because a battle occurred on those hills beyond the river. In most places, you can't even see the hills because of towering cutbanks that block your view. What you see on this side is flat, green valley floor, a slow-moving, small river, and cottonwood trees and wild rosebushes. If it's a hot June day, you might walk down to the river and sit in the shade of the cottonwoods and listen to the faint swirl of the water (I don't suggest you try this without permission, because the land is privately owned). Stay there for twenty minutes, an hour. Imagine that it's a large camping site and families and friends are picnicking, working on crafts, putting up foodstuffs, conversing, maybe gambling. Imagine that it's an immense campground filled with eight thousand people and that relatives have to walk or ride two or three miles to visit other relatives—if they can find them. (As one Lakota elder put it: "It took them maybe four days to find their relatives someplace among different bands.") Imagine children playing in the water or kicking a ball made of rags and skin or riding their ponies through camp. Imagine young men flirting with young women; boys having a contest to see who's the best archer; girls playing games with sticks and hoops, or playing make-believe with dolls; mothers cutting meat into thin flat strips to hang on the drying rack or going out to look for berries; husbands cleaning their muskets—the lucky few their new repeating rifles—or making a new bowstring by rubbing and twisting wet sinew through the eye sockets of a buffalo skull. Then imagine old ones, the keepers of the stories, as they visit with one another, recounting war honors or joking or teasing a young one who is too full of himself.

All the while it is a cloudless hot day, but down by the river, under the cottonwoods, there is a breeze and it is cool, even peaceful.

Then you hear a shout from far off. It is faint at first, hardly distinguishable from the general camp hubbub, but soon it begins to echo as more people shout. And finally you can make out the words: "Soldiers are here! Soldiers are here!" And you see an old man standing in front of his lodge, crying, "Young men, go out and fight them! You have only one life!"

But you are sitting on the bank of a slightly off-color river and what you really hear is magpies and an occasional meadowlark, or a cow calling her calf to remind you that you are here, now, nearly in the twenty-first century, a long time from that day that the alarm was raised among the lodges of that camp.

It is a different perspective. And as you look up at those cliffs across the river you can almost imagine the terror that visited the peaceful village. You can almost imagine that you are there.

5

Soon after Sitting Bull's Sun Dance on the Big Bend of the Rosebud, the enormous village struck camp and began to move farther up the creek, first south, then west. The horses and travois filled the valley from side to side and stretched out for several miles. The thousands of travois poles dug furrows in the dry earth as though the valley floor had been plowed up. Dust rose in great plumes among and behind them. Indians have reported that when the camp moved, the Cheyennes, who led the procession, would have had their lodges pitched and supper eaten by the time the Hunkpapas, the band at the rear, reached the new campsite. All around, on hills and ridges, in the valley front and rear, mounted parties of fighting men kept a lookout for the soldiers. When the bands camped at night, other warriors kept watch from the surrounding hills. Scouts, or wolves, were sent out to cover the nearby countryside, to report any movement anywhere.

Each day brought new arrivals from the agencies in the Dakotas. Families and small groups of relatives from all the bands, even some small bands from the eastern Dakotas, Yanktonais and Santees, had gotten word and left their territories to come west for the last great get-together. Inkpaduta, the chief of the Santees, rode at the head of these eastern newcomers, although it is not clear that he was entirely welcome. It was Inkpaduta who, in 1862, in an effort to stem the tide of trespassers in his country, led the Santees to slaughter as many as 750 white settlers in what became known as the Minnesota Massacre.

President Abraham Lincoln sanctioned the hanging of thirty-eight of Inkpaduta's warriors. They were hanged in the town square of Mankato, the largest mass execution in the country's history, but Inkpaduta escaped to the west, thus drawing the soldiers' violent attention to the western Sioux, the Lakotas, who were peaceful at the time. Nevertheless, Sitting Bull, always a gracious host, allowed the Santees and Yanktonais to join his Hunkpapa camp circle.

The steady flowing river of people and animals left the Rosebud where the creek turned south again to enter a narrow canyon. The people followed a small creek west toward a natural divide in the Wolf Mountains. Several scouts had ridden ahead to make sure the way was clear and safe from enemies. But the only enemies this group was concerned with were the white soldiers. No enemy tribe could stand up to them.

After the scouts signaled the all clear, the bands began the arduous, daylong movement up and over the divide. As each band reached the top of the pass, they could see clearly in the distance the broad green valley of the Greasy Grass, or Little Bighorn, River. They could also see, off to their left, the promontory known as the Crow's Nest, where Custer's scouts, several days later, would try to point out to the general these very Indians' encampment, and their enormous horse herd.

That night the many bands of Sioux, Cheyennes, and Arapahos camped on Ash Creek, sometimes called Sundance Creek, later named Reno Creek by the whites, a tributary of the Little Bighorn. It was here that Custer's troops would later come upon the famous "lone tipi."

After the bands set up camp and cooked their dinner, and the usual evening activities of dancing, courting, visiting, and telling stories began, the sound of shouting and thundering hooves came from one end of the camp. It was a group of scouts, and they told of many soldiers to the south, less than a sleep away.

The Indians in the camp that night knew that these soldiers were part of a summer campaign to kill as many of them as possible and drive the survivors to the Great Sioux Reservation. Because the Indians had not observed the impossible January 31 deadline to be on the reservation, the U. S. government was not in the mood to negotiate any further peace with them or treat them as peaceful people. To be fair, Sitting Bull and Crazy Horse and the other "free" Indians would not have negotiated with the whites under any circumstances. They had been leading a quiet life out on the northern plains, far from the whites. They were on land that had not been ceded to the United States in the 1868 treaty—in other words, they were there legally, hunting, raising their familes, minding their own business. When the January 31 deadline passed, Sitting Bull and Crazy Horse knew that the soldier chiefs would be looking for a confrontation. And the "free" Indians were not about to settle for a life on a reservation, living by the white men's rules, beholden to them for a handout. As the Lakotas would say, "It is a good day to die," meaning that they would rather die as free people than live in captivity. The U. S. Army would attempt to oblige them.

The plan, devised by Phil Sheridan, along with Generals Terry, Crook, Gibbon, and Custer, the participants, was very simple—a three-pronged attack, or a pincer movement, which would surround the Indians, leaving them no escape route. General Terry's Dakota column, spearheaded by Custer's 7th Cavalry Regiment, would attack from the east; General Gibbon's Montana column, with his infantry and cavalry, would support them from the west; and General Crook's Wyoming column, whose soldiers the scouts had just seen, would attack from the south.

If the plan looked good on paper, it was certainly farfetched in reality, given the state of communications at the time. Although Terry, Gibbon, and Custer got together on the Yellowstone River a few days before Custer's march up the Rosebud on his way to the Little Bighorn, they had no idea where Crook was. And Crook, already in the field, could only guess that the plan was proceeding. The likelihood that all three columns would come together at once was remote, especially since the planners did not know exactly where the Indians were. It is almost astonishing that the plan worked as well as it did, in that all three battalions had some contact with the Indians. Unfortunately for the soldiers, the results were catastrophic.

In a letter to General of the Army Sherman, Sheridan allows, "The organization of these commands and what they expect to accomplish has been as yet left to the Department Commanders. I presume the following will occur: General Terry will drive the Indians toward the Big Horn valley, and General Crook will drive them back toward Terry, Colonel [sic] Gibbon moving down on the north side of the Yellowstone to intercept, if possible, such as may want to go north of the Missouri to the Milk River."

Perhaps the biggest flaw in the pincer movement was Sheridan's belief that a large group of Indians could not stay together for more than a week because they would need an enormous amount of meat and other food, and the thousands of horses would graze an area around such a settlement down to nothing. Therefore, each prong would be fighting relatively smaller groups of Indians caught in the surround. Sheridan did not believe that the three columns would meet and attack an enormous village at the same time, but individually, they could attack the "hostiles" in numbers more closely approximating those of the battalions. The survivors would be only too happy to surrender and scurry off to the reservation. But the Indians, over seven thousand strong at the time of Custer's attack, did stay together and whipped Crook first, then Custer. Only Gibbon's command escaped unharmed. By the time they arrived on the scene the Indians had used up most of their ammunition and arrows and chose to leave the area. Sitting Bull felt they had punished the soldiers enough.

In reality, the campaign against the Indians had been in jeopardy almost from the start. The summer campaign was supposed to have been a winter campaign, launched several months earlier. But due to extreme weather (the very weather the Indians were supposed to brave to come to the reservation to surrender) and several foul-ups, the Dakota column could not get out of Fort Abraham Lincoln in Dakota Territory. By the time Sheridan made the decision to attack the Indians in their winter camps (hoping for a series of Washitas), both railroad and steamship companies had shut down service to Fort Lincoln for the winter. The Dakota column could not get enough provisions to keep them in the field for more than a few days.

But perhaps the biggest foul-up concerned General Custer. Although he had been promised the Dakota command and was the most experienced Indian fighter among the northern commanders, Custer had become involved (as a witness) in a scandal which revolved around the selling of licenses for post sutlerships and reservation trading posts and had helped implicate Secretary of War William Belknap as a main culprit. This was just one of many scandals that rocked President Grant's administration. But what made this one special was that it involved Grant's own brother, Orvil. Orvil, it turned out, was essentially the bagman for Belknap and his cronies.

A congressional inquiry was called, and Custer was summoned east to give testimony which further blackened the eyes of Belknap and Orvil. Grant was incensed. In a series of moves designed to humiliate Custer, Grant refused to see the young general in Washington, then had Custer arrested when he left Washington for not paying a courtesy visit on the President and, most important, relieved Custer of his command of the Dakota column. In fact, he forbade Custer from accompanying the expedition in any capacity. It was only through the intercession of Custer's superior officers, including Sherman, Sheridan, and Terry, that Grant relented and let Custer ride at the head of his 7th Cavalry but not at the head of the Dakota column. That honor would go to General Terry, who didn't want it.

In spite of the Dakota column's difficulties, both the Wyoming and Montana columns conducted separate operations in the winter and early spring of 1876. Crook, as described, marched north from Fort Fetterman and on March 17 attacked the Cheyenne village on the Powder River. He did not strike a telling blow and was forced to withdraw back to Wyoming empty-handed. The Indians even stole their horses back. Gibbon was even less effective in the field. He blew two opportunities to strike large villages on the Rosebud and the Tongue River because his troops could not cross the Yellowstone River, a feat that Indians, women and children included, performed with regularity.

Now the Lakota and Cheyenne leaders on this night of June 16 assembled in the large council lodge and heard the scouts, who said the Rosebud was black with soldiers—led by Three Stars, General Crook—and their allies, the Crows and the Shoshones, or Snakes. They were upstream near the headwaters of the Rosebud and heading this way. They had many guns, many horses and supply wagons. There was much talk in the council lodge, but even more chatter among the young warriors who surrounded the lodge. Many of them had gotten their horses and were riding around the perimeter, shooting weapons, shouting, working themselves into a lather. Many had gone to their own lodges to paint up and dress up and tie on their war medicine. The *akecita*, the police society, had a difficult time reining them in.

Finally, Crazy Horse agreed to lead a party south to the soldiers' camp. He and the war chiefs of the many bands saw that a fight was inevitable, and rather than let the young men speed off in small groups to be killed, the chiefs organized a party of 750 men and managed to control them during the night-long march. This was incredible. So many of the men came from the agencies to fight soldiers, to gain honors, to count coup, to capture weapons and horses.

Crazy Horse, Tasunke Witko, who led the attack at the Rosebud, nine days before the Battle of the Little Bighorn. Ledger drawing by Amos Bad Heart Bull. Crazy Horse never allowed anyone to take his photograph. *University of Nebraska Press*

General George Crook, the "loser" of the Battle of the Rosebud, photographed in his usual field dress, a rank soldier's overcoat. *Little Bighorn Battlefield National Monument*

Many of them had never fought before. Many of them were scared but needed to go to war. Others hated the longknives and couldn't wait to charge in among them, killing as many as they could. And there were the Crows and Snakes, longtime traditional enemies, who needed killing. All of the young men, battle-scarred or not, were eager for individual honors—the recognition they had always fought for.

And yet they rode south as a unit, flanked by the *akecita* to prevent young bloods from racing ahead, crossed over the Wolf Mountains to the valley of the Rosebud, through the night, until at dawn, on June 17, 1876, exactly three months after Crook's March 17 attack on the Sioux/Cheyenne village which united the Sioux and Cheyenne bands, they were assembled below a ridge, stretching their legs, eating pemmican and dry meat, and preparing for war. John Stands in Timber describes these preparations before the Battle of the Rosebud:

> Many had ceremonies to perform and ornaments to put on before they went into war, and they knew it would not be long. So the chiefs gave the order and the warriors howled like wolves to answer them, and scattered here and there to begin picking out their shields and warbonnets and other things they used. Not too many had warbonnets though. More used mounted birds or animals and different kinds of charms.
>
> There were many ways to perform ceremonies on the body. The warriors depended on being protected by the power that came from them. They could ride close to the soldiers and not be harmed. Some were wonderful medicines, like the mounted hawk of Brave Wolf's that he was given after fasting at Bear Butte. He would tie it onto the back lock of his hair and ride into a fight whistling with a bone whistle. Sometimes on a charge the bird came to life and whistled too, when they came close to the enemy in hand-to-hand fighting. Many mentioned that bird. On the other hand, a man without power of some kind did not go in close that way. He did not dare.

While these ceremonies were performed, Crazy Horse, in a spotted calfskin war cape, a manifestation of the hailstone vision of his thunder dream, and the other war leaders climbed to the crest of the ridge from where they could look down the other side into the shallow valley of the Rosebud.

The calfskin cape that Crazy Horse wore was a new addition to his wardrobe. Usually, he rode to battle in a breechcloth and moccasins and nothing else. He painted his body with white spots, hail-stones, and one cheek with a red jagged line, a lightning bolt. He tied a pebble behind an ear and a red hawk on his head. He sprinkled a handful of dust on both himself and his horse before battle for protection from bullets and arrows.

In 1854, when Crazy Horse was twelve or thirteen, he had had a dream after a disturbing incident which helped to bring about all-out war between his people and the whites. The Indians on his part of the plains had managed to live at peace with the whites, except for a few incidents, ever since the whites began to come into their territory. But the more the Indians, the Sioux and Cheyennes and Arapahos, saw of the whites the less they liked them. They saw the wagon ruts of the Oregon Trail dig deeper into their mother earth. They saw the great buffalo herds being split into a north and south herd, both herds avoiding the white pioneers, who slaughtered them at every opportunity. They saw the grass and trees disappearing along the trail. They saw forts being built to protect these travelers. And they saw the military presence everywhere. It is no wonder that the Indians would become increasingly angry at what the whites were doing to their country.

The incident happened at a trading post near Fort Laramie in Wyoming. The facts are sketchy and often conflicting, depending upon the source, but the incident involved a Minneconjou Sioux named High Forehead and a cow owned by a Mormon. High Forehead, for whatever reason, shot the cow, which made the Mormon angry. Some reports say the tribal elders attempted to reimburse the man for his cow, but things got out of hand. A young lieutenant, fresh from West Point, decided to handle the incident by bullying and punishing the Indians. Lieutenant John Grattan wanted to show them who was the boss. He had the equipment—a twelve-pound field piece and a mountain howitzer. And a company of soldiers. And a drunken interpreter named Auguste Lucien.

Accounts of the confrontation are clouded by confusion, but essentially a shot was fired by an unknown party and Grattan opened up with his heavy guns.

When the incident ended, Grattan, all thirty-one of his men, and the interpreter were dead. One Indian was mortally wounded—a chief named Conquering Bear. After ransacking the trading post, the Indians fled north. They buried Conquering Bear along the way.

Although most of the people thought they had done the right thing to the bullying Lieutenant Grattan, the incident seriously disturbed the youthful Crazy Horse, who was named Curly at the time. He seemed to sense that things were going to be different now, that the whites were not going to let this incident pass and in fact would use it to drive the Sioux farther from their country.

While the people were moving north, Curly left them and climbed a high butte, where an Oglala eagle catcher had dug his pit and caught eagles every year. Curly lay down and stared up at the blue sky. He tried to think of what had just happened and what it meant to the future of his people, but mostly he tried to have a vision. He fasted, he went without water, he lay on piles of pebbles, he put sharp stones between his toes to keep from sleeping. He lay there for three days, but no vision came. No animals, no birds, not even an insect came to help him. He began to think that he was not destined to have a vision, that he was somehow different from his people.

And he was. He was light-skinned, light-haired, slight. Even as a man he did not cut a physically imposing figure. He was five foot nine inches tall, with a narrow face and sharp nose. He wore no ornamentation in camp. He did not braid his hair but wore it loose and long. He was a strange youth who would grow into a strange man. He never sacrificed before the medicine pole, an almost unheard-of thing for a Plains Indian. He never took part in sings and dances. He passed through the village without recognizing people. He stayed away from camp for long periods of time, even in winter. Throughout his life, Crazy Horse was as mysterious to his own people as he is to us today. Unlike his contemporaries, he never allowed anybody to photograph him.

But up on the bluff, young Curly felt only weakness and a growing sense of despair. At the end of the third day, he arose and walked down to get his horse and make his way back to camp. But when he came to the low place where his horse stood, he was too weak and dehydrated to go on. He sat down with his back against a cottonwood tree—and he dreamed.

He dreamed of a horse moving through a sacred world—it was the real world behind this one. A man was riding the horse. The horse did not touch the ground, and the man was still, only the buckskin fringes of his moccasins stirring as he rode. In the dream were sky, trees, grass. The horse was so light on the earth it seemed to float. The man rode without effort. Then the horse changed colors, many different colors. The man wore blue leggings and a white buckskin shirt. He did not paint himself. He wore a small brown pebble behind his ear.

The man rode the changing-color horse through enemy shadows; all the time streaks came toward him like arrows and bullets, but they never hit him. They disappeared. And he was riding through his own people. They tried to touch him, to grab him, but he shook them off and rode on. Then he was in a thunderstorm and the man had a lightning streak on his face and hailstones on his body. The storm disappeared, and the people were grabbing at him again, making noises, and overhead a small hawk with a red back flew, crying. And that was the end of the dream.

He was awakened by his father, who had come to look for him. His father was angry, for he had been gone for three days without telling anybody. But as his father berated him, Curly saw a small red-backed hawk circling overhead.

Curly did not tell anybody about this dream, because he could make nothing of it. The significance eluded him. Finally, when he was sixteen, his father took him away from camp for a man-to-man talk. His father was worried that Curly was too different, too solitary. People were talking about this strange boy. With much reluctance, Curly told his father about his dream, and his father sat and thought for a time. Finally he said, "You have been given a great vision, and you cannot move the load of it from you. The man on the horse is what you must become."

And so Crazy Horse became the man in his vision. He dressed like the man—he wore a pebble behind his ear and a red-backed hawk on his head. He painted his face and body with lightning and hail. The magic of his vision would prevent him from being hit by enemy fire (although Crazy Horse was wounded at least twice, once in battle against the Snakes, and once by a jealous husband). As the man in the dream, Crazy Horse would have to make tough decisions for his people, to lead them sometimes where they did not want to go.

A short time later, his father, who was named Crazy Horse, gave that name to his son. His father henceforth went by the name of Worm and was a highly respected holy man among the Oglalas.

And now, Crazy Horse, the son, was a leader and was in fact leading 750 Sioux and Cheyenne warriors against the thirteen-hundred-man battalion of General Crook.

Because the country of the Rosebud was broken by pine-covered ridges and deep coulees, Crazy Horse and the war leaders could not clearly see the soldiers' camp. Crazy Horse ordered some scouts on horses to cross down the other side of the ridge to have a better look, but they immediately ran into a party of Crow scouts. The sound of gunfire was more than the waiting young men could stand. They jumped on their horses and sped up and over the ridge.

In the valley, the soldiers scrambled for their weapons and horses and began to deploy themselves to meet the charge. The Crows and Snakes, already mounted, rode forth and broke the brunt of the charge, while the soldiers, some on foot, others on horseback, returned fire, knocking down Sioux and Cheyenne horses and wounding some of the young men. But another wave of horsemen swooped down from the ridge, and the Crows and Snakes retreated back to safety. Then the soldiers on horseback counterattacked, driving back the second wave.

The battle raged all day, back and forth, now one side taking the offensive, then the other. Charge and countercharge. Even though the army had almost twice the number of fighters, counting the Crows and Snakes, they could not repulse the waves of enemy attackers forever. It was a hot fight, the air thick with gunsmoke, with much hand-to-hand combat.

Jack Red Cloud, resplendent in flowing warbonnet and carrying his father's silver-plated Winchester, which had been a gift from the Great Father in Washington, was knocked from his horse by three Crows and beaten, laughed at, and taunted. They took away his rifle and sent him back to his allies, thoroughly disgraced. He became a further object of shame with his fellow warriors because he had not retrieved his war bridle after his horse went down, a customary action that conveyed disdain for the enemy. Jack, weeping openly, found another horse, slipped away, and rode all the way back to Red Cloud Agency in Nebraska.

At another point, a Cheyenne named Chief Comes in Sight had his horse shot out from under him and was surrounded by the enemy. He had just begun his death song when a Cheyenne rider swept down the ridge, through the enemy line, and held out a hand to the warrior. He grabbed it and swung aboard, and they galloped off to safety. The rider was his sister, Calf Trail Woman, who according to Kate Bighead later distinguished herself in the Custer fight by being the only woman to take the offensive against the soldiers. Because of her act of bravery at the Rosebud, the Cheyennes forever referred to this encounter as the battle "Where the Girl Saved Her Brother."

Crazy Horse had developed many new fighting techniques in his years of fighting other Indians and the whites, but he now tried an old ploy that Indians had used against each other forever. He and a large group of warriors quit the attack and retreated slowly down the

Rosebud as though their horses were played out and they themselves had lost the fighting spirit. General Crook sent a detachment of men to ride them down, but just as the soldiers were about to ride into a narrow canyon, their scouts turned back and advised them to do the same. The scouts recognized the action as a decoy maneuver to lead the troops into an ambush. Crazy Horse had become well known for this trick. He had used it many times since the Fetterman Massacre in 1866, when he and a couple of other Indians had lured Captain Fetterman, who had boasted that he could defeat the entire Sioux Nation with a single company of cavalrymen, out of Fort Phil Kearney in Wyoming and into an ambush that killed him and all eighty of his men.

The maneuver didn't work this time, but it did split Crook's forces, a strategic error, and basically took the fight out of them. The casualties were mounting on both sides, and Crook, who was becoming known for his caution in perilous situations (as opposed to the reckless Custer, who enjoyed the danger to himself and his troops), decided enough was enough. Even though his forces had stood off the Indian attack, even gaining a slight advantage, he gathered his men into a defensive position and waited for the Indians to quit the field.

The battle had lasted all day, and the men and horses on both sides were exhausted. The Indians were virtually out of ammunition and arrows, they had lost many men and horses, and they had many wounded to take care of, and so, after seeing Crook's forces were not going to attack anymore, they did withdraw. They cut poles from among the slender pines and made travois to carry the wounded, then they began the long journey back to camp. That night was quiet in the camp as the medicine people tended to the wounded and the others mourned the dead. For such a hot fight, the casualties were surprisingly light. Crazy Horse later said that the Indian dead numbered thirty-six. The whites lost nine troopers and one Shoshone scout. The disparity in the numbers of casualties can be attributed to the superior firepower and numbers of the army and its allies.

The following morning, June 18, the Indians moved camp down Ash Creek to the Little Bighorn, a few miles south of the location of the camp Custer's troops would attack seven days later. That afternoon, scouts rode in with word that Crook's forces were retreating to the south. That night the Indians held a victory dance, now certain that they could fight off anything that the Americans could throw at them.

But what would have happened if the Indians had been decisively defeated? Or if they had not gone to meet Crook's troops? Many in the camp were against sending such a large party of warriors to fight the general's troops on the Rosebud. They feared that the camp would be left unprotected. What if another force attacked them while the fighting men were gone?

One thing is clear—Three Stars' forces would have been attacked by Sioux and Cheyenne warriors, no matter what. The young men were itching for a fight, and nothing could have stopped them—not their band chiefs or war chiefs, not Sitting Bull or Crazy Horse, not even their mothers. Chiefs were only listened to when they had a good idea. Chiefs usually had good ideas, and that is what made them chiefs and allowed them to remain so—that and their past history of bravery and wisdom. In this case, the chiefs realized that they could not restrain the young men, and so they knew—at least, Crazy Horse knew—that the only way to keep these young men from being slaughtered by the well-armed troops was to organize them and lead them.

Crazy Horse also had an idea about how to fight the soldiers—and this idea led the Indians to success in both the Battle of the Rosebud and the Battle of the Little Bighorn. It was a simple idea, but the effect was evident. Prior to these two battles, the Indians tended to circle around the enemy on their horses, a moving circle, offering themselves as targets to sharpshooters and making it difficult for the warriors themselves to get off accurate shots. Crazy Horse early on saw the flaw in this maneuver, and he generally stopped, even got off his horse, to get a killing shot in. Now he and the war chiefs managed to hold the warriors in check, then sent them forth in waves from several directions, directly at the soldiers—attack and retreat, attack and retreat—until the soldiers were fighting in smaller groups, each group defending a smaller part of the battlefield. By retreating, the Indians managed to draw some of these groups forward, thus exposing them to attack from a different angle. Although the Indians did not kill off a lot of these soldiers, they kept them on the defensive much of the time. Consequently, they dealt a serious blow to the morale of these experienced Indian fighters. And stopped them dead in their tracks.

Crook's troops retreated to their base camp on Goose Creek, near present-day Sheridan, Wyoming, to lick their wounds and to hunt and fish. Crook's military campaign against the Sioux and Cheyenne was now one long vacation. Crook himself had other things on his mind—in one afternoon he caught seventy trout.

But if this man the Sioux and Cheyenne called Three Stars had defeated the Indians, he might have continued his march north. He might have come upon the big village—he undoubtedly would have. He had good scouts who were as aware of the movements of the Sioux and Cheyennes as they were of his. If he had attacked the camp, he might well have sent the Indians scattering throughout the countryside. He had a large number of experienced, well-armed, well-provisioned troops who had received very few casualties at the Rosebud battle. He also had Crow and Snake allies who had fought with great heart. It is highly possible that he could have broken the back of the greatest sustained resistance to the white invasion that occurred in America. And Custer might have become President of that America instead of winding up naked and dead on a grassy hillside in Montana.

On the other hand, had Crook attacked the village, he and his entire command might have been rubbed out. Indians were desperately fierce when they were protecting their women and children. Custer found this out at the Washita.

It must be recorded here that the military, in all its Indian campaigns, was constantly frustrated by the mobile Indians and the ease with which they avoided pitched battle. It was thought that if the army could ever get the Indians to stand and fight, a very small number of well-supplied, well-armed, well-disciplined white soldiers could defeat a great number of savages—to the point of surrender or annihilation. Custer was not alone in this belief. Arrogance on the part of the military commanders was never in short supply.

Custer, when he would attack the village on the Little Bighorn, would not know what had happened to Crook only eight days earlier. The cautious Crook did not attempt to send scouts north to warn Custer and his superiors that the Indians not only were prepared to defend their women and children but were in an aggressive temper. (To be fair to the scouts, it would have taken a mighty brave man to attempt such a journey, as he would almost certainly run into groups of hostile warriors—but then again, scouts were paid to do that kind of work.) The Indians were in no mood to surrender to Custer's puny group of 647 officers, troops, and civilians when they had just driven back twice that number on the Rosebud—with fewer warriors than those amassed at the Little Bighorn. To say that the Indians were confident is an understatement.

So Crook, who was part of the largest military campaign against the Indians in frontier history, withdrew to Wyoming for some serious R&R, without warning his fellow commanders up north, Generals Terry and Gibbon, that he and his troops were out of it. The celebrated three-prong or pincer attack on the Indians at the Little Bighorn would not materialize.

Crook wrote later, in his annual report of September 25, 1876, three months after Custer's ill-fated attack at the Little Bighorn, that his actions on the Rosebud were justified: "The number of our troops was less than one thousand [over thirteen hundred, actually, including Indian allies and civilians], and within eight days after that the same Indians met and defeated a column of troops nearly the same size as ours [actually only half the size], including the gallant commander, General Custer himself. I invite attention to the fact that in this engagement my troops beat these Indians on a field of their own choosing, and drove them in utter rout from it as far as the proper care of my wounded and prudence would justify. Subsequent events proved beyond dispute what would have been the fate of the command had the pursuit been continued beyond what judgement dictated." Crook's creative accounting was matched only by his capacity for shading the truth.

On the morning of June 22, five days after the Battle of the Rosebud, Custer led his 7th Cavalry in review before Terry and Gibbon (Custer's own idea) before striking off at twelve noon up the Rosebud to find Sitting Bull and Crazy Horse. It would take him two and a half days to reach Sitting Bull's Sun Dance site. It would take him another night and half a day to reach the village on the Little Bighorn.

Custer's orders were to locate the Indians, then wait for the rest of the troops, but there was a kicker in General Terry's orders, which are quoted here in full:

The Brigadier General commanding directs that, as soon as your regiment can be made ready for the march, you will proceed up the Rosebud in pursuit of the Indians whose trail was discovered by Major Reno a few days since. It is, of course, impossible to give you any definite instructions in regard to this movement, and were it not impossible to do so the Department Commander [Terry] places too much confidence in your zeal, energy and ability to wish to impose on you precise orders which might hamper your action when nearly in contact with the enemy. He will, however, indicate to you his own views of what your action should be, and he desires that you should conform to them *unless you shall see sufficient reasons for departing from them* [emphasis added]. He thinks that you should proceed up the Rosebud until you ascertain definitely the direction in which the trail above spoken of leads. Should it be found (as it appears almost certain that it will be found) to turn toward the Little [Big] Horn, he thinks that you should still proceed southward, perhaps as far as the headwaters of the Tongue, and then turn toward the Little [Big] Horn, feeling constantly, however for your left, so as to preclude the possibility of the escape of the Indians to the south or southeast by passing your left flank. The column of Colonel Gibbon is now in motion for the mouth of the Bighorn. As soon as it reaches that point it will cross the Yellowstone and move up at least as far as the forks of the Big and Little Horns. Of course, its future movements must be controlled by circumstances as they arise, but it is hoped that the Indians, if up the Little [Big] Horn, may be so nearly inclosed by the two columns that their escape will be impossible.

The Department Commander desires that on your way up the Rosebud you should thoroughly examine the upper part of Tullock's Creek, and that you should endeavor to send a scout through to Colonel Gibbon's column, with information of the results of your examination. The lower part of this creek will be examined by a detachment from Colonel Gibbon's command. The supply steamer will be pushed up the Bighorn as far as the forks of the river if found to be navigable for that distance, and the Department Commander, who will accompany the column of Colonel Gibbon, desires you to report to him there not later than the expiration of the time for which your troops are rationed, unless in the meantime you receive further orders.

Contrary to much popular opinion, it is clear from the phrase "unless you shall see sufficient reasons from departing from [the orders]" that Custer was given the leeway to improvise depending on what he ran in to. And it should be made clear that, based on prior experience, the army commanders were more afraid that the Indians would escape the trap than that they would be found in such overwhelming numbers that they could defeat Custer's 7th Cavalry. Terry did not know of Crook's retreat.

Custer was not a fool who rode headlong into his own death—or if he was, much of the blame for such an action must rest on his fellow officers' heads. But Custer did make a vital error—he did not reconnoiter the village on the Little Bighorn and the surrounding terrain. And, as previously noted, it was not the first time he had made this mistake. At the Washita, in the attack on Black Kettle's Southern Cheyenne village, he had not sent scouts out to determine the strength of the Indians or even the numbers of Indians. So Custer, who had also been accused of the same lack of reconnaisance before his impulsive charges in the Civil War, had learned nothing from his previous mistakes. Perhaps he did not feel that caution was a necessity. After all, he had earned a reputation for being lucky during his mad charges into rebel lines: "Custer's Luck." And his luck held at the Washita. He had suddenly become the most famous Indian fighter in frontier history after that massacre. But his impatience with proper reconnaisance, borne of a constant fear that the Indians would escape him, eventually would lead to disaster.

Now Custer was leading his command of thirty-one officers, 566 troopers, and fifty scouts and civilians—the proud 7th Cavalry, which had become the flagship unit of the Indian wars—and a large support train of pack mules laden with supplies and ammunition up the Rosebud to try his luck against the Sioux and Cheyennes, who were just a few days away. He had his brothers, Tom and Boston, and his brother-in-law, Lieutenant James Calhoun, and his nephew, Autie Reed, with him. He had a civilian reporter, Mark Kellogg of the *Bismarck Tribune,* which sent his dispatches along to the *New York Herald.* (Custer himself, not to be outdone, sent three anonymous dispatches to the *Herald.*)

Custer had declined the use of Gatling guns as too cumbersome. And he had his men leave their sabers behind because they created a very loud rattle when the horses trotted, a dead giveaway. He wanted to surprise the Indians, "catch them napping," as he is reported to have said. But perhaps his biggest act of hubris in this particular instance was to decline the offer of four companies of the 2nd Cavalry. He wouldn't need them to fight these Indians, he said.

As Custer rode away at the head of his troops, General Gibbon called out to him, "Now, Custer, don't be greedy, but wait for us." Custer waved and called back, "No, I will not." An ambiguous answer, at best.

And so this small army of soldiers and civilians began their pursuit of Sitting Bull's traveling village, which by now, with nearly two thousand fighting men, had reached their final campground on the Little Bighorn. Several officers and many of the Indian scouts had serious misgivings about the operation, but Custer was ebullient, as he always was when he anticipated good hunting and much fighting. Farther up the trail, only a few hours before his death, he would tell his officers, "The largest Indian camp on the North American continent is ahead and I am going to attack it."

6

George Armstrong Custer, as he marched off to the Little Bighorn, had an attitude toward Indians that might be described as ambivalent—or, at least, confused and confusing. On the one hand, he professed great admiration for the Indians' ability to live in harmony with the land and to fight with great courage and cunning. On the other hand, he harbored ill-disguised contempt for them as a people:

It is to be regretted that the character of the Indians as described in [James Fenimore] Cooper's interesting novels is not the true one. But as, in emerging from childhood into the years of a maturer age, we are often compelled to cast aside many of our earlier illusions and replace them by beliefs less inviting but more real, so we, as a people ... have been forced ... to study and endeavor to comprehend thoroughly the character of the red man. So intimately has he become associated with the government as ward of the nation, and so prominent a place among the questions of national policy does the much mooted "Indian question" occupy, that it behooves us no longer to study this problem from works of fiction, but to deal with it as it exists in reality. Stripped of the beautiful romance with which we have been so long willing to envelope him, transferred from the inviting pages of the novelist to the localities where we are compelled to meet with him, in his native village, on the war path, and when raiding upon our frontier settlements and lines of travel, the Indian forfeits his claim to the appellation of the *"noble* red man." We see him as he is, and, so far as all knowledge goes, as he ever has been, a *savage* in every sense of the word . . . one whose cruel and ferocious nature far exceeds that of any wild beast of the desert. That this is true no one who had been brought into intimate contact with the wild tribes will deny. . . . it is not surprising that by many the Indian is looked upon as a simple-minded "son of nature," desiring nothing beyond the privilege of roaming and hunting over the vast unsettled wilds of the West. . . . This view is equally erroneous with that which regards the Indian as a creature possessing the human form but divested of all other attributes of humanity, and whose traits of character, habits, modes of life, disposition, and savage customs disqualify him from the exercise of all rights and privileges, even those pertaining to life itself.

Taking him as we find him, at peace or at war, at home or abroad, waiving all prejudices, and laying aside all partiality, we will discover in the Indian a subject for thoughtful study and investigation. In him we will find the representative of a race whose origin is, and promises to be, a subject forever wrapped in mystery; a race incapable of being judged by the rules or laws applicable to any other known race of men; one between which and civilization there seems to have existed from time immemorial a determined and unceasing warfare—a hostility so deep-seated and inbred with the Indian character that in the exceptional instances where the modes and habits of civilization have been reluctantly adopted, it has been at the sacrifice of power and influence as a tribe and the more serious loss of health, vigor, and courage as individuals.

Custer wrote this "thoughtful study" in his only book, *My Life on the Plains,* published in 1874 after having appeared serially in *The Galaxy,* a highbrow journal similar to today's *Atlantic Monthly* and *Harper's.* The book itself is an account of Custer's and the newly formed 7th Cavalry Regiment's adventures on the southern plains from 1867 to 1869, chasing Indians, occasionally catching a glimpse of them, and once massacring them. In spite of what he says about James Fenimore Cooper's novels, Custer indulges himself in considerable romance about the frontier west. And perhaps a little hard-nosed and self-serving sensationalism:

The terrible fate awaiting the unfortunate trooper carried off by the Indians spread a deep gloom throughout the command.

All were too familiar with the horrid customs of the savages to hope for a moment that the captive would be reserved for aught but a slow lingering death from torture the most horrible and painful which savage, bloodthirsty minds could suggest. . . . Never shall I forget the consummate coolness and particularity of detail with which some of the Indians engaged in the affair related to myself and party the exact process by which the captive trooper was tortured to death; how he was tied to a stake, strips of flesh cut from his body, arms, and legs, burning brands thrust into the bleeding wounds, the nose, lips, and ears cut off, and finally, when from loss of blood, excessive pain, and anguish, the poor, bleeding, almost senseless mortal fell to the ground exhausted, the younger Indians were permitted to rush in and dispatch him with their knives.

Custer was following a tradition in his mock-reluctant but juicy description of Indian savagery. In their efforts to get the government and public opinion behind them, many military leaders, including General Phil Sheridan, described such fiendish torture, as well as incidents of white women being raped so heinously by hundreds of warriors that they were not worth the rescuing but were better left with their Indian tormentors. All of these military men pretended to be loath to burden polite society with such detailed accounts but did it anyway. The red menace was out there howling for scalps.

But who were these savage creatures who were more animal than human? And were they people "whose cruel and ferocious nature far exceeds that of any wild beast of the desert," as Custer asserts?

Almost all of the clichés about Plains Indians are true: They rode pintos (as well as bays, buckskins, blacks, whites, sorrels, and Appaloosas); they signaled with hand mirrors and smoke; they cut telegraph lines so the whites couldn't signal each other; in situations requiring stealth, they called to each other in the voices of the owl, the coyote, the chickadee, but they whooped and hollered during an attack; they wore beaded or quillworked buckskin, or sometimes just a breechcloth and moccasins. They wore feathers in their hair, or whole bonnets of feathers. They had visions, dreams, war medicine. They counted coup on the enemy. They used bows and arrows and lances but preferred the white man's firestick. They held council in war lodges. They climbed trees, even telegraph poles, to have a look around. They lived in tipis, in villages of tipis, always in a circle, because the sacred hoop encompassed all life—theirs, the animals', the trees', the stones'. Tipi openings faced the east, because that is

Custer, prolific writer and author of *My Life on the Plains*, with his wife, Elizabeth, in their Fort Abraham Lincoln home. Custer is writing beneath a photograph of his favorite soldier—himself. *Little Bighorn Battlefield National Monument*

A Ute warrior and young boy on horseback, 1871. *Smithsonian Institution*

The Arapaho camp of
Cut Hair's band.
*Smithsonian
Institution*

Feather Head, a Lakota
woman, 1860s.
*Smithsonian
Institution*

where Sun Chief rose to begin his sacred journey. They danced to the sun at the summer get-together, they made offerings, they endured self-torture; the Sioux sacrificers gazed directly at the fiery sun and did not go blind.

All Plains Indians performed the Sun Dance. Although this ceremony varied slightly from tribe to tribe, the purpose remained the same: to give thanks to Sun Chief, to beg his forgiveness for transgressions, to initiate young men and women into adulthood, to ask him to look upon them with favor in the coming year. If the Sun Dance wasn't performed exactly as the originators had prescribed, if the medicine pole didn't stand straight, or if the medicine woman or the virgins weren't virtuous, great calamity might come to the people. But always the people did it right and felt renewed and good.

Other ceremonies, while smaller, were equally important. When the pipe carrier opened his bundle, he had to lift out all the items and sing a song or tell the story of each. Sacred tobacco had to be smoked to the four directions. Sweet grass had to be burned. Chosen assistants acted out the animal stories.

Each tribe had sacred bundles. The Cheyennes had their sacred arrows and sacred medicine hat. The Sioux had their sacred pipes. The Blackfeet had their sacred beaver bundles. Many of these bundles contained physical objects manifesting the tribe's origins—a sacred digging stick, an elkskin robe—or simply stories of how that sacred bundle came to be and what it meant to the people and how it must be maintained and handed down so the hoop would not be broken.

As sacred as the Sun Dance or any of the bundles was the buffalo. Indians hunted the buffalo, or *pte* as they called him, and considered him their staff of life. They killed the buffalo and made offerings to the buffalo's spirit so he would be generous to them the next time. They used virtually all the parts of the buffalo: hoofs and phallus for glue, tails for flyswatters or ornaments, horns for spoons, cups, or gunpowder flasks, tanned hides for clothes and lodge covers, raw hide for parfleches and bowstrings and saddle covers, beard hair for lariats, halters, bridles, and saddle padding, intestines for making sausage, dewclaws and scrotums for rattles, skulls for religious ceremonies, tongues for the same purpose or as a delicacy, unborn calves for bags to carry pemmican, berries, and tobacco, bones for sled runners, dice, even paintbrushes, dung for fire fuel, and finally meat as the staple of their diet.

Before the Plains Indians obtained the horse in the early eighteenth century, they used the buffalo jump as their primary method for killing buffalo. The buffalo jump, or *pishkun,* as the Blackfeet called it, was a simple device, usually a cliff or a high bluff but sometimes just a sharp incline down into a coulee. The trick was to encourage the buffalo to charge to the precipice and keep on going. The buffalo didn't have to be killed by the fall, because there were people at the bottom finishing them off with arrows, lances, and clubs. Getting the buffalo to begin their stampede required skill and precision. Warriors wearing buffalo robes, moving slowly, keeping low, would get behind the herd and at a signal would jump to their feet, waving the robes, yelling, screaming, and the buffalo would take off at a dead run in the other direction. Buffalo are very fast and quick, and they have a tendency to move in unison, in waves, like a school of fish. People and objects, by predesign, would already be stationed on either side of the stampeding buffalo, narrowing the animals' path, as in a funnel, until all the buffalo were bunched together, running for their lives, straight over the edge of the precipice.

When the killing was done, everybody, even men, who usually left such tasks to the women, would move among the animals skinning them, butchering them, taking choice pieces of meat. This was one time when the Indians didn't use all of the buffalo for their various utility. The people left much meat to rot in the hot sun. Perhaps it wasn't good conservation practice, but who cared? There were millions and millions of buffalo on the plains. They would never go away. What was left became food for the great chain of carrion-eaters—the bears, coyotes, and badgers, the eagles, ravens, and magpies, the maggots, the worms.

During these early days the Indians depended on large scruffy dogs as their beasts of burden. These dogs pulled travois, packed with the people's belongings. The people carried on their backs what the dogs couldn't. Needless to say, the Indians traveled light—their shelters were simple, almost improvised from place to place when they changed camp, depending on what materials were available. Usually they consisted of a few skins sewn together, propped up with the travois poles, a crude predecessor to the large roomy tipis of the horse Indians. Since these early Indians had no horses or guns, they lived a feast-or-famine lifestyle, living high off the buffalo they killed in the buffalo jump or by the more tedious method of deceit in which they again would cover themselves with buffalo skins and try to fool the not very intelligent animals into thinking they were short buffalo. If they could do this, they could get close enough to kill at least one buffalo, maybe more. Often they killed deer or antelope or bighorn sheep or bears. But much of the time, they lived off mice and gophers and porcupines and badgers and prairie chickens and sage hens, and other small animals and birds; some of the Indians in the more arid regions ate insects. They dug roots—wild onions, turnips, camas, wild iris, and bitterroot—and picked fruit—sarvisberries, buffaloberries, elderberries, rose hips, chokecherries, wild plums, cactus buds, and crab apples. They dried the roots and fruit and meat for winter, when food was even more scarce, often nonexistent. It was a tough life, but most of them survived. Their diet was actually very healthy when all these things were available.

Then the horse, large and fast and frightening, galloped out onto the plains, offering great promise but initially acting as an agent for hostility. The tribes that had acquired the horse earlier, the smaller and less aggressive mountain and basin tribes, suddenly found a new power against their old tormentors, the Plains Indians. They rode in among their enemies, fast and mobile, shooting arrows, trampling, clubbing heads. Revenge was sweet, but short-lived.

Each group of Indians were so surprised when they saw their first horses, they tried to make up words to describe them. The Blackfeet, who saw their first horses in about 1730, called them "elk-dogs," which is a pretty good description. The horse looked something like an elk and could be domesticated to carry or drag things like a dog. It has been suggested that the Indians first employed the horse as a pack animal. This may have been true for a short while, but then somebody, a foolhardy youngster perhaps, climbed up on the back of one of these beasts and discovered something wonderful.

The horse originally came with the Spaniards in the very early sixteenth century when they invaded Mexico (not long after Columbus made land on the Windward Islands in the Caribbean Sea in the name of Queen Isabella and proceeded to kill and enslave the people who welcomed him). From Mexico, after conquering the Mayas and Aztecs, the Spaniards rode up into the territory that is now Arizona and New Mexico. They had been told that this territory contained vast amounts of gold, cities of gold, the Seven Cities of Cibola, gold which the Spaniards sought to send back to Spain. Of course, there was no gold to be easily had, or at least not cities of gold, in the desert southwest. But the Spaniards did establish mission forts, especially among the Pueblo people. One of the largest was called Santa Fe. Although the Pueblo people were mainly farmers, they were surrounded by nomadic hunters who raided the pueblos on a routine basis. The Comanches, Kiowas, and Apaches later found the mission forts worth raiding. As early as 1705, the Comanches were striking the New Mexico settlements, stealing horses, sometimes driving off whole herds.

It didn't take long for the trade system to include these new creatures which could carry a man or a load on their backs. The Comanches began to drive horses northwest into the Great Basin country of present-day Utah, southern Idaho, and southwestern Wyoming. They traded with the Utes and the Shoshones. Gradually horses reached the Nez Perce, Salish, and Kutenai peoples in the mountains of northern Idaho and western Montana. Soon the Blackfeet out on the plains of Montana had them. When Lewis and Clark, in 1805, came through this northwestern area on their way to the West Coast and back, they bought horses from many of these tribes. At a greatly inflated price.

Another route for the diffusion of horses to the Plains Indians was more straightforward. The Kiowas and later the Comanches drove horses from the southwest into the central plains of Colorado and Nebraska. There they traded horses for goods with the Arapahos and Cheyennes, who in turn traded horses northward into the Dakotas. On the surface, it is surprising that the tribes in the Dakotas that established the biggest trade in horses were the agricultural people, the Arikaras, Hidatsas, and Mandans, all tribes who lived in settlements along the Missouri River. On the other hand, it is natural that the southern traders would bring their horses to these particular Indians—they knew where these tribes were at all times, and these tribes had goods that the southern Indians wanted. It seems that the most natural exchanges occurred between the settled agricultural people and the nomadic hunting people. Thus it would seem that the swap would be horses for grains and beans and tobacco.

But in the case of the upper Missouri tribes, they had other things to offer. Because they were close to Canada, they often traded with British and French companies. Unlike the Spanish, who strictly forbade the Indians to own guns, these northern Europeans willingly traded guns and ammunition to the relatively peaceful agricultural tribes (or to any other Indian who had something of value). Thus, the most important exchange between the southern tribes and the northern tribes was horses for guns. Actually, in those early days, neither of these commodities was available in great abundance— demand far exceeded supply. But enough guns and horses became available so that they made a significant inroad into Plains Indian

culture. Later on, horses were available in large numbers, but guns and especially ammunition remained rare and much valued. Indians learned somewhat later how to make lead balls and reload spent cartridge shells.

The Lakotas in this period of the mid-eighteenth century were not a big factor in intertribal conflicts. They were nomadic, on foot, their only domesticated animal the dog. And because in the dog days the Indians had to scatter to forage for food, the Sioux were not concentrated in large, mobile bands, as they were later.

So, the nonthreatening Lakotas got their first horse through trade with the agricultural Indians on the Missouri River. They in turn traded horses to their eastern relatives, the Dakotas and Yanktonais. In a relatively short time, the Sioux, who outnumbered all other tribal groups within a thousand miles, dominated the northern plains.

Plains Indians and horses were truly made for each other. Imagine the vastness of the plains, the "big open," mile after mile of rolling dry country, of hot sun or blistering blizzards, of great buffalo herds and antelope off in the distance, always staying a little out of reach; then imagine a family or a small group of families and their travois dogs walking slowly across this open, largely shelterless landscape that was much the same in all directions. Imagine the women with infants on their backs, and small children and old people trying to keep up, the crisis of stepping on a prickly pear cactus, or worse, a rattlesnake. Then imagine the hunters going out on foot in the teeth of a roaring blizzard because there was no more food in the winter camp. Imagine famine, starvation. It happened often.

Then imagine how the horse would effect the social and economic structure of these wandering people. Small groups became larger, lodges became larger. Divisions between rich and poor became more prominent. Men with large horse herds could afford to take more wives. More wives meant more buffalo skins prepared for trading. It took at least four women to prepare the number of hides a single horseback hunter could provide. More children meant more help to acquire more horses and to work around the lodge when they grew up. As children they represented a man's wealth—he could afford them. Indians came to be impressed with wealth, and a large herd of horses became a symbol of that wealth. Young men risked their lives to take horses from other tribes. To steal horses was not only a means to obtain wealth but a chance to display courage and cunning, virtues which impressed potential young wives.

The horse, in practical terms, meant that the Indians could follow the buffalo herds closely. They could strike camp and find new herds within a day or two. A good buffalo runner was much faster than a buffalo. With their bows and arrows, hunters could kill as many buffalo as they needed or wanted (the early muzzle-loaders the Indians had acquired from the white man were almost worthless in the buffalo chase, because they were impossible to reload at a full gallop). Then they could load the meat and hides on packhorses and carry them a long distance back to camp. Also, as the Indians throughout the warm months accumulated dried meat, berries, and roots, they could carry them on pack animals right into winter so that they could eat well even during the cold, stormy times. And they accumulated possessions. Medicine bundles became larger and more complex; tipis, which in the pre-horse days were made from four to seven skins, now grew to twenty, thirty, even up to forty skins for council lodges. Furniture and bedding, cooking utensils, flour, sugar, and coffee, changes of clothes, religious articles, things that a family did not *need* for day-to-day life, such as war bonnets, burial moccasins with beaded soles, brass jewelry, and elaborate paint kits, became part of their traveling households.

A horse could pack two hundred pounds of material on its back or drag three hundred pounds on a travois. A large dog could pack less than forty pounds on its back. A horse could travel over twenty miles a day comfortably, while a dog could go only five or six miles. A horse ate grass, abundant on the plains, while a dog needed meat, always in short supply. Dogs fought each other, and so had to be strung out a good distance from each other while the group was on the move, while horses were relatively peaceful among themselves.

Perhaps more than anything, the horse brought new excitement into the lives of the Plains Indians. Suddenly they could move as fast as the wind, they could chase down enemies and game, which before the arrival of the horse would have been only an empty wish. Above all, they could control these beasts, they could ride them, make them do their bidding. And they became highly skilled in horsemanship.

Almost all of the soldiers who came to fight them, from generals to privates, remarked on the expertise of the Indian horsemen, how horse and man were almost one. One stunt which most impressed them involved the Indian way of fighting. An Indian would slide down to the side of his horse, hook one heel in the ribcage on the other side of the backbone, hook another beneath the horse's belly, throw one arm around the horse's neck, and manage to fire a rifle, handgun, or even a bow and arrow from beneath the horse's neck at the enemy. Although this fancy stunt impressed the soldiers, they lived to tell the tale, because it was next to impossible to get off an accurate shot. This is one of the foolish tactics that Crazy Horse frowned upon. He was a practical man.

Nevertheless, the horse gave the Indian freedom and mobility and power. And the desire to show off.

Indians loved pageantry—whether going out on a horse-stealing raid or coming home with scalps after a successful war party, they would paint themselves and their horses, put on their best clothes, and parade through the village. Or they would show up on a ridge, hundreds of them, just like in the movies, to display their might to passing wagon trains, railroad workers, or small cavalry units—quite often posing just before an attack. Sometimes this pageantry was more organized and sophisticated, such as the time wave after wave of painted warriors on their best horses galloped up to and around the Black Hills peace commissioners. Even the threatening gestures, the angry shouts, the mad dashes back and forth and around the commissioners was carefully orchestrated by Crazy Horse and the other "free" Lakota leaders who did not take part in the discussions but had runners reporting to them. They wanted to make a statement not only to the commissioners, but to the reservation Indians about the wisdom of selling the Black Hills. They did it in the most flamboyant style they could think of.

Such a display, which made the commissioners and their soldier escorts tremble in their boots, was effective not only as a statement but as a threat to life and limb. The whites were truly at the Indians' mercy. This kind of demonstration gave the newspapers and the cheap novels of the period plenty of ammunition in their portrayal of the Indians as brute savages, whose only recourse to reasonable discussion was violent posturing. Readers as far away as New York and Europe had developed an image of howling bloodthirsty fiends who would stop at nothing until all the settlers were skinned alive and their women repeatedly violated. It was always this image of white women being defiled by red men that struck the most outraged chorus of responses.

Yes, the Indians scalped, tortured, and mutilated their enemies. Their enemies included other tribes with whom they had longstanding conflicts, white settlers who were stealing their land, and soldiers who constantly sought to kill them.

Tribal warfare was traditional and continual. Usually the battles were centered on revenge, a kind of nonstop revenge, war parties going back and forth between tribes. The Sioux hated the Crows and Shoshones, or Snakes. The Crows hated the Sioux and Blackfeet. The Blackfeet hated the Crows and Snakes and Assiniboins. Always, they sought to kill each other, to count coup, to humiliate, to steal women and horses, to avenge the death of warriors who had been killed in a previous battle. Sometimes alliances were formed to present a more powerful force. The Sioux and Cheyennes and Arapahos were such an alliance. The Arikaras, Hidatsas, and Mandans formed an alliance. The Crows and Snakes presented a united front when possible.

Most tribal battles involved a lot of skirmishing, a lot of coup counting, with very few casualties. Indians were not out to annihilate each other, but to exact revenge or cover themselves with war honors. In most instances, it was better to humiliate the enemy than to kill him. A Blackfeet account tells of a party of horse raiders who stole into an enemy camp one night and made off with some buffalo runners. One of the raiders found a sentry sleeping at the base of a ledge near the edge of camp. The warrior pissed on the sentry from the ledge, then stole off into the darkness. This feat was talked about in the Blackfeet camps for years to come. The Blackfeet got off with the horses, and the drenched sentry had to explain to his chiefs what happened. It was almost better than counting coup. It gave the whole tribe a chuckle.

Of course, warfare was more serious than that. It was important to lift the enemy's hair, both as a warning to the enemy and as a morale-booster to the scalper, his party, and other tribesmen. Nothing delighted a waiting camp more than to see scalps on the lances of returning warriors. These scalps were passed around, talked about, laughed at, sometimes thrown into the fire or given to the dogs in disdain. Often the hair decorated a lodge or was sewn onto a war shirt. White men's hair was taken but was less desirable because it was usually short. Some of the white men were balding and weren't worth scalping. But scalping was an institution among the Plains tribes. A scalp was a trophy of war, just as it became for the whites.

Torture, and the mutilation of bodies dead and alive, was, and is, more problematic, if only because it is odious to civilized society. Throughout the years, those cultures which have "seen the light" have been horrified by the desecration of bodies committed by barbarians of other cultures. We think of the Nazis in World War II who justified torture and mutilation of live bodies for "scientific" purposes. The communists in Russia, especially under Stalin, committed

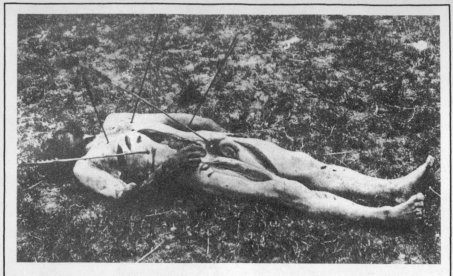

Sergeant Frederick Wylyams, killed and mutilated by a Cheyenne or Sioux band near Fort Wallace, Kansas, in 1867. He was photographed by Dr. William Abraham Bell, a close friend. *Smithsonian Institution*

Ralph Morrison, a hunter, who was killed and scalped by Cheyennes near Fort Dodge, Kansas, in 1868. The photograph was taken within an hour of his death. *Smithsonian Institution*

similar atrocities on ethnic groups. The Khmer Rouge beheaded and chopped the limbs from innocent people and left them by the thousands in the killing fields of Cambodia. The military did the same in El Salvador. Thousands of Moskito Indians died in such a horrible fashion. African leaders, in their beribboned military costumes and with their weapons supplied by the United States, Russia, France, and Israel, continue to kill and mutilate their tribal enemies.

European tribes beheaded their foes, posting the heads along roads or at the town gates as a grisly warning to those who would oppose them. The Catholic Church in Europe, especially Spain, during the Inquisition tortured and mutilated those who it thought were possessed by the devil—or those it simply wanted to get rid of for political reasons. The Puritans in America burned, crushed, and drowned people almost gratuitously in their effort to root out witchery. Thousands, probably millions, of people have been treated in a similar fashion by the religious right of all cultures.

Soldiers who go to war commit unspeakable acts to their enemies. Homer tells us that in the Trojan War, Achilles dragged Hector's mutilated body behind his chariot for twelve days. From the time of the Slaughter of the Innocents to My Lai in Vietnam, war has created a callousness toward human life to such a degree that torture and mutilation have become accepted practices. Witness the Serbs in their treatment of the Muslims, torturing and mutilating men, raping women to death—all in the name of ethnic and religious purity. Virtually all warfare has been conducted for such contrived principles as ethnic and religious purity.

On November 29, 1864, a former Methodist preacher and Civil War officer, Colonel John Chivington, led two regiments of Colorado militia in a dawn attack on a sleeping camp of Southern Cheyennes at Sand Creek. This group of Indians was led by Black Kettle, who survived the attack only to be killed four years later in another dawn surprise led by General George A. Custer on the Washita River in Oklahoma.

The reason given for Chivington's attack was a familiar one. Indians had been raiding, stealing horses and cattle, killing settlers. Whether the attack by Chivington's hundred-day volunteers caught the right Indians is not even debatable. They did not. It has been stated that these Colorado volunteers' enlistment was about up and they wanted some action. Because of their inefficiency in punishing Indians they were derisively called the "Bloodless" 3rd Cavalry.

Black Kettle had been given an American flag at a treaty council in 1861 by the Commissioner of Indian Affairs. The chief had been told at that time that as long as the flag flew over his village his people would be safe.

It is known that some of Chivington's junior officers reminded him of this promise. Evan S. Connell, in *Son of the Morning Star,* quotes the violent Chivington as replying: "I have come to kill Indians, and believe it is right and honorable to use any means under God's heaven to kill Indians!" He is reported to have added: "Scalps are what we are after.... I long to be wading in gore!"

And soon he was. Even after Black Kettle himself came out of his lodge waving the American flag, Chivington's troopers shot men, women, and children indiscriminately. There are many accounts, not only those of Indian survivors but also those of the troopers themselves, of soldiers taking deliberate aim at fleeing children. A Major Scott Anthony remembered the murder of a three-year-old: "I saw one man get off his horse at a distance of about seventy-five yards and draw up his rifle and fire. He missed the child. Another man came up and said, 'Let me try the son of a bitch. I can hit him.' He got down off his horse, kneeled down, and fired at the little child, but he missed him. A third man came up and made a similar remark, and fired, and the little fellow dropped."

When the killing ended, soldiers went from body to body, scalping them, cutting off ears and fingers to get at jewelry, cutting out the genitals of men, women, and children, arranging the bodies in suggestive postures. A Lieutenant James Connor stated in testimony that he did not find a single body that had not been mutilated. He went on: "I also heard of numerous instances in which men had cut out the private parts of females and stretched them over the saddlebows and wore them over their hats while riding in the ranks."

By way of justification for such acts, several men said they found scalps, which they identified as belonging to whites by the color of the hair, hanging from lodgepoles, a couple of them fresh. "The skin and flesh attached to the hair appeared to be yet quite moist," one said. It doesn't appear that there were many of these scalps, but by the time the militia got back to Denver the number had grown to dozens of white scalps—as well as a blanket woven from white women's hair.

Chivington's troop's last act of heroism was to display a hundred Indian scalps on the stage of a Denver theater. They were greeted by thunderous applause. The Bloodless 3rd became celebrated as the "Bloody Thirdsters."

The Indians committed their share of atrocities, of torture and mutilation. There had been many accounts in the eastern newspapers of such acts, but they were isolated, small instances, quickly forgotten in the bustle of the industrializing nation. The frontier newspapers were more alarmed. These killings were happening too close for comfort. In 1869, the *Helena Weekly Herald* reported: "That we are on the verge of a general Indian outbreak no sensible man who understands the situation can deny. The pleasant and innocent amusement of butchering and scalping the pale-faces is believed by some likely soon to begin in good earnest."

But the Plains Indians were equally outraged by the notion that an invasion force of whites was seeking to conquer them, perhaps annihilate them, certainly take their land, kill all their buffalo, and reduce them to prisoners on reservations where they would be forced to deny their religion, their culture, their traditional methods of supporting themselves—in short, take away their way of life as they had practiced it for centuries. They had learned at Sand Creek, the Marias, and the Washita that the whites would stop at nothing to bend the Indians to their will. The arrogant invaders would not stop until the Indians were forced to adopt the ways of the white man—or were executed.

Eastern Indians had already been slaughtered and the survivors imprisoned on reservations for centuries. None other than Christopher Columbus wrote to the King and Queen of Spain about the Tainos who welcomed him to the New World: "So tractable, so peaceable, are these people that I swear to your Majesties there is not in the world a better nation. They love their neighbors as themselves, and their discourse is ever sweet and gentle, and accompanied with a smile; and though it is true that they are naked, yet their manners are decorous and praiseworthy." Then the Spaniards, in their search for gold, proceeded to loot and burn villages and kidnap hundreds of men, women, and children to be sold into slavery in Europe. Within a decade, whole tribes had been annihilated, thousands of people killed.

But this was just the beginning. The English-speaking white men arrived in Virginia in 1607 and received the same welcome as Columbus's Spaniards by the Powhatans. Within a few years, thanks to the superiority of English weapons, their numbers had been reduced from eight thousand to less than a thousand. When the white men landed at Plymouth, Massachusetts, in 1620, they were welcomed and saved from starving to death that first winter by the

Pemaquids and Wampanoags, who shared their corn with them and taught them how to fish. In the next several years, the whites took more and more land from the Indians, who were only too willing to help these strangers. In 1675, Metacom, leader of a confederacy of eastern tribes, dubbed King Philip by the whites, attempted to lead his people from the brink of extinction. But the guns of the colonists proved too strong and the Indians were defeated, killed, pushed farther into the wilderness, and several of them were captured and sold as slaves. King Philip was beheaded and his head was publicly exhibited at Plymouth for several years.

For the next two centuries the whites pushed west, slaughtering and imprisoning Indians in their way. The Mohicans and Raritans in New York, the Five Nations of the Iroquois, the Senecas, the Ottowas, the Shawnees, the Miamis, the Sauks and Foxes, the Winnebagos, Potawatomis, and Kickapoos, the Chickasaws, Choctaws, Creeks, and Seminoles were attacked. Whenever and wherever they were encountered they were termed savages and disposed of.

Perhaps Americans remember best the fate of the Cherokees. These highly civilized, friendly people had taught white settlers how best to survive in the lush Carolina region of the southeast. But with the press of white settlers who wanted even their treaty lands, they became victims of a law proposed by Andrew Jackson, a military leader whose army had already killed thousands of Cherokees, Creeks, and Choctaws, soon after his election to the presidency of the United States in 1829. This law, enacted in 1834, was called "An Act to Regulate Trade and Intercourse with the Indian Tribes and to Preserve Peace on the Frontiers." Under the terms of this act, all of the United States west of the Mississippi "and not within the States of Missouri and Louisiana or the Territory of Arkansas" would be Indian country. All eastern Indians who still held territory the white man wanted would be moved there. As a bogus compensatory gesture it was stipulated that no white man could enter this Indian country.

In the fall of 1838, all the Cherokees were rounded up by U.S. soldiers and driven westward to the Indian Territory in Oklahoma. It is difficult for most Americans to imagine what it must be like to be forced to leave your chosen country en masse—your ancestral country, the country the Great Spirit had blessed, the home where all your people had lived and were happy and died and were buried— forever. Perhaps a small clue might be found in what the Cherokee people called the journey: the Trail of Tears. During this winter forced march, one out of every four people died of disease, cold, or hunger. The survivors found themselves in a strange, arid landscape.

The United States broke its law almost immediately when thousands of soldiers marched through Indian Territory to go to war with the Spaniards of the southwest. After winning the war in 1847, the United States took all the territory from Texas to California.

In 1848, gold was discovered in California, and thousands of gold-seekers crossed the Mississippi into Indian country. Thousands more went north to settle in Oregon, while many ended up in the southwest. Wagon trails became permanent ruts in the fragile earth of the plains.

By this time, the U. S. government was not interested in enforcing the law which prohibited whites from entering Indian country. In fact, they saw the Indians as an impediment to westward expansion. What to do?

Invent Manifest Destiny, of course. The whites had not only the right but the duty to expand their horizon westward. It was God's will. God also told them to tame the Indians, to civilize them, and if they refused His generosity, to kill them. Nothing could stand in the way of destiny.

And so the floodgates opened and the war with the Plains Indians began, a war which would not come to a close until 1890, when a band of Ghost Dancers was massacred at Wounded Knee.

But the Indians had lost the war long before Wounded Knee. By 1860 there were approximately 300,000 Indians left in the continental United States out of an estimated one million at the time the colonists landed in Virginia and New England. By way of contrast, there were 31 million whites in 1860—and they were still coming. By 1890, thirty years later, the year of Wounded Knee, the population of whites had doubled to 63 million. And by 1900, there would be only 237,000 Indians left, most of them on reservations in the west.

And so it is not difficult to understand that in their increasingly rare victories over the aggressors the Plains Indians would vent their sorrow and rage in the one way they could which would give them a small satisfaction—they mutilated the bodies of the *men* who had come to kill them.

But even in their horrible acts there was a purpose, a purpose which makes much more sense than gratuitous slaughter: It was clear to the Indians that their enemies would be there in the world behind this one, the real world, and an enemy without arms or legs or a head could do them no harm there. They wanted to live in peace when they joined their ancestors. Custer and his troops at the Little Bighorn were just another threat to this peace.

Who was the Indian? Perhaps, as Custer so eloquently stated in *My Life on the Plains*, "Stripped of the beautiful romance with which we have been so long willing to envelope him ... the Indian forfeits his claim to the appellation of the *'noble* red man.'" True. The Indian was not a cliché. The Indian was a providing family man, a protective mother, a teaching grandparent, a child learning to survive in a changing world. To this day, children are taught by their parents to survive the neglect and the many injustices heaped upon them by the new world order. And to remember their people's lives on the plains. These are not noble red men. Nor savages. These are Native Americans. Human beings.

A Bannock family of the Sheep-eater band camped on Medicine Lodge Creek in Idaho, 1871. Photo by William Henry Jackson. *Smithsonian Institution*

At approximately 12:15 on the afternoon of June 25, 1876, General George Armstrong Custer, hot on the trail of the traveling village of Lakotas and Cheyennes, crossed the divide between the Rosebud and the Little Bighorn valleys and split his command into three battalions. Captain Frederick Benteen was to lead his three companies on a sweep south to reconnoiter from the hills east of the Little Bighorn River. He was to prevent any Indian escape upriver. If he found fleeing Indians he was to "pitch in" to them, and send a courier to notify Custer immediately. If he found no Indians he was to rejoin the other two battalions as quickly as possible. Major Marcus A. Reno was to lead his three companies down the south side of Ash Creek (later named Reno Creek) to its mouth, cross the Little Bighorn, and attack the enemy camp from the south. Custer would take his own five companies (210 men and officers) along and behind a ridge to the east, first riding parallel to Reno's advance battalion on the north side of Ash Creek, looking to find the far end of the village, where he would make his own attack.

Custer was full of high energy this day, conferring with the scouts one minute, his officers the next, riding among the troops, buoying their spirits. Custer was ready to kill Indians. He had been waiting for this moment ever since his successful attack on the Southern Cheyenne village on the Washita eight years earlier.

As the three battalions separated to go their own ways, the temperature was already nearing a hundred degrees. The men had not slept the night before; they had marched in darkness, stopping only at dawn to make coffee from a stream of brackish water. The Indian scouts, Arikaras and Crows, had scouted ahead all night and had spent much of their time on their tired ponies talking of Custer's foolishness in preparing to attack such a large village. At the same time, they were committed to help destroy their powerful enemies.

At 2:15, Custer called Reno over to an abandoned campsite east of Ash Creek. A lone tipi stood, and within the tipi lay a dead Lakota warrior, Old She Bear. He had been mortally wounded a few days earlier in the successful attack by the Lakotas and Cheyennes on the command of General George A. Crook. It was at this point that Custer gave Major Reno orders to lead out in preparation for a charge. According to Reno, Custer's adjutant, W. W. Cooke, came to him with Custer's orders: "To move forward at as rapid a gait as prudent and to charge afterwards, and that the whole outfit would support me." Meanwhile, the Arikara scouts painted themselves for battle and for

Battle of the Little Bighorn, as drawn by Amos Bad Heart Bull.
University of Nebraska Press

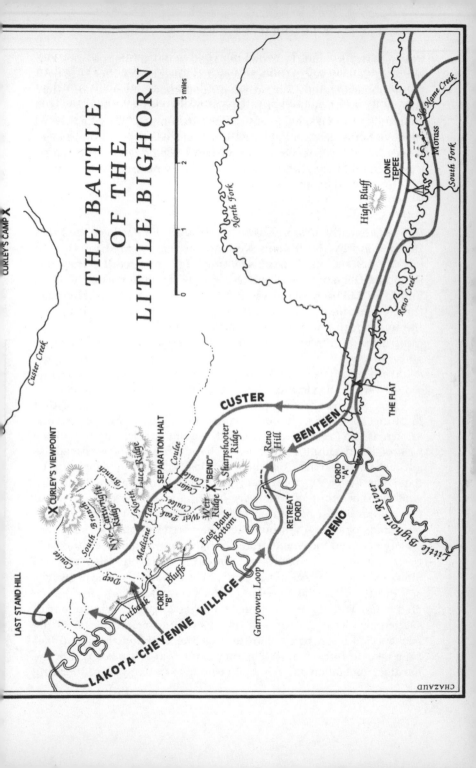

CURLEY'S CAMP **X**

Custer Creek

THE BATTLE
OF THE
LITTLE BIGHORN

3 miles

0   1   2

North Fork

South Branch

CURLEY'S VIEWPOINT **X**

Nye-Cartwright Ridge

North Luce Ridge

SEPARATION HALT **X**

Cedar Coulee

Coulee

Sharpshooter Ridge

Deep Coulee

South Branch

Medicine Tail

Weir Peak

Weir Ridge **X** "BEND"

Reno Hill

East Bank Bottom

CUSTER

BENTEEN

High Bluff

LONE TEPEE

No Name Creek

Morass

South Fork

THE FLAT

Reno Creek

LAST STAND HILL

Deep Coulee

Cutbank

Bluffs

FORD "B"

RETREAT FORD

FORD "A"

LAKOTA-CHEYENNE VILLAGE

Garryowen Loop

RENO

Little Bighorn River

CHAZAUD

death. Both they and the Crows felt they would all die that day. Earlier, Half Yellow Face, a Crow, had said to Custer: "You and I are both going home today by a road we do not know." Even before that, Bloody Knife, an Arikara, had signed to the sun with his hands: "I shall not see you go down behind the hills tonight." They had seen a massive horse herd and smoke from hundreds if not thousands of lodges far in the distance, and they knew they did not have a chance. Custer thought they were cowards. And now he ordered the battalions forward, Reno leading out.

One of the many mysteries which surround the Battle of the Little Bighorn is why the Indians were not better prepared for the 7th Cavalry's attack on their village. Only eight days earlier they had fought off General Crook's thirteen-hundred-man force on the Rosebud. They had been told by reservation Indians who were arriving at the big camp daily that there were soldiers to the east. Scouting parties and hunting parties were constantly leaving and returning to camp from all directions. Custer's Crow scouts, about eight miles ahead of Custer's last camp on the morning of the 25th, said they could see smoke from the army campfires. If any Sioux or Cheyenne scouts were in the vicinity, they should have seen the smoke too.

And, as a matter of fact, there were Sioux parties in the area that morning. The Crow scouts, on the promontory in the Wolf Mountains known as the Crow's Nest, observed two Sioux riders not far to the west of them, riding right toward them. An attempt was made to ambush these warriors, but the scouts lost sight of them down on the flat. Then they saw a group of six other Sioux hunting buffalo nearby. And another group of four were hunting at the base of the small mountains, not far below the Crow's Nest. There were other sightings of Indians by the Crow scouts, and they became convinced that the enemy had seen the smoke from Custer's camp and were riding back to warn the village. Mitch Boyer, one of Custer's scouts, had seen two Sioux within 150 yards of the camp. He watched them sneak away.

But the final evidence that Custer's command had been discovered came with the news earlier on June 25 that a detachment of soldiers had located a party of Indians on the back trail. One of the packers had lost a box of hardtack on the trail and the squad had been sent to retrieve it. When they arrived at the place where the hardtack had fallen off, they saw a couple of Indian youths breaking open the pack and eating the hardtack. The soldiers fired on them, and one of the Indians, a boy of ten or eleven named Deeds, fell dead, but the other galloped away.

Custer, who had been angry with the Crow and Arikara scouts for suggesting that his command had been discovered, now had to face the fact that the Indians would know within an hour or two not only that he was in the vicinity but precisely where he was. It was at this point that Custer decided he had to attack the village as soon as possible. Normally, army strategy dictated that the best time to attack Indians was at dawn. Large gatherings of Indians usually went to bed after much late-night feasting and dancing and courting and woke up late in the morning. The early-morning attacks had worked at the Washita and Sand Creek, and at the attack on the Blackfeet on the Marias River, and at the Cheyenne village site on the Powder River earlier that year.

Custer had originally planned to lay over under concealment all day on the 25th and attack at dawn on the 26th. If "Custer's Luck" held, the rest of General Terry's Dakota column and General Gibbon's Montana column would arrive at about that time from the west and the Indians would be caught in a loose surround. (Of course, this would require extraordinary luck, and not even Custer would count on it.) But now that he was convinced that his troops had been discovered, all previous plans were thrown to the wind in favor of an immediate attack. As always, in true military mind-set, Custer was afraid that the Indians would escape. This attack would occur, by necessity, at midafternoon, a time when the camp was up and alert and presumably preparing to flee or fight.

So why did Reno's charge into the south end of the village where the powerful Hunkpapas had their camp circle come as a surprise? Sitting Bull, the headman of the Hunkpapas and overall chief of the gathering, had been visiting with friends in a council tipi in the center of the camp. Crazy Horse, at the other end of the village, was seeing acquaintances in the Cheyenne circle. Young warriors were fishing or hunting, women were out digging turnips, others were just sitting around, doing sitting chores, waving buffalo-tail fly brushes over napping children, reliving the revelries of the night before. All were in a peaceful mood.

It was customary for Indians to picket their best horses close to their lodges at night to prevent them from being stolen by enemy thieves. But at dawn on the 25th, the horse wranglers drove these horses first to water, then to the large herds on the hills west of camp. So the only horses in the immediate vicinity of the camp belonged to the police, the *akecita*.

Only moments before Reno's attack, the surviving one of the youngsters who had found the hardtack pack rode into camp to tell what happened. At about the same time, an Oglala who was leaving the village to go back to Red Cloud Agency saw a cloud of dust down the valley, then the blue coats of the soldiers. He whirled around and galloped through camp, shouting, "Soldiers coming here! Soldiers coming here!" The women who were digging turnips also hurried into camp, crying out their warning.

The camp became a turmoil of people running, screaming, shouting, gathering weapons. Young men rushed out to the horse herds to gather family horses. Old men yelled advice. Women and children started to run to the hills on the west side of camp. Dogs ran among the lodges, barking. The few horses in the south end of camp grew skittish, making it difficult to mount them.

By now Reno's columns of twos, then fours, had fanned out in full charge position and the sounds of their rifles echoed throughout the camp, bullets striking tipis, buzzing around the Indians "like angry bees," as one would later put it.

The day before, a Cheyenne prophet, Box Elder, had sent a crier around the camp circles, warning the people to keep their horses close to their lodges because the soldiers would come the next day. A Sans Arc had issued the same warning on the 24th. Another Cheyenne had howled like a wolf and a wolf had answered him. That meant fresh meat in camp, dead meat, soldiers. And then there was Sitting Bull's Sun Dance vision—soldiers falling into camp. Then why were the Indians not prepared for this attack?

There have been explanations. The most common is that since the Indians had beaten Crook so badly only eight days before, the Indians did not think the soldiers would be anxious to tangle with them again so soon. Their scouts had watched Crook retreat to the south. They did not know that the eastern column of soldiers was so close (even though they had been warned repeatedly), and they did not know that it was led by Custer, who, unlike many of his contemporaries, would rather fight Indians than eat.

Another explanation that has been offered is that the Indians were in a purely defensive state of mind. They were not looking for a fight, they were looking only to defend their village, and consequently were not as alert or aggressive as they normally would be. It does seem odd that their roving scouts had not picked up smoke from Custer's campsite or seen the dust kicked up by more than six hundred horses and mules. And too, while Custer's troops marched down Ash Creek, they flushed a party of forty Sioux. Fred Gerard, Custer's interpreter, is reported to have said, "Here are your Indians, General, running like the devil." Reno's attack came forty-five minutes later, around 3:00 P.M., surely giving the Sioux party ample time to warn the village and mobilize the warriors. Historian Stephen E. Ambrose thinks that the Lakotas did not see Reno break off from Custer's column and cross the Little Bighorn to attack the south end of the village. They were still tracking Custer's movements.

Although no full explanation has been given for the Indians' lack of preparedness, perhaps a logical speculation would be that the Sioux and Cheyenne leaders knew of the army's penchant for attacking at dawn and had expected the fight to occur the next day. Certainly they didn't expect to be attacked in midafternoon. And perhaps they were just complacent in their strength. Their numbers had been growing by the day and were still growing, almost hourly. In any case, Reno's charge caught the Indians "napping," as Custer is reported to have exclaimed.

But there were a few horses in camp, and a rather cautious counterattack was launched by a few warriors. Although they did not venture too far out from the Hunkpapa camp circle, these warriors managed to break Reno's charge, which could have swept quite a way through the confused village and possibly have given Custer a chance to attack from the northern end and create more confusion. But the faint-hearted Reno ordered his men to dismount and form a skirmish line, a fatal mistake for the overall success of the mission. It should be noted here that even as Reno charged down the valley, he was nervously looking around for Custer's troops, who had disappeared behind the bluffs to the east. On a purely human level, Reno and his troops were shocked when they finally saw the size of the village they were charging. They would have been slaughtered if they had tried to charge into it.

Reno's skirmish line consisted of squads of four—three shooters and one horse holder. The holders took the horses away toward the river, thereby reducing Reno's strength by one-fourth, an incredibly drastic reduction in firepower. But the men were cool at this point and did their job with a fair degree of efficiency.

Custer, meanwhile, was heading north behind some tall bluffs on the east side of the river. He was looking for a way down to cross the river and attack the village in its northern reaches. At one halt he galloped over to the top of a high bluff and saw for the first time the huge size of the village. He also saw Reno's 140 troops charging that village. When he rejoined his command he ordered a Sergeant Knipe of Company C to ride back and find the pack train and tell the commanding officer to come quick with extra ammunition packs. Then he moved farther north before riding to the crest of another bluff to view the action. What he saw was Reno's dismounted troops holding their own for the moment at their first skirmish line. Again he rejoined his troops and ordered a trumpeter, Giovanni Martini, to ride back with a message. Custer's adjutant, W.W. Cooke, not trusting the Italian immigrant's command of English, wrote out the order: "Benteen. Come on. Big Village. Be quick, Bring packs. P.S. Bring Pack. W.W. Cooke." Again Custer rode north, desperately concerned with the overwhelming numbers of Indians but somewhat reassured that Reno was keeping them occupied for the time being. Custer still had visions of a northern assault which would confuse and panic the Indians. At this point, Custer was still on the offensive.

But Reno was not doing well as more mounted warriors arrived, shooting into the skirmish line, holding the soldiers at bay. Reno had taken most of the Arikara scouts with him, and they were deployed along the western flank. As more and more Sioux and Cheyenne warriors arrived, the Arikaras began to fall back, eventually mounting up and galloping away from the village. When they recovered their courage, they would become more interested in stealing horses than in fighting their traditional enemies.

As the fight grew hotter, Reno could see that the Indians were getting around the flank that the Arikaras had abandoned and were actually behind the soldiers, so he ordered a "charge" (as he would later put it to a military court of inquiry) into the timber along the river. Here the soldiers found a cutbank which they could use for a breastwork, shooting over the top at the Indians. They were in a good defensive position for the moment, but the Indians just kept coming.

As the Sioux and Cheyennes retrieved their horses from the large herds west of camp, the warriors prepared for battle, not a quick and easy task for some, especially not for Wooden Leg, a young Cheyenne: "I quickly emptied out my war bag and set myself at getting ready to go to battle. I jerked off my ordinary clothing. I jerked on a pair of new breeches that had been given to me by an Uncpapa [Hunkpapa] Sioux. I had a good cloth shirt, and I put it on. My old moccasins were kicked off and a pair of beaded moccasins substituted for them. My father strapped a blanket upon my horse and arranged the rawhide lariat into a bridle. He stood holding my mount. 'Hurry,' he urged me. I was hurrying but I was not yet ready. I got my paints and my little mirror. The blue-black circle soon appeared around my face. The red and yellow colorings were applied on all of the skin inside the circle. I combed my hair. It properly should have been oiled and braided neatly, but my father again was saying, 'Hurry,' so I just looped a buckskin thong about it and tied it close up against the back of my head, to float loose from there." Presumably less vain, the seasoned warriors, more concerned with repelling Reno's attack, wore breechcloths and moccasins and perhaps their leggings and shirts.

Sitting Bull wore his everyday clothes: a fringed buckskin shirt embroidered with green porcupine quills, with tassels of human hair attached to the shoulders; leggings and moccasins and a red breechcloth; a single eagle feather upright in his hair; braids wrapped in otter skins. He carried a butcher knife in a black sheath tucked under his belt. Although short and stocky, he must have cut an imposing figure with his narrow piercing eyes, and a thin-lipped scowl on his red-painted face.

Which brings up another mystery surrounding the Battle of the Little Bighorn: Where was Sitting Bull during the fight? Depending upon which scholar you read, he was making medicine in his tipi, he was riding at the front of his warriors shouting, "Brave up, brave up," he was riding herd on the women and children in the center of camp, or he was cowering behind them. These various accounts of his whereabouts were furnished by Indian people who were in the village. Some of them are honest recollections, but some are inspired by adulation or jealousy. Contrary to popular perception, Sitting Bull was not beloved by all, and his appointment as chief of the gathering did not sit well with some. Gall, a Hunkpapa war leader who fought as fiercely and bravely as any Indian during the battle, was induced by a scheming Indian agent to later brand Sitting Bull a coward, which, of course, is absurd. Sitting Bull, although a holy man as well as a chief, had counted more war honors in his younger days than any of his contemporaries. After the Hunkpapas surrendered four years after the battle, the agent declared Gall the chief of his people and Sitting Bull a coward and troublemaker. Sitting Bull's kin, however, placed the chief at the head of his warriors during the battle.

The truth is that Sitting Bull was forty-two years old at the time of the battle, an advanced age for a warrior. By contrast, Gall was twenty-nine, prime fighting age. Sitting Bull had gone through the self-torture of the Sun Dance earlier that month, cutting fifty strips of flesh from each arm and dancing for a day and a half before finally fainting from fatigue, pain, and gazing at the sun. And he was a chief, not an active war leader.

The most probable sequence of Sitting Bull's movements, based on the majority of accounts, is that he was mounted shortly after Reno's attack, shouting encouragement—definitely not instructions, as some scholars have suggested, since Indians of that time in the heat of battle were not inclined to listen. Then he made his way through the village, gathering women and children and old ones, persuading them to stay put in the safety of the village, or just west of the village, near the hills. Wooden Leg, a Cheyenne warrior, makes a case for this latter action: "I suppose [Sitting Bull] was helping the women and children and old people, where he belonged. He had a son in the fight. Any man having a son serving as a warrior was expected to stay out of battles and give the son his chance to get warrior honors. . . . I do not know of any other tribal chiefs or old men having mixed into the battle. . . . I have no ears for hearing anybody say he was not a brave man."

It didn't take long, perhaps fifteen minutes, for the warriors to put Reno and his troops on the run from the trees near the river. The fighting grew closer and hotter until the Indians were virtually mingling with the troops. It was at this point that a warrior's bullet struck Bloody Knife, the only Arikara scout left, in the head, splattering brains and blood all over Reno's face. And it was here that Reno came apart, shouting orders to mount up, to dismount, then mount again. This last order was not heard by a large number of the troops, and they became aware that this was the plan only when they saw Reno galloping upriver, a handkerchief tied around his head. Among the troops left in the timber was the badly wounded Negro interpreter, Isaiah Dorman. He was married to a Sioux woman and was known by most of the Hunkpapas as On Azinpi or Teat. According to some accounts, an old woman was about to shoot him when he begged for mercy: "Don't shoot me, Auntie. I'll be dead soon enough, anyway." Then when a group of warriors were about to kill him and strip his body, Sitting Bull himself rode up and said, "Don't kill that man! He is Teat. He used to be a friend of our people." Sitting Bull gave him a drink of water with his own drinking cup of polished buffalo horn. After his drink, Teat died. Later, his body was found, stripped and mutilated, "a picket pin through his balls."

"Lonesome" Charley Reynolds, the scout who had ridden day and night through hostile Lakota and Cheyenne country with the news of the gold discovery in the Black Hills in 1874, was also killed in the timber when he tried to make a break to catch up with Reno.

Gall and One Bull, both Hunkpapas, led the fight against the soldiers in the timber, the Indians rushing at them again and again, blowing their eagle-bone whistles, firing their weapons, screaming, clubbing, until the troopers panicked and raced their horses upstream. One Bull and his brother, White Bull, were nephews of Sitting Bull and did the fighting for the family. It was traditional for young warriors to defend their family's honor, and both youngsters counted many coups that day, jerking soldiers from their horses, striking them, taking their guns and ammunition and horses.

Gall, who fought the longest and the hardest of any warrior that day, also lost the most—his wife and children were killed by the soldiers. Nevertheless, it was Gall who led the pursuit of Reno's troops, who were galloping toward the ford they had crossed to begin their attack on the village. But their big American horses were just about used up, and the Indians were in among the stragglers, shooting them, clubbing them from their horses. In desperation Reno made a turn toward the river, and the men followed, jumping their horses from a four-to-six-foot bank into the river. It took remarkable horsemanship to stay mounted during the jump and then in the fast swirling water. Many of the troopers fell from their horses, either on the bank or in the water. They were killed where they fell, many in hand-to-hand combat in the river. Even Black Elk, a mere boy, got into the act. A warrior told him to get off his horse and scalp one of the wounded soldiers: "I got off and started to do it. He had short hair and my knife was not very sharp. He ground his teeth. Then I shot him in the forehead and got his scalp."

But most of Reno's troopers made it to the other side and managed, through fear and adrenaline, to climb a high, steep bluff on the other side. At this point, the Indians left off their pursuit. Sitting Bull is reported to have said, "Let them go! Let them live to tell the truth about this battle." And so the Lakotas busied themselves stripping the bodies on the bank and back in the timber. Meanwhile, the troops, dazed and frightened, regrouped on top of Reno Hill, where they would lie under siege for a day and a half.

Incredibly, a number of soldiers and scouts managed to hide out in the brush down by the river after Reno's retreat. Some, including scout George Herendeen, who was almost trampled in his hiding

Gall, a Hunkpapa Lakota warrior who led part of the final attacks up Last Stand Hill. *Smithsonian Institution*

Reno's panicked retreat back across the Little Bighorn River, drawn by Amos Bad Heart Bull. *University of Nebraska Press*

place by Sioux warriors, were able to rejoin Reno in a couple of hours after most of the Indian warriors left. Others, including Lieutenant Charles C. DeRudio, post interpreter Fred Gerard, and Pikuni scout Billy Jackson, hid out until the night of the 26th. Gerard and Jackson reached Reno's position at 11:00 P.M. DeRudio came a short time later.

Crazy Horse, when the battle began, was at the far end of the village, some three miles away. According to most Indian reports, he immediately rallied his Oglalas and Cheyennes and sent them off to get their horses and paint up. He prepared for battle by painting his face with a lightning streak and his body with hailstones, in accordance with his dream. He tied the red-backed hawk on his head and sprinkled gopher dust on himself and his horse, to make them impervious to bullets. It was a trick that had worked many times for him in the past. When all were prepared they raced through the village to the point of Reno's attack. By the time they arrived, Reno had been repulsed, the timber battle had been fought, and the soldiers were racing toward the place where they forded the river. At best, Crazy Horse only got in at the tail end of this particular battle. From the time Reno attacked at 3:00 P.M. to the time he climbed the bluff in full retreat, the fight had lasted a little over an hour.

But while the Indians were stripping the bodies, they heard shooting. The shooting was far off and not heavy, but in the momentary quiet, the warriors became alert. Then a messenger rode up, pointing back down the river, shouting of another attack, this time at the north end of the village.

Gall quickly gathered his Hunkpapas and galloped off through the cottonwoods between the village and the river, while Crazy Horse and his Oglalas raced north through camp, picking up other warriors who had also heard the shooting. Women in camp trilled as the horses pounded by. Crazy Horse, the inspirational leader, encouraged his men: "Ho-ka hey! It is a good day to fight! It is a good day to die! Strong hearts, brave hearts, to the front! Weak hearts and cowards to the rear!" By now all of the warriors had caught their horses and finished making war medicine, and the fighting force numbered nearly two thousand.

Custer's intention at the ford where Medicine Tail Coulee empties into the Little Bighorn is widely disputed. Some scholars suggest that his entire five companies charged the ford in an attempt to enter the village from the north and east, then swing south through the village to meet up with Reno. As noted, Custer had told Reno before his charge that the whole outfit would support him, but what Custer really had in mind was a separate attack on the village wherever he could find access down the steep bluffs, preferably as far north as possible. That access site was Medicine Tail Coulee.

Other historians believe that Custer had divided his command into two battalions of two and three companies and that he sent the two-company battalion to the ford to test the Indian resistance. This is the view that has gained much current support from testimony gathered from the Crow scouts (all of whom survived) and the Cheyenne and Sioux warriors, and from archaeological evidence.

The Crow scouts—White Man Runs Him, Goes Ahead, Hairy Moccasin, and Curley—were released from duty at Cedar Coulee, a juncture farther up Medicine Tail Coulee. (The two other Crow scouts, White Swan and Half Yellow Face, had gone into the valley fight with Reno, and they also survived.) Mitch Boyer, the scout and translator for Custer and the 7th Cavalry, spoke Custer's words: "You scouts need go no farther. You have guided Son-of-the-Morning-Star here, and your work is finished." Boyer is reputed to have added, "We are all going to die today." All of the scouts, except Curley, obeyed and rode off, taking a roundabout way to Reno Hill to join the besieged soldiers. Because the hills were now swarming with small parties of Lakotas and Cheyennes, the Crow scout felt they would be safer with the soldiers.

The seventeen-year-old Curley, who later became something of a haunted man because of all the interviews he gave and the seeming discrepancies each time he told his story, stayed with Custer and Mitch Boyer until the fighting got too hot; then he took Boyer's advice to leave and rode off to the east, concealing himself in coulees and ravines. Along the way he came upon a dead Sioux warrior, with the warrior's pony standing nearby. Curley took the Indian's red blanket, his Winchester and cartridges, and the pony. Later, he found another loose pony, which he also drove before him. He watched much of the battle with field glasses from a ridge about a mile and a half directly east until it became clear to him that Custer was going to be defeated; then he rode away to warn Generals Terry and Gibbon, who were coming up the Bighorn River from the north, of the disaster.

It is only recently that Curley's testimony has been given a great deal of credence. In fact, most Crow, Sioux, and Cheyenne accounts of the battle had been dismissed as unreliable by early historians. Robert Utley, the noted historian, puts his finger on the problem in his

Custer's cavalry column fighting at the Battle of the Little Bighorn in a ledger drawing by Red Horse, a Miniconjou Dakota, in the late nineteenth century. *Smithsonian Institution*

Curley, the last Crow scout to leave Custer. He claimed to have watched much of Custer's final battle, and his story remained controversial for the rest of his life. Years later, Gall told him that he must have turned into a bird that day because that was the only way he could have left the battlefield alive. *Little Bighorn Battlefield National Monument*

foreword to John S. Gray's excellent *Custer's Last Campaign*, which includes an analytical account of the 7th Cavalry's movements from the time it left the Yellowstone on its march up the Rosebud to its crossing into the Little Bighorn valley and the subsequent battle and its results, complete with graphs and time/motion studies. Utley writes:

> Indian testimony is difficult to use. It is personal, episodic, and maddeningly detached from time and space, or sequence and topography. It also suffers from a language barrier often aggravated by incompetent interpreters, from the cultural gulf between questioner and respondent, and from assumptions of the interviewer not always in accord with reality. Curley's testimony is a prime example of the blind interviewer leading the seeing witness, for in Gray's estimate Curley accurately saw, remembered, and reported. Guided by erroneous assumptions, however, interviewers quizzed Curley on Custer's movements toward the Sioux village, then bent the responses to fit those erroneous assumptions. The results, distorted by the interviewers rather than Curley, have baffled students ever since and earned Curley low marks as a witness. Gray penetrates the fog, makes sense of Curley's testimony, shows him to have been at Custer's side all the way to Calhoun Hill, where the final half-hour of the Last Stand began, and validates his claim to have watched the end from a distance.

An example of the scorn Curley suffered involves the red blanket. Historian Mardell Plainfeather says:

> Even the fact Curley had a blanket that day has been ridiculed. Some writers criticize [that] it would border on the absurd for anyone to possess a blanket considering the thermometer registered near 100 degrees at the Little Bighorn. It was not unusual for Curley, or a Sioux, to have a blanket. In fact, Plains Indian people relied upon blankets for a variety of reasons and always had one on hand, no matter what the temperature was, especially in traveling. Blankets were used for saddle padding, for sudden rainstorms, for chilly summer nights, and for signaling the village as they returned home. During the Battle of the Little Bighorn, the Sioux waved blankets to frighten the horses of Custer's men.

Curley's testimony includes much crucial (and now validated) detail on Custer's troop movements, including Custer's descent down

Medicine Tail Coulee, his scouts' report that Reno had been defeated and had climbed the bluffs to the east side of the river in retreat, and Custer's separation halt at Cedar Creek where he divided his troops into two battalions, sending companies E and F down to the ford and taking companies C, I, and L east and north along Luce Ridge and Nye-Cartwright Ridge and across upper Deep Coulee, and finally ending up on Calhoun Hill, the southernmost point of Battle Ridge. Curley went with Custer's companies and had a good view of what happened down at the ford.

Curley's account also belies the belief of some historians that Custer led the troops down to the river and was the first to fall, mortally wounded by Cheyenne gunfire. Custer came nowhere near the river.

But it is true that companies E and F, under Captain Yates, did make it to the ford. Many Indian accounts describe a well-organized detachment of soldiers on gray horses actually getting into the water. This was Company E, the "gray horse troop," the most noticeable of all the companies because of the horses' color. Time after time, Indians described the movements of this company, led by Lieutenant Algernon Smith, Yates's subaltern, all over the battlefield until the very end.

And it is true that the Cheyennes were the first ones to repulse this movement at the ford. Only a very few Cheyennes were left in this part of the village. All the others went with the Sioux to the southern end to fight Reno's initial assault. But these few Cheyennes held the Americans at bay until reinforcements arrived—which raises a couple of questions.

Why did Custer divide his already inferior forces into two battalions? Wouldn't it have been more prudent to keep the five companies together, to present a united front whether on the attack or on the defensive? And why didn't the two companies at the ford cross the river and attack the few Cheyenne defenders? John Gray provides the best guess to both these questions. The companies were sent to the ford "to *pretend* to attack, as a *feint* or threat, for even a semblance of an attack on the Indian women and children should draw the warriors from Reno's endangered battalion, allowing it to regroup in safety; it might then join Benteen and/or the packtrain and provide backup for a stronger Custer attack.... Meanwhile, Custer's main force could seize a holding position on the north rim of upper Medicine Tail Coulee, where it could wait a little longer for reinforcements and ammunition.... This high rim also overlooked the valley, enabling Custer to keep an eye on [Captain] Yates's feint and the Indians' reaction to it...." Custer's main plan may have been to fight a holding action at the ford and on the ridge until he could make an aggressive attack by crossing the river farther downstream, then charging back up along the flats to the village.

Custer did not know that Reno had been thoroughly discouraged and that Captain Benteen, having gotten the message from trumpeter Martini to "Come on.... Bring packs," disobeyed orders by stopping to help the wild-eyed Reno. Custer's five companies would have to go it alone. And now they were split into two separate fighting units.

Custer, who had always relied on "Custer's Luck" in his previous hell-for-leather battles in the Civil War and on the frontier, had done everything wrong in this particular engagement with the Indians. He had not scouted the village or the terrain. He had seriously underestimated the Indians' strength and resolve. He had not listened to his scouts, who had pointed out time and again that the village was immense. He had divided and weakened his forces at every point along the attack route.

As the Cheyenne defenders fired from clumps of brush on the village side of the river, moving and yelling to create the impression there were a large number of Indians, companies E and F moved away to the north, almost leisurely, to high ground on the northwest side of Deep Coulee. Only one trooper, whose horse had bolted across the river, was missing. It has been reported that four mounted Cheyennes, three of them identified as Bobtail Horse, Roan Bear, and Buffalo Calf, crossed the river to harass the soldiers. Custer's battalion on Luce Ridge and Nye-Cartwright Ridge poured heavy fire on the four warriors and on those others across the ford. At this point, both Yates and Custer felt they had time to organize a defensive posture and await reinforcements. But suddenly, hundreds of warriors, led by Gall, arrived from the Reno fight, splashed across the river, and pursued Yates's companies. Some rode up Deep Coulee on his right flank. Others crossed farther downstream to attack his left flank.

Caught in the crossfire, and with Indians shooting from the ford, Yates had nowhere to go but up to Calhoun Hill, where Custer's battalion awaited him. Yates set out skirmish lines while he and his troops labored up the hill, with Indian sharpshooters all around them, to reach the reunion point. Casualties began to mount up.

With so many mounted troops and Indians, the hillsides became

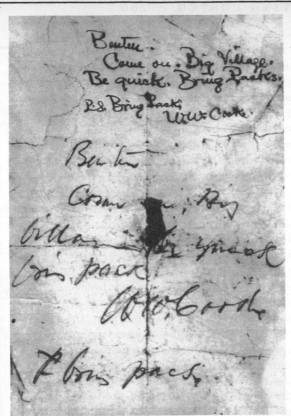

Custer's Last Note, written to Captain Benteen in hopes of hurrying reinforcements. *Little Bighorn Battlefield National Monument*

The Battle of the Little Bighorn, drawn by Amos Bad Heart Bull. *University of Nebraska Press*

thick with dust and smoke from the guns. The noise of the rifles, hoofbeats, whinnying and screaming and shouting echoed across the battlefield. The united battalions threw up a heavy fire, which stopped Gall's forces momentarily, killing and wounding several of them. Many of the Indians had dismounted, leaving their ponies in coulees and ravines, and were on foot now, crawling and darting from sagebrush to yucca to clumps of long grass, always moving uphill. Those on horseback again charged the troops, shooting and yelling, waving robes and blankets to frighten the horses. And most of the horses broke loose from the horse holders and stampeded toward the river, taking the troopers' extra ammunition in their saddlebags. The Indians prized the big American horses for their stamina and strength and fine lines and welcomed them with open arms. The horses, many of them wounded, welcomed the cool water shimmering beneath the relentless sun.

Crazy Horse had not yet appeared on the field. Most of the fighting with Reno and Custer took place without him. But he was leading a large group of Oglalas and Cheyennes downstream to cross the river and attack from the north. When he did show up a short time later, the troops were done for. They were completely surrounded, most of their horses had been driven off, and they found themselves on a naked ridge, vulnerable from all sides.

It is at this point that the troopers panicked. White Bull, a Cheyenne, said that the white men acted as if they were intoxicated, or "beside themselves," shooting wildly in the air. The Indians on foot were picking them off with guns and bows and arrows. Many of the Sioux and Cheyenne warriors found the bows and arrows more effective than guns. They could shoot the arrows without standing up and exposing themselves to return fire. Kate Bighead, a Cheyenne woman who had crossed the river to sing brave-heart songs for her fighting nephew, observed this tactic: "The Indian could keep himself at all times out of sight when sending arrows. Each arrow was shot far upward and forward, not at any soldier in particular, but to curve down and fall where they were. Bullets would not do any harm if shot in that way. But a rain of arrows from thousands of Indian bows, and kept up for a long time, would hit many soldiers and their horses by falling and sticking into their heads or their backs."

Under such heavy pressure, the companies began to break up, some running here, others running there, but always in a pattern of disorganized retreat to the north, then to the west. Now the mounted warriors closed in and began to ride them down, Gall's forces from the south and west, Crazy Horse's men from the north and east. Although several of the troopers were shot, the Indians, true to warrior tradition, preferred to use clubs and hatchets whenever possible, riding close and counting coup in a fairly heavy-handed way. One of the Sioux warriors said, "It was just like hunting buffalo."

At least one modern-day authority agrees with this assessment of the troopers' behavior. Richard Fox, an archaeologist who holds a Ph.D. from the University of Calgary and teaches at the University of South Dakota, has come up with a theory which disputes a widely held belief that Custer's troopers fought a controlled action against the Indians, even up to the point of their deaths. According to many historians and buffs, they set up skirmish lines, retreated in order, obeyed their officers' commands, conducted the best fight possible under the circumstances. Their actions are often favorably compared to those of Reno's troops, who retreated from the valley fight in wild disarray and generally just tried to save their own skins. And, of course, the two leaders are compared: Reno was a coward and a drunk, a poor leader who panicked in the valley fight; Custer, on the other hand, was credited with being a strong leader who inspired his men with his derring-do and who fought a strong tactical fight.

According to Fox, however, Custer's troops panicked almost immediately when the Indians attacked in force. They bunched together in helpless clusters, shooting wildly in all directions until their guns were empty. Then many of them took off running, making it easy for the horseback Indians to pursue and kill them. Others stayed in their bunches and allowed themselves to be killed. In fact, Fox uses the term "bunching" to describe this very human, pitiable reaction to a killing force.

It is difficult to argue with Fox's conclusion. In August 1983, a grassfire swept upslope from Deep Ravine near the Little Bighorn and quickly consumed most of the Custer battlefield site. Although this fire was considered something of a (natural) disaster at the time, it turned out to be of enormous benefit to Fox and a team of archaeologists and volunteers. The site, suddenly denuded of knee-high grass, yucca, and sagebrush, offered a clean slate on which to study the battle through the distribution and locations of artifacts. Using a grid system, metal detectors, and controlled excavation, Fox and his volunteers were able to track the development and conclusion of the battle, including tracing shell and bullet patterns as the fight progressed. For instance, he traces shot patterns from where he found large concentrations of shell casings to where he found large concentrations of bullets that matched the shell casings, thereby establishing the locations of the shooters and their targets. Since the cavalry used only two weapons, the .45 caliber Springfield single-shot carbine and the .45 caliber Colt single-action six-shot pistol, it was relatively easy to trace the flight lines of their bullets. But the Indians used every type of gun imaginable, from obsolete muzzle-loaders to modern repeating rifles, such as the Winchester Model 1873 and .44 caliber Henry.

Nevertheless, Fox manages to recreate the movements of the battle for the first time through solid archaeological evidence. He concludes that "the battalion disintegrated. Prior to collapse, fighting appears to have been subdued. Disintegration [of order] occurred early and spread to remaining battlefield sectors. The flow was generally from south to north. There was little or no organization and very little resistance during this process." This is not a pretty picture of the famed 7th Cavalry, and Fox's conclusion is bound to be disputed by Custer buffs and historians alike. Myths of heroism, from the Charge of the Light Brigade to Custer's Last Stand, do not die easily.

While the companies of the southern positions were being overrun, Custer led his regimental headquarters command, which included his brothers, Captain Tom (who had won a Medal of Honor in the Civil War) and Boston (nominally a civilian "scout" who had never been in that country), and his nephew, Autie (a true civilian who had come to watch Custer whip the Indians), and stragglers from other companies to the far north end of Battle Ridge, to Custer Hill.

By now the troops were spread out all along Battle Ridge, most in small pockets. Those troops on Calhoun Hill were the first to fall. Then the Indians simply rode down the nonresisting troops between Calhoun Hill and Custer Hill. The grave markers today (although often erroneously placed) reflect the direction of the battle and the distribution of the dead soldiers.

There are two groups of gravestones that verify that not all the soldiers died on the ridges. One large group of markers stands at the bottom of Custer Hill to the west, indicating that forty-five or more soldiers, most on foot, had left Custer Hill early in the fighting, according to Indian sources, in a mad dash to reach the river, to find cover in the trees and brush. They didn't come close. They stopped, and those few on horses dismounted and formed a very brief skirmish line. This group probably included the remnants of E Company, the famed gray horse company, although by that point in the battle all the horses were mixed up. These troopers then ran into Deep Ravine, a large, steep ravine that empties into the Little Bighorn. There they were slaughtered like sheep in a pen. The scout and interpreter Mitch Boyer was among those killed at this location, which has been dubbed the South Skirmish Line. A smaller group of fourteen widely scattered markers lie a few hundred feet downslope to the west of Custer Hill. According to Indian accounts, fifteen to twenty soldiers broke and ran toward Deep Ravine near the end of the fighting. White Bull, Sitting Bull's nephew, helped kill them. Big Beaver recalled this development and also recalled that there was no movement left on Custer Hill. Custer and his small group of forty officers, soldiers, and civilians were already dead. "Custer's Last Stand" was not the last of the fighting.

One of the most controversial elements of the battle is testified to by Cheyenne informants. Several of them said that many of the soldiers killed themselves or each other. Wooden Leg says of the South Skirmish Line fight: "All around, the Indians began jumping up, running forward, dodging down, jumping up again, down again, all the time going toward the soldiers. Right away, all of the white men went crazy. Instead of shooting us, they turned their guns upon themselves. Almost before we could get to them, every one of them was dead. They killed themselves." At another part of the battlefield, Wooden Leg is disappointed that the skirmish is over: "By the time I got there, all of the soldiers there were dead. The Indians told me that they had killed only a few of those men, that the men had shot each other and shot themselves." Turtle Rib, a Minneconjou Sioux, saw some of the soldiers shoot each other. He also witnessed, along with others, one soldier break away on a fast horse and gallop away from the battle. Turtle Rib was one of those giving chase, and he says the soldier, on his strong American horse, was pulling away when he took out his pistol and shot himself in the head. Foolish Elk, an Oglala, confirms this.

Kate Bighead saw the fight on the South Skirmish Line: "I think there were about 20 Indians to every soldier there. The soldier horses got scared, and all of them broke loose and ran away toward the river. Just then I saw a soldier shoot himself by holding his revolver at his head. Then another one did the same, and another. Right away, all of them began shooting themselves or shooting each other. I saw several different pairs of them fire their guns at the same time and shoot one another in the breast. For a short time the Indians just stayed where they were and looked."

It may be true that some of the soldiers killed themselves or each other in suicide pacts. One of the first things veteran Indian fighters told recruits was to "save the last bullet for yourself" rather than fall into the Indians' hands. But most Indian accounts do not mention suicide. They say that the soldiers panicked and shot wildly into the air until their guns were empty. Then the Indians killed them. But even today, many Cheyenne elders will insist that the soldiers killed themselves and each other.

A smaller point of controversy involves the participation of "suicide boys." These were literally Indian boys, below fighting age. They made the announcement that they were suicide boys, and after some ceremony, they were paraded through camp so that others might know their names, then sent to do their task, which was relatively simple: to charge into the soldiers' lines, to engage them in hand-to-hand combat, to distract them from more organized older warriors, and to pump up the morale of the Indian people. Needless to say, these boys would meet their maker covered with glory. And it was certain that they would meet their maker. But did they exist? Only a couple of accounts, including Stands in Timber's, mention them. And it seems unlikely that the fiercely protective Indian parents would allow their young sons to participate in such a lethal activity.

Did the Indians know that they were fighting Pe-hin Hanska (Lakota), or Hi-estzie (Cheyenne), both of which mean Head Hair Long or Long Hair? The vast majority of Lakotas did not know Custer by sight. The Northern Cheyennes did not know him. Some of the few Southern Cheyennes did know him from the Battle of the Washita in 1868. But only Kate Bighead indicated that he was recognized. She related that two Southern Cheyenne women told her that they recognized his corpse and pushed an awl into each of his ears to "improve his hearing, as it seemed he had not heard what our chiefs in the South said when he smoked the pipe with them. They told him then that if ever afterward he should break that peace promise and should fight the Cheyennes the Everywhere Spirit surely would cause him to be killed."

A curious relationship developed between Custer and the Southern Cheyennes after the massacre on the Washita, which occurred in November 1868. Custer returned the following spring and smoked the peace pipe with the Cheyenne chiefs, Medicine Arrow and Little Robe. That is when the chiefs warned him to keep the peace. They emphasized their warning by knocking the tobacco ash out on his boot at the conclusion of the ceremony. Then they allowed Custer and his troops to take them to Fort Sill.

Kate Bighead remembered that time: "I saw Long Hair many times during those days.... I was then a young woman, 22 years old, and I admired him. All of the Indian women talked of him as being a fine-looking man. My cousin, a young woman named Me-o-tzi, often went with him to help in finding the trails of Indians [to get them to surrender].... All of the Cheyennes liked her, and all were glad she had so important a place in [his] life. After Long Hair went away, different ones of the Cheyenne young men wanted to marry her. But she would not have any of them. She said that Long Hair was her husband, that he had promised to come back to her, and that she would wait for him. She waited seven years. Then he was killed."

In *My Life on the Plains,* Custer himself acknowledges a ceremony in which he and Me-o-tzi (or Mo-nah-se-tah, as she was also called) held hands while a Cheyenne woman said some solemn words. To his surprise (or so he claimed), he discovered that he had just become the nineteen-year-old Me-o-tzi's husband. Although he professes nothing more than a passing admiration for the girl, his description of her is glowing:

> Little Rock's daughter [Me-o-tzi] was an exceedingly comely squaw, possessing a bright, cheery face, a countenance beaming with intelligence, and a disposition more inclined to be merry than one usually finds among the Indians. She was probably rather under than over twenty years of age. Added to the bright, laughing eyes, a set of pearly teeth, and a rich complexion, her well-shaped head was crowned with a luxuriant growth of the most beautiful silken tresses, rivaling in color the blackness of the raven and extending, when allowed to fall loosely over her shoulders, to below her waist.

Such a description seems to indicate a sexual attraction, but whether it was acted upon is conjectural. Rumors circulated—that an army doctor caught Custer and Me-o-tzi in the act of making love, for instance—and a child was born to the young woman shortly after she met Custer. The time frame was all wrong and the infant looked purely Cheyenne, but the rumors persisted. Another rumor had it that Me-o-tzi had another child shortly thereafter and it had curly blond hair. Yet another rumor circulated—this one may have been true—that both George and Tom Custer were treated for gonorrhea during those idyllic days on the southern plains. Several troopers of the 7th Cavalry were treated for this malady. Whether the troopers caught it from the Indian women or brought it themselves is subject to debate.

The strange thing about this Custer–Southern Cheyenne relationship is that it was peaceful, if not downright friendly. Custer had just massacred the relatives and friends of these Indians, yet many of them speak of him admiringly. At least the women did, which speaks to Custer's charisma.

And now this charming young man (he was still only thirty-seven at the Little Bighorn) was about to die. Surrounded by forty of his staunchest loyalists on Custer Hill, he blazed away with his two English self-cocking Bulldog pistols and octagonal-barreled Remington Sporting Rifle. He may even have had a dog with him—in some accounts a greyhound, in others a bulldog. Custer always had dogs with him on his expeditions. In the quiet dark before the attack on the Cheyenne village at Washita, Custer ordered all the troops' dogs killed, including two of his own, to prevent their alarming the Indians.

Custer's favorite horse, Vic, a sorrel with a blaze face and white socks, probably had been run off or killed for breastworks at Little Bighorn. Although many 7th Cavalry horses ended up with Lakota and Cheyenne owners, the only *known* survivor, human or animal, of the Custer forces was a horse belonging to Captain Miles Keogh named Comanche. When Comanche was found, he was in pretty bad shape, suffering from at least seven wounds. Nevertheless, he managed to make the trip on the steamship *Far West* back to Fort Lincoln along with the rest of the wounded. He lived for fifteen more years and now stands stuffed under glass at the University of Kansas.

In addition to his brothers and nephew, Custer had his physician and several officers of the five companies with him. Why these officers were all there on Custer Hill remains a mystery, as their companies were scattered all over the length and breadth of the battlefield. Some historians have speculated that they were conferring with Custer's headquarters command. Others say that their troops had already been killed or had become unmanageable in a military sense. It could have been that they left their helpless troops and rode to the safest position, Custer Hill. The final fighting probably began a little after 5:00 P.M.

Indian time and white time differed in those days, not only in terminology, but in actuality. White time is based on units of time—seconds, minutes, hours, days, weeks, months, years. Clocks and calendars keep track of these units. Indian time was relative and often based on imagery, or a time of day when a certain common event took place—such as the evening meal or the time to water horses or the time to dig turnips. Indians followed the movement of the sun across the sky to determine the length of the day and the approximate time of day. Similarly, they followed the phases of the moon to determine longer periods of time—the moon of ripening berries; the moon of shedding ponies. They kept winter counts to keep track of years. Each symbol on the winter count determined a particular year—the year of smallpox; the year of the white buffalo; the year of the great fight with the *wasichus* on the Little Bighorn.

Many of the Indian informants say the battle started at midday, about the time the horses were customarily watered. By white time, Reno charged the southern end of camp shortly after 3:00 P.M.

The Indians were quite certain that the final attack in the Custer battle lasted only a short time, although many talk of the long part of the fighting, which was the long-range shooting while the Indians were sneaking up on the companies, most of them on foot. Two Moons said the battle "took about as long as it takes for a hungry man to eat his dinner." The widow of Spotted Horn Bull said, "It was done very quickly. What was done that day was done while the sun stood still and the white men were delivered into the hands of the Sioux." An old Cheyenne, recalling the battle, said the fight took as long as it takes the sun to travel the width of a lodgepole, fifteen to twenty minutes. All of them are speaking of the final phase of the battle, when the troops were surrounded.

John Gray, in *Custer's Last Campaign,* plots the whole of the battle, from Reno's charge to Custer's demise, in very convincing time/motion studies. According to him, Custer's part in the battle lasted from 4:08 (when his three companies left the separation halt in Medicine Tail Coulee) to 5:25 (when the battle ended). The heavy part of the battle took thirty-five minutes.

According to Captain Godfrey, an officer in Reno's command who had been sent with the burial detail on June 28, "All the bodies, except a few, were stripped of their clothing, according to my recollection nearly all were scalped or mutilated, and there was one notable exception, that of General Custer, whose face and expression were natural.... When I arrived there General Custer's body had been laid out. He had been shot in the left temple and the left breast. There were no powder marks or signs of mutilation. Mr. F. F. Girard [Fred Gerard], the interpreter, informed me that he preceded the troops there. He found the naked bodies of two soldiers, one across the other and Custer's naked body in a sitting posture between and leaning against them, his upper right arm along and on the topmost body, his

Dead and mutilated members of Custer's 7th Cavalry, drawn by Red Horse. *Smithsonian Institution*

"Long Hair," Custer, with short hair and in civilian clothes in 1872. Note the receding hairline, one possible reason that his scalp was not touched after his death at the Little Bighorn battle. *Little Bighorn Battlefield National Monument*

right forearm and hand supporting his head in an inclining posture like one resting or asleep." This is a rather romantic portrait of the fallen hero, but it should be noted that the Indians had stripped his body and were doubtless responsible for Custer's posture. It should also be noted that there were other bodies on Custer Hill that hadn't been mutilated. The idea advanced by some that the Indians left only Custer's body unmutilated out of respect for the great warrior is absurd. Only a few of the Southern Cheyennes could have recognized him, and it is doubtful that, even had they wanted to, they could have protected Custer's body from the angry Lakotas and Northern Cheyennes. Custer was the "chief of the thieves" who were stealing Indian lands. The idea that Indians recognized him by his flowing locks is equally absurd. Custer had gotten his hair cut before the expedition left Fort Abraham Lincoln in North Dakota. Long hair got dirty and was impossible to keep groomed in the field. That Custer hadn't been scalped by the Indians was not out of respect—he was growing prematurely bald and what hair he had left was cut short. Long Hair's scalp was not worth taking.

It is difficult to imagine what these bodies looked like. Captain Weir, also on that burial detail, exclaimed, "Oh, how white they look!" But only the parts of them that had been covered up could look so white. Their faces and other exposed parts were grimy with dust and gunpowder. The dust was so thick during the battle, Kate Bighead said, that she almost choked. A Sioux warrior, Good Fox, said, "All these others say they saw what happened but all I saw was one big cloud of dust."

What is abundantly clear is that the bodies were horrible to look upon. Tom Custer seems to have particularly incurred the wrath of the Indians—or perhaps only one Indian. In the winter of 1874 he had personally arrested Rain-in-the-Face, a Sioux warrior, in a trader's store at Standing Rock Agency for murdering two men, a sutler named Baliran and a veterinarian named Honsinger, who were illegally in Indian country. Rain-in-the-Face managed to break out of the Fort Lincoln guardhouse and rejoin his people, but he was angry and vowed to eat Tom Custer's heart someday. At the Little Bighorn, Tom Custer's heart was missing. He lay facedown, arrows bristling in his back, his entrails leaking out of him, all his scalp removed, the back of his head so smashed it looked flat. He was recognized by the burial party only by his tattoos: the American flag, the goddess of liberty and his initials, T.W.C.

Rain-in-the-Face became an important culture villain in the

Captain Tom Custer, George's brother, the winner of two Medals of Honor during the Civil War. He was so badly mutilated at Little Bighorn that his body was identified by a tattoo on his arm. *Little Bighorn Battlefield National Monument*

Rain in the Face, a Hunkpapa Sioux who was once arrested by Tom Custer—and who later boasted that he had cut out Tom Custer's heart on the battlefield and eaten it. He later said that he had made the story up for eager newspaper reporters. *Little Bighorn Battlefield National Monument*

nineteenth century. Journalists and poets, including Longfellow, singled him out for his savagery. Elizabeth Custer called him an "incarnate fiend." But it seems he was no more or less fiendish than any of the other savages. In his later years he became a reservation raconteur, sometimes admitting, sometimes denying that he cut out Tom's heart. He also claimed, on more than one occasion, that he had killed George Custer. On other occasions, he denied it.

Who did kill Custer? A man named Hawk said he did. Nobody else said he did. Old Cheyennes told Thomas B. Marquis that a Southern Cheyenne named Brave Bear did it, but they were only joking; they had elected Brave Bear as the culprit because the white reporters wanted a name. Of course, there are other names.

Sitting Bull's elder nephew, White Bull, tells how he killed Custer:

> I charged in. A tall, well-built soldier with yellow hair and mustache saw me coming and tried to bluff me, aiming his rifle at me. But when I rushed him, he threw his rifle at me without shooting. . . . We grabbed each other and wrestled there in the dust and smoke. It was like fighting in a fog. . . . I lashed him across the face with my quirt, striking the coup. . . . But the tall soldier fought hard. He was desperate. He hit me with his fists on the jaw and shoulders, then grabbed my long braids with both hands, pulled my face close and tried to bite my nose off. I yelled for help: "Hey, hey, come over and help me!" Bear Lice and Crow Boy heard me calling and came running. These friends tried to hit the soldier. But we were whirling around, back and forth, so that most of their blows hit me. They knocked me dizzy. I yelled as loud as I could to scare my enemy, but he would not let go. Finally I broke free. He drew his pistol. I wrenched it out of his hand and struck him with it three or four times on the head, knocked him over, shot him in the head and fired at his heart. I took his pistol and cartridge belt.

Stanley Vestal, who offers this account in his book *Sitting Bull: Champion of the Sioux,* takes White Bull at his word.

Although none of the other Indians would say with certainty who killed Custer, Medicine Bear, a Cheyenne, claimed he counted the third coup on the body. He said the first and second coups were counted by Two Moons and Harshay Wolf.

The butchery and mutilation occurred immediately after the battle. Young boys rode among the bodies, shooting arrows into those that still moved. Then the women came, with hatchets, knives, and stone marrow-bone hammers. According to Iron Hawk, a Hunkpapa who was fourteen at the time, the business wasn't all grim: "The women swarmed up the hill and began stripping the soldiers. They were yelling and laughing and singing. I saw something funny. Two fat old women were stripping a soldier, who was wounded and playing dead. When they had him naked, they began to cut something off that he had, and he jumped up and began fighting with the two fat women. He was swinging one of them around, while the other was trying to stab him with her knife. After awhile, another woman rushed up and shoved her knife into him and he died really dead. It was funny to see the naked *wasichu* fighting with the fat women."

Not all had such a good time. Black Elk recalls his father and uncle, in a rage over the death of the uncle's son, butchering a fat *wasichu*, whose "meat looked good to eat, but we did not eat any." Despite the fact of Rain-in-the-Face's vow to eat Tom Custer's heart and Black Elk's description of the fat soldier's meat, the Sioux, Cheyennes, and Arapahos were not cannibals.

But they did mutilate the corpses horribly. Wooden Leg says, "I went with other Cheyennes along the hills northward to the ground where we had killed all the soldiers. Lots of women and boys were there. The boys were going about making coups by stabbing or shooting arrows into the dead men. Some of the bodies had many arrows sticking in them. Many hands and feet had been cut off, and the limbs and bodies and heads had many stabs and slashes. Some of this had been done by the warriors, during and immediately after the battle. More was added, though, by enraged and weeping women relatives of the Sioux and Cheyennes who had been killed. The women used sheathknives and hatchets."

John Stands in Timber, whose grandparents were at the Little Bighorn when Custer attacked the camp, was a little more circumspect: "I never heard who damaged the bodies up there. I asked many of them, and most said they did not go [from the village to the battleground]. A few said they had seen others doing it. They did scalp some of the soldiers, but I don't think they took the scalps into camp. The ones who had relatives killed at Sand Creek came out and chopped the heads and arms off, and things like that . . . those who had relatives at Sand Creek might have done plenty. . . . But I think many never admitted what they did. At least nobody would tell the details of what was done to those soldiers' bodies."

Black Elk, who later became an Oglala holy man, was not so reticent in summing up the Indians' feelings toward their adversaries: "I was not sorry at all. I was a happy boy. Those *wasichus* had come to kill our mothers and fathers and us, and it was our country. . . . the soldiers were very foolish to do this."

Among the trophies brought into camp was the battered head of an Indian, a head with graying hair. Two young sisters brought it in, swinging it by the hair like a rag doll. The Sioux and Cheyennes normally parted their hair in the middle and braided it, or left it long and flowing, like Crazy Horse. The Crows cut their hair short in front and left it long and ruffed in the back. But this head's hair was in neither of these styles. Of course, the Sioux recognized the style as that of the Corn Eaters, the Arikaras, their hated enemies. But one woman recognized the head. It was the head of Bloody Knife, Custer's favorite scout. It was also the head of the woman's brother; moreover, it was the head of the girls' uncle. The girls were the woman's daughters. Bloody Knife's sister is reported to have said, "Gall has killed him at last!" Custer had sent the Arikara with Reno in the valley charge, and it was Bloody Knife's brains that splattered Reno, causing him to panic and lose control.

Bloody Knife was only half Arikara. He was Hunkpapa on his father's side and had lived with the Hunkpapas into his early teens, at which time his mother left the band to return to her own people. She took Bloody Knife with her and left his sister with her Lakota father. Most of the Lakotas did not like Bloody Knife as a boy. He was beaten by other boys and particularly incurred the wrath of a young Gall, although no one knows why. A couple of accounts of Bloody Knife as a man mention that his lip seemed always curled with disdain and that he ridiculed and scorned the white men. Perhaps he was that way as a boy. Or perhaps he was treated badly because he was half Corn Eater. Custer enjoyed his company, despite the Arikara's contempt for the general's shooting, and awarded Bloody Knife a silver medallion.

While stripping the soldiers, the Indians found many things amazing. One of the most amazing to them was simply the color of Isaiah Dorman's skin. These Indians had never seen a naked black man up close. Another soldier had gold fillings in his teeth. The Indians were puzzled. They had seen lots of gold, but why would a man put it in his teeth, unless it was the man's personal medicine? Black Elk, who wanted a soldier's uniform and was stripping a corpse, was pushed aside by an older warrior. Instead of getting his uniform, Black Elk had to content himself with a round gold object that he put around his neck: "At first it ticked inside, and then it did not any more. I wore it around my neck a long time before I found out what it was and how to make it tick again." Rising Sun, a Cheyenne, found a similar device, but when it quit ticking, he threw it away in disgust.

Another object that interested the Indians was a small, round, flat case with a needle. If held properly, the needle floated and always pointed toward the north. Since the bodies of the dead troopers lay in this direction, many thought the object pointed only toward white men, and therefore that was how they always found each other.

Among the other things the Indians found were knives, guns, bullets, gloves, boots (the Indians cut the tops off the boots and made sturdy bags of them), military insignia, guidons, flags (including Custer's battle flag), rings, coffee, tobacco, binoculars, McClellan saddles (only the old men thought these would be useful), and religious ornamentation, including at least one scapular belonging to Captain Miles Keogh.

The green picture paper found in leather packets did not excite the warriors. They threw it away or gave it to children to play with. They kept the wallets.

According to Wooden Leg, several of the metal bottles carried by the troopers contained a strong liquid, holy water, which some of the Indians drank. Because it was so strong and difficult to swallow, many of the warriors speculated that it was this holy water that caused the soldiers to go crazy and shoot themselves and each other. Others thought that the soldiers did not have time to drink too much and that their foolish actions must have been caused by the prayers of medicine men.

After the battle, the Sioux and Cheyennes carried their dead and wounded back down to the village. Many of the Indians were killed by friendly fire. Lame White Man, the Southern Cheyenne chief, whom the Sioux did not know too well, was probably mistaken for an Arikara scout. He was found dead and scalped in the vicinity where the Sioux had been fighting. Another Sioux was greatly embarrassed to find that he had scalped one of his own and offered the scalp to the victim's parents. Many more Indians were killed by accident, getting into the line of fire, or being caught in a crossfire by their compatriots.

But it was the soldiers' rifles, particularly in the early part of the battle, that caused the great majority of the Indian deaths. Much has been made by firearms "experts" of the inadequacy of these .45 caliber Model 1873 Springfield carbines, standard issue to all soldiers (short barrels for the cavalry, longer barrels for the infantry). Some even suggest that these guns' sad performance contributed to the defeat of Custer's troops, that the Springfields were inadequate to the task of repeated hot firing, that, among other things, their shell extractors did not work properly. Proof of this would be gouges on copper cartridge casings where a soldier would have to use a knife or some other sharp instrument to pry the shell out. The truth is that virtually all of the army Springfields fired properly and the shell extractors worked just fine. In fact, Richard Fox found that the Indian weapons, because of age, condition, or lack of cleaning, were just as prone to misfiring or jamming as the soldiers' weapons. Split shell casings were found, suggesting that the cartridge was the wrong caliber for the weapon. Many shell casings show three or four firing-pin strikes; such multiple strikes indicate that the Indian turned the bullet several times trying to get the firing pin to touch off the primer which would ignite the powder and send the bullet on its way. This perseverance suggests that bullets were precious to the Indians. In any case, the mechanical performance of the weapons involved was not a factor in the outcome.

Some Indians reported that they saw the soldiers throwing these guns away. One school of thought has it that the guns jammed and became useless. Another school suggests that the soldiers panicked when the fighting became close and threw away perfectly usable rifles. Whatever, these rifles proved effective in the long-distance fighting, where most of the Indian casualties occurred.

While the Indians were finishing off Custer's command, several of them noticed on a hill three and a half miles away another group of white men. A great cry arose and several hundred warriors leaped on their ponies and took off in the direction of these soldiers. Their blood was boiling now, and they weren't going to rest until all the white men in the vicinity paid with their lives for this attack on the Indian village. If any of them, especially the reservation Indians, had misgivings at the start of the battle, they were gone now. Their medicine was strong and they were fighting for a righteous cause.

The hill was later named Weir Point, and the white men were the remnants of Reno's command, augmented by Benteen's fresh battalion, who had topped the hill to look for Custer. But look was all they did. When they saw the hundreds of mounted Indians galloping toward them, they turned back to Reno Hill—not without great difficulty, for the Indians did catch up with them, forcing them to fight a close-quarters rearguard retreat. But they did make it back to their position on Reno Hill with surprisingly light casualties and spent the rest of the afternoon, all that night, and the major part of the next day under siege.

As darkness fell over the hills and valley along the Little Bighorn, the literal smell of blood was high. But the spirit of the Indians had changed from triumph to sorrow. Too many of their sons and husbands, friends and relatives, had died or been mortally wounded that afternoon. It is estimated that between sixty and one hundred Indians were killed. That night the drums beat steadily, and the wailing of the women filled the air. The noise from the village sounded to the troopers like "a wild victory dance." But the women had cut their hair and gashed their legs in mourning. Perhaps the victory ended for the Indians that night. Although the siege, and the hope for wiping out these remaining soldiers, continued through the next day, the fighting was desultory for the most part, with occasional heavy firing, but more often light potshotting.

One incident occurred on that night of the 25th that gives an insight into Reno's state of mind. According to W. A. Graham, in *The Custer Myth,* Lieutenant Edward S. Godfrey, one of Benteen's officers, related a story at an Order of Indian Wars dinner in 1930 or 1931: "Benteen had confided to [Godfrey] . . . that on the night of the 25th of June . . . Reno had conferred with [Benteen] as to what to do; whether, outnumbered as they were, they should stand and fight it out, or whether they should make a run for it under cover of the darkness. Their losses were already heavy, both in men and animals, and they had many wounded men beside. If they stayed and fought, the odds were against them. . . . On the other hand, if they could get away during the night, they had a good chance to save themselves, destroying or abandoning to the Indians everything that would not serve in making their escape. Here Benteen interrupted Reno to interject: 'But the wounded; how would you move the wounded?' Reno replied, 'Those who can ride can be mounted and go; those who cannot ride we would have to leave.' Benteen's reply was 'No, Reno; you can't do that.' " To abandon wounded men to the savagery of the enemy was unthinkable in any war; to leave them for the Indians was despicable. But that this conversation took place at all is based solely on Benteen's word. And Benteen (and Godfrey) had enormous contempt for Reno.

The next day, the 26th, brought pretty much the same thing. Occasionally the Indians would feint an attack, would step up their firing activity and move in closer. In response, the soldiers mounted

Captain Frederick Benteen (seated in the middle), who hated
Custer, relaxing with other 7th Cavalry officers. *Little Bighorn
Battlefield National Monument*

two counterattacks, at Benteen's insistence that something positive needed to be done. But the counterattacks only drove the near Indians away from the besieged soldiers' perimeter. When the soldiers withdrew, the Indians moved closer again.

The Sioux and Cheyennes came and went as they pleased—back to camp for a bite to eat or a nap, then returning to the surround. The besieged soldiers were trapped beneath a searing sun with no cover from above and little cover in front of them. But they made themselves as small as they could in their shallow depressions with tins of hardtack and saddles and whatever else they had piled between them and the Indians.

The only surviving doctor out of the three who had accompanied the expedition moved from one wounded soldier to the next, performing his impossible tasks. The wounded begged for water. The horses and mules in the center of the deployment became unruly with thirst. The stench of decaying flesh was inescapable. It would be only a matter of time before Reno and Benteen's troops would have to expose themselves in an attempt to break the siege; then the final battle of the Little Bighorn would begin.

But a miracle happened. In the late afternoon, the soldiers saw a cloud of smoke down by the village. Then a curtain of smoke arose between themselves and the village. The Indians had lit a long fire, indicating some sort of activity. The soldiers were puzzled. Some thought they meant to burn out the white men. Others thought it might be a signal.

After a time the smoke cleared and the soldiers saw the entire village moving away from them. The lodges had been struck and folded and were resting on the tipi poles being dragged by horses. Women were riding the horses, and old ones and children were walking or riding on the travois. Before them and around them, the warriors rode guard, many of them looking off to the north as they rode west and south.

The soldiers cheered the incredible sight. Sergeant Charles Windolph said, "It was like some Biblical exodus; the Israelites moving into Egypt; a mighty tribe on the move." Reno recalled, "Between six and seven P.M. the Indians came out from behind the clouds of smoke and dust and we had a good view of them as they filed away in the direction of the Bighorn Mountains, moving in almost perfect military order. The length of their column was fully equal to that of a large division of the Cavalry Corps of the Army of the Potomac, as I have seen it on its march." But the soldiers kept their positions, just in case it was a trick.

It was not a trick. Sioux and Cheyenne scouts had seen Generals Terry and Gibbon and their battalion coming up the Little Bighorn from the north. Many of the warriors wanted to attack this column and settle the whole score, but wiser heads, including Sitting Bull, convinced them that saving the women and children and old ones was more crucial. In fact, Sitting Bull had wanted to leave Reno's command alone, so that Reno might tell his superiors what had occurred that day, in the mistaken belief that if the white chiefs knew that the 7th Cavalry had attacked an entirely peaceful camp, they would be more lenient in their response.

The relief force would not reach Reno Hill until the late morning of the 27th, two days after the initial fighting. Lieutenant Bradley, chief of scouts of Gibbon's column, was the first to reach the bedraggled survivors. Because Reno and Benteen still had no clear idea of what had happened to Custer, that was the first question. They had seen a fight, but were driven back before they could learn its outcome. According to Lieutenant Godfrey, in his narrative of the battle, ". . . the general opinion seemed to prevail that [Custer] had been defeated and driven down the river, where he would probably join General Terry, and with whom he would return to our relief."

Although the main column of relief troopers had marched north along the west side of the river, down in the valley, Bradley had crossed the river and ascended the hills to the east. From there, he rode directly to Reno's emplacement. According to Godfrey, ". . . Lieutenant Bradley, 7th Infantry, came into our lines, and asked where I was. Greeting most cordially my old friend, I immediately asked: 'Where is Custer?' He replied: 'I don't know, but I suppose he was killed, as we counted 197 dead bodies. I don't suppose any escaped.' We were simply dumbfounded. This was the first intimation we had of his fate. It was hard to realize; it did seem impossible."

Curley, the young Crow scout who was the last to leave Custer's command, had ridden for two and half days (three sleeps) before he found the steamboat *Far West* tied up on the Bighorn River, near where the Little Bighorn and Bighorn rivers join. The steamboat had been Terry's and Gibbon's headquarters and supply ship. Captain Grant Marsh of the *Far West* had taken the boat thirteen miles upstream beyond this point the day before when an army officer refused to believe that the smaller river was the Little Bighorn. Consequently much time was lost before the captain and the officer realized the error and steamed back down to the confluence the next day. If things hadn't been so serious, this disappearance of a steamship on the small river would have been comic.

The captain and some other men, including a barber, were fishing about a mile from the boat when a young Indian on horseback signaled peace to them from the opposite bank. He had three ponies and the red blanket that he had taken from the battlefield. One of the men later wrote, "He wore an exceedingly dejected countenance, but his appetite proved to be in first-rate order." Curley, first by signing (none of the white men spoke Crow), then by drawing on the ground, then on paper, tried to get his message across. The drawing was of two concentric circles, the inner circle representing troops, the outer circle the Indians. The white men could only understand that there had been a battle, but they didn't understand the outcome. They also didn't trust the young scout.

In fact, the men of the *Far West* wouldn't know what happened until one of Terry's scouts, a Muggins Taylor, arrived the next day, the 29th, with dispatches from Terry. They were to prepare the boat to receive wounded soldiers. They were also to provide Taylor with a fresh mount so he could forward the dispatches to Fort Ellis and the nearest telegraph.

It is plain that if the steamboat hadn't overshot the confluence of the two rivers, and if the soldiers had been able to understand Curley, they would have been aware two days earlier of what had happened on the Little Bighorn. It is more than likely that Curley would have reached the steamboat on the 27th if it had been where it was supposed to be.

It is not clear what were the consequences of this two-day delay. It seems that nothing would have changed if things had gone perfectly. Generals Terry and Gibbon had already taken their column south to find the 7th Cavalry. And in fact they did find the dead bodies of Custer's command and the live bodies of Reno's command. But they had to stay that night of the 27th and spent all of the next day, the 28th, burying the dead. They didn't get started back to the boat until that evening and didn't arrive until 1:00 A.M. on the 30th. The litters carrying the wounded men were awkward and had to be repaired periodically, making for a slow march (for some reason the army rejected the idea of carrying the wounded on travois, the simplest and most comfortable method of transporting cargo).

Thus Curley's three-day odyssey had been in vain. His news of Custer's death would have changed nothing. But the fact that he stuck with it so doggedly makes it truly heroic. If he had known what the white men thought of him then and what future historians would think of his story, perhaps he would have thought twice about this fierce loyalty.

For the record, the *Far West,* carrying fifty-four wounded soldiers, made it down the Bighorn to Fort Pease at the mouth of the Bighorn River; then it steamed down the Yellowstone to its confluence with the Missouri, then down that river to Fort Abraham Lincoln near Bismarck, North Dakota. The boat left Fort Pease at noon on July 3 and delivered the wounded to Fort Lincoln at 11:00 P.M. on July 5.

General Terry's report, under the wing of his adjutant, went along with the boat to be telegraphed all over the country. That report of the Custer disaster would keep the United States of America buzzing for weeks to come. It completely ruined the centennial celebration, including the Great Philadelphia Exposition, a tribute to technology, with its displays of heavy machinery and assembly lines of sewing machines, a chewing-tobacco machine, Krupps cannons, McCormick reapers and combines, silkworms, ice cream, clocks, carpets, and perfumes. The dozens of machines in Machinery Hall were all powered by a single monstrous machine, the Corliss engine. Even though the country was still in the midst of a great depression, the Philadelphia Exposition was designed to encourage the populace to look ahead, to think of the bright future of a great industrial nation.

But two days after Independence Day, on July 6, the *Bismarck Tribune* carried what it called the first account of the Custer Massacre. (Actually, two Montana newspapers, the *Bozeman Times,* on July 3, and the *Helena Daily Herald,* on July 4, beat the *Tribune* to the punch. Furthermore a very sketchy news flash of the disaster had reached the east by July 4. But the Bismarck paper carried a more complete account.)

According to the *Tribune,* its correspondent, Mark Kellogg (the only newspaper reporter present at the Little Bighorn), had sent an earlier dispatch which stated: "We leave the Rosebud tomorrow and by the time this reaches you we will have met and fought the red devils, with what result remains to be seen." Of course, Kellogg, who was with Custer's command, was killed. The *Tribune* story, after an account of Reno and Benteen's gallant combined commands holding off the Indians until General Terry and reinforcements forced the Indians to strike camp and steal away, continues with its narrative of Custer's fate:

> Lt. Bradley reported that he had found Custer dead, with one hundred and ninety cavalry men. Imagine the effect. Words cannot picture the feeling of these, his comrades and soldiers. Gen. Terry sought the spot and found it to be too true. Of those

The Custer family dead at Little Bighorn. Photos of George surrounded by brothers Tom (upper right) and Boston (lower right), nephew Harry Armstrong Reed (lower left), and Lieutenant James Calhoun, his sister Margaret's husband. *Little Bighorn Battlefield National Monument*

brave men who followed Custer, all perished; no one lives to tell the story of the battle. Those deployed as skirmishers lay as they fell, shot down from every side, having been entirely surrounded in an open plain. The men in the companies fell, with their officers behind them in there [sic] proper positions. General Custer, who was shot through the head and body, seemed to have been among the last to fall [there was no evidence of this], and around and near him lay the bodies of Col. Tom and Boston, his brothers, Col. Calhoun, his brother-in-law, and his nephew young [Autie] Reed, who insisted on accompanying the expedition for pleasure, Col. Cook and the members of the non-commissioned staff all dead—all stripped of their clothing and many of them with bodies terribly mutilated. The squaws seem

---

FIRST ACCOUNT OF THE CUSTER MASSACRE.

TRIBUNE EXTRA.

Price 25 Cents.   BISMARCK, D. T., JULY 6, 1876.

MASSACRED

GEN. CUSTER AND 261 MEN THE VICTIMS.

NO OFFICER OR MAN OF 5 COMPANIES LEFT TO TELL THE TALE.

3 Days Desperate Fighting by Maj. Reno and the Remainder of the Seventh.

Full Details of the Battle.

LIST OF KILLED AND WOUNDED.

THE BISMARCK TRIBUNE'S SPECIAL CORRESPONDENT SLAIN.

Squaws Mutilate and Rob the Dead

"NO OFFICER OR MAN OF 5 COMPANIES LEFT TO TELL THE TALE."
Headlines in the *Bismarck Tribune* herald the massacre of Custer's 7th Cavalry. *Little Bighorn Battlefield National Monument*

to have passed over the field and crushed the skulls of the wounded and dying with stones and clubs. The heads of some were severed from the body; the privates of some were cut off, while others bore traces of torture, arrows having been shot into their private parts while yet living, or other means of torture adopted. . . .

"The body of [correspondent] Kellogg alone remained unstripped of its clothing, and was not mutilated. Perhaps as they had learned to respect the Great Chief, Custer, and for that reason did not mutilate his remains they had in like manner learned to respect [!] this humble shover of the lead pencil and to that fact may be attributed this result. . . .

The *Tribune* account goes on to put an interesting spin on reality:

The Indians numbered at least eighteen hundred lodges [closer to one thousand] in their permanent camp, while those who fought Crook seem to have joined them, making their effective fighting force nearly four thousand [less than two thousand]. These were led by chiefs carrying flags of various colors, nine of whom were found in a burial tent on the field of battle [Lame White Man was the only chief killed]. Many other dead were found on the field, and near it ten squaws at one point in the ravine [not true—evidently the work of Ree [Arikara] or Crow scouts [since white men did not kill squaws].

The Indian dead were great in number [about sixty to one hundred Indians were killed], as they were constantly assaulting an inferior [in number] force. The camp had the appearance of being abandoned in haste. The most gorgeous ornaments were found on the bodies of the dead chiefs and hundreds of finely dressed and painted robes and skins were thrown about the camp. The Indians were certainly severely punished [!].

I have quoted the *Tribune* article at length because it reflects the quality of journalism of the day. First, it is clear that there is no attempt at impartiality in the account. Second, in portraying the Indian fighters as "red devils" and "screeching fiends, dealing death and destruction," the article is intended to inflame passion and horror and to dehumanize the Indians. Third, in stating that the officers and men of the 7th Cavalry deployed themselves properly, the article intends to portray the soldiers as calm, brave, and fighting to the death, whereas Captain Benteen, on viewing the battlefield two days later, states that the soldiers reacted in "clear panic" and did not conduct themselves as courageous soldiers of the United States Army. And finally, in describing the mutilation and torture of the soldiers in such bloodthirsty terms, the *Tribune* account failed to provide even a clue as to why the Indians treated the soldiers as they did. To do so would be to admit that the Indians had some justification for their fierce defense of the village.

We have to go back to the statements of Wooden Leg, Stands in Timber, and Black Elk to understand the mood of the Sioux and Cheyenne people, especially the women, who apparently committed most of the mutilations. According to Wooden Leg, it was the immediate fact of losing loved ones at the hands of the soldiers that led to grief and rage and the desire to avenge this loss on the bodies. Stands in Timber thinks the Cheyenne at least were still grieving over their relatives who had been killed and mutilated at the massacre on Sand Creek. And finally, Black Elk states the obvious: "These *wasichus* had come to kill our mothers and fathers and us, and it was our country...."

Nevertheless, it was the *Tribune* account, picked up by the eastern newspapers, that millions of this country's citizens read, and they reacted with horrified outrage.

Ironically, the Indians back on the Great Sioux Reservation, through riders and signals, knew about the rubbing out of the soldiers long before the whites did. Many miles to the south, Crow and Snake scouts, under General Crook, knew what had happened on the Little Bighorn within hours. They told Crook that the 7th Cavalry had been wiped out, but they would not tell him how they knew this—literally, with smoke and mirrors and moccasin telegraph.

The Sioux and Cheyennes, upon leaving their large camp on the Little Bighorn, headed west to the benchland above the valley; here they turned south, traveling as rapidly as a town can. Mourning families left behind their tipis, including burial lodges in which Sioux warriors were interred. The Sioux buried their dead, so to speak, in lodges, whenever possible. The Cheyenne dead were taken to the western hills to be buried there, with their weapons and fine clothes, beneath ledges, in crevices or beneath piles of rocks. Some of the lodges left behind contained furniture, meat, cooking pots, robes, weapons, and ornate clothing, including the clothing the dead warriors were buried in. Terry's relief column, as well as Reno's and Benteen's troops, found some fine souvenirs, many of which turned up in collections several years later. The Indians and soldiers took away each other's clothes and personal effects like pals trading treasured items at the end of summer camp.

In their haste, many Indian families took only their tipi covers, leaving the skeletal lodgepoles and brushy wickiups as evidence of the enormous camp.

Black Elk remembered the journey: "We fled all night, following the Greasy Grass. My two younger brothers and I rode in a pony-drag [travois], and my mother put some young pups in with us. They were always trying to crawl out and I was always putting them back in, so I didn't sleep much."

The Indians stopped that night for a short rest, then resumed the march under darkness. They continued the exodus the next day, the 27th (the same day Lieutenant Bradley discovered the naked, mutilated bodies of Custer's command), then set up camp in the late afternoon near present-day Lodge Grass. Here they celebrated their victory with kill dances and coup stories and feasting; but not all celebrated. The mourning families and their friends kept to their lodges, and the leaders held a council to determine the future. Already, the camp had the atmosphere of separation.

But a funny thing happened at this camp. A cry arose, "Here come the soldiers!" Warriors scrambled for their weapons and women went to protect their babies. But the "soldiers" turned out to be a group of young warriors, who had been acting as scouts covering the back trail. They were all dressed in military uniforms—tunics, hats, soldier rifles, big American horses—and they were having a little fun by charging the village.

The large group continued south to the north face of the Bighorn Mountains. Here, some of the warriors surprised a scouting party sent by the relaxing Crook to discover the location of the Indians. Only by abandoning their horses and supplies were the scouts able to escape and make their way back to Crook's camp in Wyoming.

Most of the Sioux and Cheyenne turned east to the headwaters of Rosebud Creek. For several sleeps they traveled down the Rosebud, sending out hunting parties and scouting parties, but it was becoming increasingly clear that the large group could not stay together. According to Wooden Leg, the young Cheyenne, the large camp moved swiftly, camping only one sleep in each place. Children and old ones could not keep up the pace, meat was scarce, the buffalo herds were not in the vicinity, the horses were tired and had to range far for grazing, and the nearby soldiers could be gearing up for another attack.

The reservation Indians became nervous and began to leave in scraggly little groups. Other small groups of "free" Indians struck out on their own, to provide for themselves. But still most of the village remained. They crossed over to the Tongue River, then to the Powder River. Now they were in the immediate area where the Cheyennes, the Oglalas, and the Hunkpapas joined forces after Crook attacked the sleeping Cheyenne village on March 17. They had come full circle as a united people. They rested here for four days, the chiefs counciling, the people recounting stories of coming together, of becoming a mighty nation that had whipped the U.S. Army, of becoming a desperate people on the run. At this point, they had no more illusions of life as it used to be, of following the buffalo herds forever, of freedom. They only wanted one last summer before they were killed or put on

An UNKNOWN marker posted on the site of the battle amid horse bones, 1877. *W.H. Over Museum*

the reservation. Black Elk states: "My father told me all the fighting had not done any good, because the Hang-Around-the-Fort people were getting ready to sell the Black Hills to the *wasichu* anyway, and that more soldiers were coming to fight us. He said that Three Stars [Crook] was on Goose Creek and that many other soldiers were up on the Yellowstone, and that these would come together and have us between them."

The chiefs decided that the bands and tribes should separate, go their own ways in pursuit of the buffalo and flight from the soldiers—or back to the agencies. So the remainder of the large camp split up, some going north, some east, some west, and some southeast to the Great Sioux Reservation to give themselves up.

The people said their goodbyes, Sitting Bull and Crazy Horse, who had called the people together—"We will have good times!"—wished each other well, and the greatest party of Indians ever on the plains was no more.

For the record, Black Elk's father was not quite right—the Hang-around-the-fort Indians were not getting ready to sell the Black Hills. The United States government was getting ready to take them. After the Custer "massacre," the government was in no mood to treat the Sioux and Cheyennes kindly—or even fairly.

On September 7, 1876, a commission arrived on the reservation led by George Manypenny, a former Commissioner of Indian Affairs, to "negotiate an agreement" whereby the Indians would relinquish the Black Hills and the unceded territory in Montana and Wyoming. The deal the commission gave the Indians was territory for food. Put another way, the government threatened to cut off all rations to the agencies if the Indians did not agree to give up the Black Hills. The Indians were to give them up or literally starve to death. Another provision of the agreement was that the Indians would send a delegation to look over the Indian Territory in Oklahoma. The government wanted to terminate the Great Sioux Reservation and send the people to that chunk of ground, which was already overcrowded with displaced Indians from all over the country.

Although Red Cloud and Spotted Tail protested the lack of negotiating room, the commissioners, backed up by a company of soldiers with bayoneted rifles and a cannon, pointed to the dotted line and the agency chiefs signed. The Manypenny Commission did not even attempt to get three-quarters of the male Indians to sign, as agreed upon in the Treaty of 1868. As far as they were concerned, that treaty was now a flimsy scrap of paper. On February 28, 1877, Congress ratified the new agreement, and the sacred Black Hills, Paha Sapa, became the property of the United States of America.

I returned to the Custer Battle-
field National Monument in the fall of 1990. I was feeling a little
apprehensive, because this trip was going to be a lot different from
my visit in 1974 and I didn't know if I was going to like it. Back then,
I had been a tourist with hardly a care in the world. Now, I was a
gainfully employed scriptwriter who had never written a script.

Paul Stekler and his associate producer, Maia Harris, had driven
out from Boston several weeks earlier, making stops along the way to
do research in state archives, historical societies, and libraries and to
make contact with the people at the monument and on the several
reservations in the Dakotas and Montana. They eventually put ten
thousand miles on Paul's old Toyota station wagon, which had a bent
coathanger for an aerial and a back end filled with books and maps
and duffel bags.

I had flown to Billings in a very loud twelve-passenger torpedo of
a plane. I had just gotten off a book tour and had barely enough time
to dump my dirty clothes in Missoula, scrounge up some clean ones,
and catch the plane. I was still fuzzy-headed from signing books, giving readings and being interviewed, and traveling.

Paul, whom I had met that summer when he flew out to Missoula, introduced me to Maia, a slender young woman with short
dark hair and large dark eyes. We shook hands politely, then we
squeezed my bag in the back and took off.

We drove out to the interstate on the edge of town and turned east and south. I hadn't been in that part of Montana for two or three years, and I was suddenly thrilled at the sight of the rolling plains filled with golden grasses under gray clouds that extended to every horizon. I came from that kind of country, but I have lived in Missoula, in the mountains, for almost thirty years. But my heart has remained in the plains country and I can take it in for hours, days, and not get bored. Paul and Maia were a little less thrilled, having crisscrossed the plains for the past several sleeps. But gradually their enthusiasm grew as we talked about the next few days, which would include much more driving, but also the opportunity to meet Indian elders and look at sites that would appear in the film. In spite of my apprehension and an occasional wave of bone-weariness, I was enjoying the country and the conversation.

About fifty miles down the interstate we came to the town of Hardin, just off the Crow Reservation. I hadn't asked what we were going to do about food and lodging that night, but I was pretty sure we were going to pull in at Hardin, get motel rooms, and find a decent restaurant. Hardin is a town of about two thousand souls, and it has these things, as well as a couple of convenience stores, a car wash, and enough bars to light up the small downtown with neon. I hadn't eaten since morning, and I was looking forward to food and a good night's sleep.

To my surprise we sailed right by Hardin and kept on going. We drove past Crow Agency, the governing center of the reservation, and a couple of miles later we were exiting at the big green sign that said "Custer Battlefield National Monument." By now I was a little surly. When we pulled into the parking lot at the visitor center I asked Paul what we were going to do about food and lodging that night. He said we were going to stay in a funky old hotel ("You'll love it") in Lodge Grass, a tiny reservation town farther down the road. Paul and Maia had been staying there the past couple of days. First we would check in at the visitor center to get a few details about our business for the next few days ironed out.

Paul, Maia, and I stepped from the car into the face of a chilly wind that had kicked up from the north. While Paul was rummaging around in the back end for something, I studied the cinder-block visitor center. It looked the same as it had in 1974—rectangular, low, institutional, a bit ratty. I remember how out of place it was in that rolling landscape, like a brick church in a wilderness area.

Inside the center, things were a bit more cheerful. There were a few people, mostly employees, books and pictures for sale, exhibitions—and Barbara Booher. I had read a small feature article about her in the Missoula newspaper when she first became superintendent of the monument—she was news because she was the first Indian woman who had attained such a lofty post in the National Park Service. That she had become superintendent of this monument to Custer's famous Last Stand was a grand irony not lost on Barbara. Of course, I respected and admired her greatly for her achievement as an Indian woman, but I wasn't prepared for her warmth and welcoming presence, which is in itself almost an irony. If you saw her walking from the parking lot to her office in the visitor center, in her crisp uniform and Smokey the Bear hat, warmth might not be the first thing that would come to mind about this woman. She sets her jaw and looks straight ahead without expression. Her walk is deliberate, unswerving. This is power. This is a woman who flies her own plane and deep-sea fishes in the icy Pacific (her last assignment before Little Bighorn was in Alaska).

Barbara Booher, former superintendent of the Little Bighorn Battlefield National Monument *Billings Gazette*

But when she puts on her civvies, a bright blouse and slacks, she smiles and laughs and tells stories and has a good time. She speaks frequently to area civic groups such as the Kiwanis and Lions, but she is more comfortable with a small group sitting around a table at the Merry Mixer Supper Club in Hardin, as we later found out.

She was interested in and very supportive of the film project, because it not only promised to tell the battle from the Indian point of view as well as the inevitable white point of view, but also would employ Indians as on-camera interviewees and as liaison people, crew people, historians—in other words, Indian people would be involved in a meaningful way. This had nothing to do with Barbara's official position as superintendent of the monument which had been erected to memorialize Custer and the 7th Cavalry. Officially, she was just helping another film crew find their way around the battlefield. Unofficially, I sensed that she felt that the Indians would not allow us to do just another Custer story.

We made arrangements to have a conducted tour of the battlefield the next day. A young summer ranger named Mike Moore, who is a military aficionado, would lead us. And we made arrangements to visit a Northern Cheyenne tribal elder whose grandfather had been prominent in the battle. Barbara asked if she could accompany us. She knew the man and, I think, wanted to see how we would conduct ourselves during the interview. We also made arrangements to visit other Northern Cheyenne and Crow elders.

It was quitting time by the end of our visit with Barbara, and the employees were putting on their coats, making small talk, shuffling to the door. Some of the employees were official Park Service with their green uniforms; others were civilians, including a couple of Crow women who sell books, maps, and reproductions of the battle to the tourists. But in the hour we had spent in the building I hadn't seen a single tourist. Business slows way down in the winter months. As we stood in the lobby for a minute or two to get our bearings and glance at the titles of the books, we were approached by a bright, attractive woman who would be of enormous help in the next few months. Her name was Kitty Deernose, and she was the curator of the museum. She was also a Crow Indian.

It was almost dusk when we stepped outside and walked to the car. A cold wind slashed across our faces, and the clouds had lowered even more. It was going to be cold the next few days, but as I stood in the parking lot, looking in all directions at the hills, the valley, the lights of the visitor center, and the barely distinguishable obelisk that is the monument, breathing in the excruciatingly pure air, this whole filming business seemed possible and exciting. It was at that moment that I thought, I am now a part of all this.

We ate at the convenience store/souvenir shop/gas station/restaurant called the Sagebrush Inn at the base of the hill. Indians from Crow Agency were gassing up their cars, buying junk food and milk, and visiting with each other. A few were in the restaurant, men with cowboy hats and big belt buckles, women in windbreakers that said Lodge Grass Indians, Crow Agency Pow Wow, children in sweatshirts and blue jeans and small colorful jackets. Like us, many of them were eating buffaloburgers and Indian tacos.

After supper, we headed south on the interstate to Lodge Grass. Half an hour later, in pitch darkness, we had exited the freeway and were driving into the small town. One thing I had noticed from the freeway was a long bank of lights on a hill behind Lodge Grass. The lights were pale white and bright and eerie. But we were too tired to investigate. We thought it was probably some sort of tribal industry large enough to warrant a night shift. The next night we did drive up the hill and found that the lights illuminated several outdoor basketball courts. The Lodge Grass Indians are one of the premier high school basketball teams in Montana. But tonight, the town itself was quiet, buttoned-up.

The Cottage Inn, where we would be staying, was indeed funky—but in a funny way. The first floor was all restaurant, rather large for such a small town and very nicely laid out. The ten or twelve tables were at interesting angles and set up for the following morning. At the far end was a large stone fireplace, which was smoke-blackened from years of use. The walls were covered with painted dishes and old photographs, various pieces of small rusty farm equipment, brittle horse tack, oil lanterns—pieces obviously collected from farms and ranches and homesteads in the area.

The woman at the check-in desk had a baby on her hip. It was her daughter's baby; she was baby-sitting. The dining room was empty and almost dark, just enough light to see the equipment and photographs on the walls. The woman told us that in the old days, families from up and down the valley used to come in just to eat dinner, that the room was even grander then. There were several large ranches surrounding Lodge Grass in those days. She spoke of imported furniture, chandeliers, fast buggies. I didn't ask if these family ranches were owned by Indians—I knew the answer. Even though the Crows, for protection from the Sioux and Cheyennes, had thrown in with Custer and the military, it wouldn't have been too long after the

Little Bighorn that the whites would be conniving to settle on the best bottomlands of the Little Bighorn valley. And the government would have colluded with these opportunists. In fact, the Dawes Act of 1887 allotted 160 acres of land to the head of each Crow household, then threw open the rest of the reservation to white settlement. The act was meant to discourage tribal living and encourage farming among the Indians. That's what the government said.

The second floor was the hotel proper, but it was more like a rooming house in an old western movie. It had none of the splendor of the dining room on the first floor. One corridor, ten rooms leading off it. Bathroom with a tiny shower stall, and a toilet on a raised platform, like a throne, at the head of the narrow stairs. Phone on a tiny table near the bathroom. Paul and Maia had the room between the bathroom and the phone.

My room was number ten, the last room at the end of the creaky corridor. It had been done in pink—pink walls, pink sink, pink bed-spread. But the price was right. Ten bucks a night.

The next morning I put on all my clothes, grabbed a pink towel, and walked down to the bathroom for a shower. I almost bumped into a man who stepped suddenly into the corridor from his room. He was old and black and wore a brown cowboy shirt, tan baggy dress pants, rodeo buckle, and high-heeled cowboy boots. He had a cowboy hat in his dark hand. He was the hotel's only other guest. We both laughed at the improbability of meeting so abruptly in the corridor of the largely deserted hotel. His laugh was deep, but nervous, as though he had spent many years getting out of people's way.

I learned that his name was Bill, that he was at least eighty-five years old, and that he was a genuine cowboy. He had been a rodeo rider in his youth and had been in the movies—nobody could re-member which ones. He had once been a sheriff or policeman on or near one of the Montana reservations. He had worked for ranchers up and down the valley for as long as anyone could remember. He now dyed his hair black to look younger so he could get work. The woman who had checked us in the night before could not remember where he came from, she only knew he had spent his winters, when there wasn't much ranch work available, in the little room upstairs. He got up early every morning, had breakfast, then left the Cottage Inn. She thought he played cards and shot the bull all day with other old cowboys—in this case, Indian cowboys. At night, he would come back and watch television (his own—the only television in the hotel) until it was time to go to sleep.

What a life, I thought. To be the only black man within miles of this tiny Montana town. I thought of Isaiah Dorman, the only black man on the Custer expedition, and I wondered how he had been treated by the officers and troopers of the 7th Cavalry. He had one thing going for him: He was married to a Sioux woman and spoke the language very well. In fact, his role with the army was as an interpreter, on the off-chance that there would be any Sioux survivors. Unfortunately, Isaiah Dorman didn't have a chance to practice his skill—he was killed shortly after Reno's charge into the village. I wondered then if Bill at one time had had an Indian wife or girlfriend. A surprising number of black men have been welcomed into western tribes, marrying Indian women, fathering children. This is not to say that all Indian people are free of prejudice. Some are downright racist toward other people as oppressed as themselves. A sad fact.

A couple of days later, Paul found out that Bill did have at least one son, who called him collect every month from prison—another sad fact.

After breakfast, we drove to the battlefield to begin our four days of touring, driving, meeting people who might be of some help, interviewing Indian elders who might be possible speakers on film. The days were long, and we returned to the Cottage Inn well after dark, hungry and exhausted, to sack lunches put out by the woman manager—sandwiches, potato chips, soda pop, and a piece of homemade pie.

Things went well enough. People were kind and helpful. We found a number of sites to film. And the interviews went well—after the first one, which was a complete disaster. This is the one Barbara Booher accompanied us on.

The man in question was a well-respected elder in his tribe. Each summer he conducted a ceremony at the battlefield that was well attended by Indian people as well as white tourists. He might even have held a holy bundle or a sacred shield in his tribe. He conducted sweats and other ceremonies at his home.

We picked Barbara up after lunch that day and drove the twenty-odd miles to his home, a fairly large, fairly modern house on a hill above Rosebud Creek. His wife welcomed us and led us into the living room, where the elder was sitting. When he stiffly unfolded himself from the easy chair, he turned out to be a tall, straight, somewhat slender man. He had a small face with small squinty eyes and a straight nose. His hair was gray and neither long nor short. He was a handsome man, and I could tell Paul was thinking of his presence and how well it would translate to film. He welcomed us, exchanged a few pleasantries with Barbara, then motioned us to sit. Paul gave him presents of tobacco and cloth (he had learned from a knowledgeable Indian woman that one presents gifts right off), then told him our story, that we were making a film about the Little Bighorn, that we wanted to present the Indian side of the whole Indian/white conflict of that period, and that we had heard he was a wise man who could tell us much about the subject. The elder listened thoughtfully, then told us that yes, he had a lot of stories, stories that nobody from the white world had heard, and now might be the time to tell them. He could tell us things about the battle that would surprise and astonish us.

And then he began a long monologue about money. At first, he seemed to be saying that he didn't care about money, that he didn't need it, that he found it distasteful when people brought up the subject of money. He wasn't like a lot of other Indians who were only interested in money. He could live without it, it didn't mean anything to him.

I thought of the paper money the soldiers had carried with them to Little Bighorn. Because Custer and the other officers didn't want the men to get drunk and get into trouble before they left Fort Abraham Lincoln near Bismarck, Dakota Territory, the men were not paid until they were well out of sight of the fort. On the trail they were each given a month's pay. And so at Little Bighorn they were wealthy men. When the Indians stripped the bodies after the battle, they found wallets and saddlebags stuffed with green paper. They threw it away or gave it to the children to play with. The girls made little dresses of it for stick dolls and the boys made saddle blankets of folded green paper for mud horses. But most of the soldiers' pay just blew away in the hot June wind.

This brief reverie was interrupted by the elder, who was now saying that unfortunately other people cared about money and so he was compelled to bring up the subject of payment for his time. Paul assured him that we fully expected to pay him, both now and when the time came to interview him on film. That satisfied the elder for a while. He again started talking about what he knew of the battle and said that we would be surprised at what really happened. He jumped up at one point and went into another room. When he returned, he had an eagle-wing fan, a pipe, which he carefully unwrapped for us, a blanket, and a flag—these items had been carried by his grandfather at the battle. By now, we were leaning forward on the sofa, prompting the old man to tell us something that no white man knew. So far, he had not told us a single thing about the battle. Wait'll those cameras get rolling, he said.

But now he wanted to see the color of our money. Fair enough. Paul pulled out his wallet and handed the elder a decent sum. The elder put it in his shirt pocket and launched into another oration on greed and how it had destroyed many trusting friendships and factionalized Indian groups. The white man's money was the cause of much unhappiness. Then his diatribe turned toward white people who always wanted something from the Indians but were not prepared to pay for it. These white people included anthropologists, historians, and moviemakers. They all wanted something for nothing.

I knew this. I had heard stories all my life about white people who used Indians, especially elders, to gain knowledge about historical events (like the Little Bighorn) or cultural aspects of tribal life or whatever was of interest to the white interviewer. These interviewers then went away to publish their books or make their films, and they never even sent a note of thanks, much less a fair fee for the Indians' time and effort. This is one of the many discourtesies that Indians resent and that contribute to an overall distrust of whites.

In fact, I had been concerned earlier about how Paul planned to compensate Indians for their time and effort on behalf of the film project. I was afraid that, being from the east, Paul might not know some of the etiquette involved in dealing with elders, and with younger men and women who had been exploited too often, too much. I had a selfish motive as well in wanting Paul to do it right—I was with him. I have a good reputation in Indian country, based on my novels and visits to many reservations to give readings or to talk with young people about the value of learning to write well so they can record their own histories, write their own poems and stories, set the record straight. I had been brought to Indian communities, both on and off the reservation, as a role model, and I didn't want to be involved in yet another exploitive enterprise that would leave the Indians with their pockets turned out, waving goodbye. I had approached the subject of courtesy and compensation delicately, but Paul had done his homework. He had talked with Indians, and with white people who had conducted business with Indians, and they had given him advice on payment.

The trouble was, this particular elder had a touch of the confidence man in him. He played us like a drum. What seemed to be idle rambling by an old man about money was cleverly calculated to make us feel guilty for asking him for a sample of his knowledge of the Little Bighorn. He accused us of wanting to acquire his amazing secrets for next to nothing. He wanted a lot of money. After all, we were moviemakers, weren't we?

Paul patiently explained the difference between documentaries and Hollywood blockbusters. He explained the difference in budgets. He explained that this was a pre-interview just to get an idea of what the person knew and how he presented it, that there would be more money down the road when the camera was actually recording the interview. He added, with a touch of frustration, that we had paid the elder fairly for this pre-interview and hadn't gotten anything useful. If we couldn't get an idea of what he knew, there probably wouldn't be a film interview.

There was a long silence. I glanced at Maia. She had a notebook in her lap, and she was making marks on it, nervous marks. The elder had been particularly gracious to her when we had all been introduced, but now I noticed that her notebook didn't have much writing in it, just the nervous marks.

Barbara Booher had been quiet during the interview, sitting off to one side on a straightback chair. Her face had taken on that impassive look, but I knew she was alert and tense, as we all were. I didn't know whether she thought that we had done something wrong or that the elder was being unreasonably recalcitrant. Normally, it wouldn't have made much difference, but we were counting on her goodwill and cooperation to make the film work. One of her goals in coming to the Little Bighorn National Monument had been to get Indian people more involved, to get them to think of the monument as a place where they could come to honor their own ancestors. Many Indian people throughout the years had come to think of the monument as a hostile place, a place where they were not welcome. Barbara wanted to turn this around, and so it was important for her to get out into the Indian community, talk with people, let them meet her, an Indian woman who understood how they felt, who wanted to make the battlefield more welcoming, more accessible to them.

Were we blowing it? Not only for ourselves, but for Barbara? By now the elder was actually pouting. It was clear that the interview had crawled to a conclusion. The elder was wrapping his grandfather's pipe, the pipe that had been at the battle, in a piece of dark cloth. Paul clicked off the tape recorder and we put our notebooks away. The elder's wife, who had been in the kitchen during the whole of the time, came into the living room, smiling—somewhat sadly, I thought.

Paul, not wanting to leave it like this, asked the elder what we had done wrong, what he wanted. Not surprisingly, the old man began to talk again about white people using Indians, not paying them enough. By now the old man had ceased to be an elder and had become simply an old man bickering over money. I knew from past experience that he had received a fair sum for his time—in fact, he had gotten a fair sum for almost nothing in return. Paul felt the same way. For the first time, he expressed his exasperation, his voice rising slightly, as he again explained who we were and what we intended to accomplish. We wanted to be fair to everybody involved in the project. What did he expect?

As we drove away from the elder's house, there was an exceedingly glum silence in the car. Paul had eventually paid the old man four times what he had budgeted for pre-interviews. As we drove Barbara back to the monument, we all seemed to be pretending that the disastrous event hadn't occurred. Although there were several silent moments in the car as we watched the tan hills, the dark pine ridges, the horses and cattle grazing in the bottoms of ravines, and the endless gray sky, we managed off and on to talk of schedules, of further meetings, of food, of weather. We didn't speak of our first interview, but I think we were all thinking, My God, what if all of the interviews are like that? My own thoughts were quite simple: that old man might have been an elder, but he was a better trickster. He had taken our money and given us thin air. Old Coyote had taught us a good lesson.

But maybe we got a small bit of revenge, albeit a pyrrhic revenge. The man had great presence and a large ego, he would have looked and sounded great on film, but we didn't use him. We couldn't afford it.

Fortunately, this interview was not typical. The others went swimmingly, and we were in high spirits the rest of the visit. We met Bill Tall Bull, the Northern Cheyenne tribal historian, who became a member of our board of advisers. He taught at Dull Knife Community College in Lame Deer. And we met Ted Rising Sun at the same time. Both men visited with us in a small room at the college. They sat silently as Paul explained what we wanted to do in the film (by now Paul had a small speech committed to memory) and how we envisioned the role of elders in the film. When Paul finished, both men sat for a moment and looked at us. Then Tall Bull spoke, and for a moment or two he voiced the same concern as the first elder had. Outsiders come to the reservation, take something, then leave. No thank-you, no offer to compensate. Paul assured him that we had heard the same stories and that we deplored such a practice. We had come prepared to do things the right way.

As Paul was talking I became aware that Bill Tall Bull was looking directly at me. Tall Bull is not tall but broad, with big forearms which rested on the table between us and a dark glowering face. It is one of those faces that look vaguely threatening in repose, but you find out later that it doesn't have much to do with the personality behind it. But right now, under those unwavering eyes, I found myself shifting a lot in my chair. When Paul finished, Tall Bull said, "I've read your books." I said something like "Oh?"—expecting the worst. I racked my brain, trying to remember if I had insulted the Northern Cheyennes in my writing. It was possible. In my first novel, *Winter in the Blood*, an old Gros Ventre lady says that the Crees are no good. She goes on to enumerate the reasons. A few months later, a friend told me I had better not go to the Rocky Boy Reservation ("Boy, those Crees are mad at you. What the hell you write that for?"). So, now I expected the worst, but Tall Bull smiled and said, "I really liked that historical one—what was it called?" *"Fools Crow,"* I said. "That's the one!" he boomed. And just like that, the ice was broken.

Ted Rising Sun, who had not spoken a word since the initial introductions, now began to talk. He is in his seventies, and although he is an elder in the tribe, he is shy and somewhat self-effacing. He has lived an incredible life. He was a war hero in both the Second World War and the Korean War. He was the most decorated Indian in the Korean War. But like many Indians who fought bravely for their country (and they make the point that it is *their* country that they were defending), Rising Sun couldn't handle the pressure of his war-hero status and hit the skids. He became a skid-row drunk in a couple of cities, literally waking up in the gutter on occasion. He lost several years of his life to cheap wine, until he bottomed out and began the slow painful climb back to the world of his people. It is such an agonizing story, such a typical story of Indian heroes, that it is difficult to listen to. But Rising Sun tells it. He survived, and he wants young Indian people to know that they can make it too. Ted is now a deacon in the Mennonite Church on the reservation, as well as being a traditional elder. A much-respected man, kind and gentle.

Ted is in the film. At one point, he tells of what happened to Chief Dull Knife (after whom the college is named) and his people after the

William Tall Bull, Cheyenne adviser for the film, and Kitty Deer Nose, curator at the Little Bighorn Battlefield National Monument. *Maia Harris*

Ted Rising Sun.
Maia Harris

Battle of the Little Bighorn. On a cold November day in 1876, five months after the battle, Dull Knife's camp on Crazy Woman Creek in central Wyoming was attacked by soldiers. Even though the Indians knew that the soldiers were in the area, they thought they were safely out of the way up the creek. At dawn the soldiers opened fire and killed many people. But the others managed to run into the hills on the other side of camp. There they watched as the soldiers burned up the lodges, the winter food, the warm clothing. Then in a chilling few seconds, Ted says, "They could hear the sound of the horses as their throats were cut." According to Ted, the soldiers cut the throats of all the Indian horses. In the film, you can hear this war hero's voice get husky as he relates this savagery. He seems to be seeing that winter camp almost as though he were there. His grandparents, who told him this story, were there.

That night, following our first day of interviews, we found ourselves eating a giant pizza in Hardin, some fifty-five miles away. We were there on some business which didn't pan out and had decided to eat something before the long drive down to Lodge Grass. The Little Big Man pizza parlor was decorated with cardboard pumpkins, black cats, and witches. It was Halloween night.

As we walked out to the car after dinner we noticed that the sky was black and sharp, a minor miracle after the horizon-to-horizon clouds of the day. In the clear air of eastern Montana, the stars multiply until the whole sky is filled with a mass of pinpoints in the blackness. It is difficult to pick out familiar constellations, because they are not alone. Off on the far horizon, a great full moon was rising.

I was in the backseat drowsily watching stars when I felt the car list to the right. I sat up, startled, but I saw a big green sign whiz by and I knew we were opposite the battlefield. Paul was taking the battlefield exit. "I've got a great idea," he said. "Let's sneak onto the battlefield." Well, it was Halloween, after all.

So we drove to the monument with our lights off and parked near the gate. The gate had been closed for the night, but we slipped through a fence and walked a crunchy gravel road near the housing compound. Barbara Booher was in one of the houses, probably doing some paperwork or watching television, or getting ready for bed, like other normal people. I was sure she could hear every crunchy footstep. Then we were in the cemetery, on the grass, near the graves, and we walked silently. I'm not a superstitious soul, I had done things like this on Halloween, but not on such a grand scale, with hundreds of graves beneath my feet and a bloody battlefield before me, and I felt very uneasy—just as I had as a kid.

Then we were in the open and the bare hills lay before us. Perhaps it was frost on the grasses, or perhaps it was the full moon's light—the entire battlefield glistened before us. Every hill, every dark ravine, every shallow coulee was edged in silver. To our left, fifty yards away, the visitor center looked both monumental and pale. Above and beyond it, on Custer Hill, the obelisk, the monument to the dead soldiers, seemed to float on the top of a swell in a sea of swells. To our right, the hills dropped down to the Little Bighorn, and we could see clearly where the north end of the immense camp had been. We could see where the Cheyenne camp circle had been, and a little south of that, Crazy Horse's circle of Oglalas. Bluffs and the long stream of cottonwoods along the river hid the rest of the camp circles. Beyond, on the valley floor, we could see dark stands of trees, soft lights of ranches, sweeping headlights of cars on the interstate, and finally the plains rolling out of the valley south and west toward the mountains.

It is difficult, if not impossible, to truly imagine the battle if you are a daytime visitor. There are too many man-made assaults on the senses. You have been to the visitor center. You have taken in all the information on the battle. There are other people around. You share their moods and observations, like it or not. You hear official voices, explaining. You hear officious voices of Custer buffs talking about calibers of weapons and what the 7th Cavalry guidon looked like. And you are always aware of metal and rubber—cars, pickups with campers, tired old vans, gleaming recreational vehicles pulling cars. Engines starting, stopping, idling. Car doors opening and slamming shut.

But at night you are alone with your imagination. Especially if the moon has lit up the battlefield for you. You can see the soldiers racing their horses up Calhoun Ridge from the ford at Medicine Tail Coulee. You can see where the skirmish lines were set, where riflemen got down off their horses to protect the rear of the retreating troopers. You can see down the hill where hundreds of Indians were crawling on their bellies, on hands and knees, darting from yucca plant to yucca plant, all the time advancing. You can see the waves of horsemen charging from the south, led by Gall, and from the north, led by Crazy Horse. You can see the soldiers, in a blind, terrified panic, running from Calhoun Hill toward Custer Hill, seeking safety in numbers.

And you can hear the continuous reports of rifles and handguns, the hiss of arrows as they rained down on the troops. You can hear shots and the thud of horses hitting the ground as they were shot by the troopers for breastworks. You can hear the thunder of hoofbeats, the whoops and yips of the warriors, the screams of the soldiers as they were hit with bullets and arrows, stone clubs and hatchets.

You can smell gunpowder, blood, dust, guts, horseshit, sage, and fear. You can also taste it, metallic on your tongue. And in the hundred-degree heat and the dust, you forget you want a drink of water, and for some, a drink will do no good. The battle is over and the women and children are coming up the hill from the camp.

The next morning we had breakfast at the Cottage Inn with Joe Medicine Crow, grandson of White Man Runs Him, one of Custer's Crow scouts. Joe lives just down the road from Lodge Grass, in a comfortable house set among the trees of the Little Bighorn River. Nearing eighty now, he is as bright and brown as a copper penny. He is a short, thick man in great shape. He wears a cowboy hat, a big belt buckle, and boots, but you don't sense that he was ever much of a cowboy; in fact, he is a Crow tribal historian, after a long career as a Bureau of Indian Affairs official. Joe is an educated man. He got his master's degree in 1939 at the University of Southern California, a time when it was rare for an Indian to go to college, much less graduate school. He started work toward a Ph.D., but the Second World War intervened and he spent the next five years in the army.

Joe has always been unique. Never one to miss an opportunity, he tried to break into the movie business in Los Angeles during his college days. He tells a wonderful story of reading in the newspapers that a film company was looking for Indians to play bit parts in an upcoming western. Joe took the streetcar down to the studio, and after much waiting around with dance-hall girls and cowboys and "Indians," he was finally called into the casting office. The man looked him up and down, told him to take off his shirt, told him to turn so he could see his profile, studied him, then told Joe that they would be in touch. Joe was happy as he rode the trolley home. After all, he was an Indian, they needed Indians, and there weren't many Indians in Hollywood in those days. A couple of weeks went by and no call. Finally, Joe went back to the casting office and asked if they had called and maybe he just hadn't been home. But the man said, "No, we can't use you." Joe said, "Why not?" "Because you don't look like an Indian—your nose isn't big enough." Joe laughs as he recalls this, and he'll recall it for anybody who cares to hear it. "So they got a bunch of Jews and Italians to play Indians 'cause they have bigger noses!"

As Joe ate his ham and eggs and took sips of coffee, he talked. He told stories, he gave information, he commented on the food, he asked questions, he talked about Custer's Crow scouts. As a young man, he knew all of the scouts and had been conducted around the battlefield by them as they described in detail the development of the battle. Joe's mind goes a mile a minute, and he's fun to be around. He is much beloved in Crow country.

After breakfast, we left Joe and drove to the battlefield for our tour. The clouds had come back, darker than ever, and the wind from the east flattened the grass on the hillsides and rocked the car with mighty gusts. The leaves were pretty much gone from the trees and bushes in the valley, giving a hard-edged, gray look to the fields. Although the Crows are known for their horses, I didn't see a single one on the drive. Apparently, they were finding what shelter they could. The only people I saw were in cars speeding along the interstate.

The next couple of hours at the visitor center were taken up with Paul and Maia's busywork. There is a lot of busywork involved in filmmaking, I discovered. Phone calls trying to make arrangements for more interviews, trying to make contact with tribal liaison people, checking in at the office back in Cambridge, checking with the cinematographer to see if he would still be free in February when we would start filming, still trying to find a sound person.

Meanwhile, I wandered around the museum, browsed the books, then walked up to the obelisk on Custer Hill, a distance of about one hundred yards. I studied the names of the dead troopers etched on all four sides of the granite monument. This monument was erected after the soldiers' bodies, what was left of them, were retrieved in 1881 from the original graves dug where they fell. It contains the names of 261 men, which includes Reno's and Benteen's dead. According to John S. Gray, the acknowledged authority on the battle, this number is two short of the actual 263 killed: "The two missing names are the same ones Reno had omitted from his July 5 [1876] roster of the dead, although they had been on the corrected regimental records for five years."

Because the work was so gruesome, and because the work detail, under Major Reno, didn't have the right tools, and because they were afraid that the Indians would return, the troopers didn't dig proper graves. They sometimes dug a shallow depression, rolled the body into it, and covered it with a few inches of dry dirt. Other times, they piled rocks on top of bodies, or simply brush brought up from the river's edge. The stench, after two and a half days under the hot sun, of the bloated white bodies and the bloated horses was almost too much to bear, and so the men worked hastily, their Christian duty to honor the dead overcome by an overwhelming urge to get the job done and get out of there. They marked the graves only of the nine of twelve officers whose faces and bodies were recognizable. They wrote the name of each officer on a piece of paper, rolled it up and put it in a cartridge shell, then pounded the shell into the top of a stake that marked a grave.

Interestingly, seven individuals, including six officers, made body counts that ranged from 206 to 212 dead and buried. Custer's five companies, plus two civilians, numbered 210, so the body counters were in the ballpark. Only one, a Major Brisbin, counted 210, but even he may have been wrong. One or two bodies were apparently missing. To this day, historians and Custer buffs argue over the exact number of bodies that were lying on the battlefield that day, and exactly where they were lying.

In early summer of 1881, a party of soldiers from Fort Custer came back, collected the bones that had been picked clean by coyotes, crows, magpies and other carrion eaters, and carried them all to the top of Custer Hill. There they dug a long trench, threw in the remains, and erected the granite monument that stands today. They carried away the remains of the officers for a proper burial in the east. All except for a Lieutenant Crittenden, whose parents, for reasons of their own, wished his body to remain there.

There is a rather large group of white marble headstones on the north side of Custer Hill surrounded by an iron picket fence. This is the place where Custer and his headquarters command, along with stragglers from companies that had already disintegrated, fell. The officers are named. The enlisted men are not. Custer's headstone is marked by a badge of brown or black paint. It is too weathered to be sure. The stone says: "G.A. Custer, Brvt Maj Gen, Lt Col, 7th U.S. Cavalry, Fell Here." Custer's remains were disinterred along with those of the other officers and shipped back to West Point for reburial with full honors.

Back at the visitor center, I was taken down to the archives where Kitty Deer Nose presides. Paul and Maia were already there, looking for material, such as diaries, letters, maps, and photographs, that could be used in the film. Kitty, with her white gloves, had just laid an original letter on the table, and Paul was ecstatic. "Look at this!" he said. "You won't believe this!"

It was a letter dated August 22, 1875, from a Mr. Abraham Buford to "My dear Custer" concerning a scheme to sell horseshoes to

An 1875 letter to Custer detailing the specifics of their Goodenough horseshoe deal. *Little Bighorn Battlefield National Monument* the army. Custer, in spite of his national fame and aquaintance with eastern bankers and robber barons, had never managed to acquire anything approaching wealth. After the Civil War, he had lost his battlefield commission as brevet major general and was reclassified a captain in the regular army. Along with the reduction in rank, his pay was drastically reduced. And so he involved himself with unscrupulous wheeler-dealers to make his fortune. Custer was either a naive hero, allowing his name to be used, or a willing schemer in these questionable enterprises. At one point, he was associated with a plot to sell stock in a Colorado silver mine that existed mostly on paper. Other schemes involved stagecoach lines and sutlerships at forts and at least one agency on a reservation. The letter from Mr. Buford concludes: "If I can have control over horse shoes &c, I mean to ask a Board [sic] with yourself as President. The Goodenough and Elastic Companies want an Officer [Custer] to go in Europe. It can be easily managed—if-if-if their [horse]shoes are actually the best— about which I am doubtful more than half the time." And so Custer was to become president of a company that would attempt to sell questionable horseshoes to the very army that Custer was a part of, which was searching for a new horseshoe contractor.

The letter seemed invaluable at the time to show another side of Custer, but it never actually made it into the film. Like many of our juicier tidbits, it got dropped because of time and space constraints. However, one of our historians, Richard Slotkin, does mention that the "Goodenough horseshoes were not quite good enough."

About two that afternoon we met Michael Moore upstairs near the entrance to the visitor center. Mike is a young man—in his mid-twenties, at most—with longish curly black hair, a black beard, bright brown eyes, and a no-nonsense manner. He is a seasonal ranger and had already left for his home in North Dakota after the tourist season but had come back to do some research and to show us around.

That cold, blustery afternoon that Mike went over the battlefield with us was interesting, if not much fun. We stopped every quarter of a mile or so, got out of the car, listened to Mike, and followed his pointing finger to the distant hills and mountains, the ravines, the valley floor, the river. Normally, I resist any discussion of that part of Montana that contains the word "bleak," but on that day the landscape was bleak. We stood beside the car, our faces red and our noses running, as Mike explained every detail so carefully that I forgot almost everything that afternoon.

As we finally drove down toward the visitor center in the late dusk, I realized how much I didn't know about the Battle of the Little Bighorn and I wondered seriously if I would ever catch up enough to be of much help in writing the script. Right at that moment, as I concentrated on seeing if my fingers would ever bend again, I had my doubts.

Paul came out to Missoula the following February and stayed with my wife and me for two and a half weeks. Although we had been working together by phone and mail for three months, Paul and I were never really on the same page. The thing I had the most trouble with in our long-distance collaborating was putting the battle into the context of what was happening in America at that time, which was crucial to making the film transcend a simple fight. Paul and I needed to sit in the same room for several days.

So we sat and we wrote. We put together a single-spaced seventy-two-page script, working day and night. Call it what you will, a wish list, a kitchen-sink script, we threw everything we wanted to into that script, knowing full well that it would be cut drastically by the time the final version of the film was put into the can, as filmmakers say. In some ways, it's like when you were a kid and you had a roomful of toys and your mother said to pick out a few favorites to take to Grandma's house. Only we had to leave many of our favorite toys behind. When the script eventually reached its final form of twenty-two pages, several months later, we couldn't even remember what toys we had planned to pack. Furthermore, most of the really fun ones had been tossed out.

At the end of Paul's stay, we drove to the Little Bighorn for the first filming session, with a stop at the state historical society in Helena to do some research on a diary we wanted to use to illustrate what life was like along the Bozeman Trail. The diary was that of a Bill Thomas, who, along with his seven-year-old son, had been killed by Indians beside the Yellowstone River.

We stopped for the night in Bozeman, where we were to pick up Dan Hart, who teaches television and film courses at Montana State University. Dan has taught many Indian students how to use video equipment and how to structure documentary stories so they can make their own films about their people. His program has been so successful that some of his former students have gone on to win awards at festivals. I have seen the films of Roy Big Crane and Dean

Bear Claw, and I am not surprised at their recognition as filmmakers. Dan himself had agreed to be a member of Paul's film crew.

Early the next morning, we were on the road, driving I-90 east to Billings. We got off the freeway once, between the tiny communities of Graycliff and Reedpoint, to look for the graves of Bill Thomas, his son, Charley, and Joe Shultz, a mule driver.

The Thomases had started for the west from the family farm in Illinois in 1866. Thomas's wife and two infant daughters had just died of pneumonia, so he decided to pull up stakes and head for Bozeman, Montana, where he had relatives. A new start. He put together a wagonload of furnishings and supplies, hired Shultz, and started west from St. Louis along the Oregon Trail. He kept a diary of the trip, which records a feeling of adventure, but few real adventures. The Oregon Trail was well protected all the way to Fort Laramie, Wyoming, a distance of six hundred miles. At Fort Laramie, the Thomases left the Oregon Trail to head north along the Bozeman Trail through Indian country. They were part of a convoy of perhaps 150 private and freight wagons, led by the famous mountain man Jim Bridger, along with two companies of infantrymen. Life along the Bozeman Trail was much more dangerous than on the Oregon Trail. The convoy passed several graves, including one which especially interested Thomas. He writes in his diary: "About a half mile's drive from camp this morning, on the hillside to the left of the road, is a grave containing the bodies of five men who were killed a few days ago by the Indians. As I passed by the grave, I saw that the wolves had made an opening to the inmates and had torn the flesh from the bodies and left their ribs exposed. Such is the haste and the depravity of man out here that he will hardly take the time to pay his last respects to the dead—but leaves them for the wild beast of the field to cry and howl over, and often feast upon. . . ." Thomas remarks on another poor soul's grave where the wolves had "gnawed the flesh from his face."

Finally, the large wagon train reached Montana, and with great difficulty—some men, mules, and oxen were swept away—forded the Big Horn River. Jim Bridger proclaimed this friendly Crow country. The Sioux territory was behind them. The military escort, with its wagons and animals, stopped at this site to build Fort C. F. Smith. The civilian freight trains, along with a few private wagons, pushed on to the Gallatin valley and the goldfields of Virginia City along a new trail that Jim Bridger had discovered which would cut off several miles of the old trail. Thomas stuck with the large party for a while, until he became impatient with the pace of the lumbering wagon train. When one of the freight wagons broke down, promising another long delay, Thomas's wagon kept going.

For five days the trip was exhilarating and peaceful. The party saw herds of buffalo and antelope, picked berries, made a nice watering hole at a spring "of the best water that I ever drank of." There they left the Bridger cutoff, dropping down into the Yellowstone valley to continue west on the original Bozeman Trail. Thomas wrote in his diary that evening: "In the afternoon we drove five miles and crossed a river [Bridger Creek]. While crossing it we lost our coffee pot. Drove three miles from there and camped for the night on a nice little branch, a few hundred yards upslope from the Yellowstone [River]. Broke our champagne bottle." It is difficult to say if this last sentence means that they broke the champagne bottle accidentally or broke it open in celebration. They were nearing their destination.

Paul Stekler and James Welch standing on either side of Bill Thomas's grave, just off Interstate 90 in Montana. *Paul Stekler*

Whatever the case, it was the last entry in Bill Thomas's diary. The next day the party was attacked by twenty Sioux warriors and killed. Thomas and his son were found dead and scalped near the wagon. Thomas had thirteen arrows in him; Charley had three. The Indians had planted several sticks, with blue-green cloth tied to their tops, around the bodies of the father and son. Thomas's diary was found near his body.

Joe Shultz was found down near the Yellowstone River. He had been fishing and had caught two cutthroat trout. He had twelve arrows in his body and was scalped.

The grave lies between the interstate and a frontage road (old Highway 10). As David Walter, in an article in *Montana Magazine,* puts it, the grave "seems incongruous, perched in the midst of the Yellowstone power corridor. Interstate 90 runs four lanes of whizzing traffic within yards of the grave site on one side, while old U.S. 10 passes just as close on the other side. North, toward the Yellowstone River—where Joe Shultz was fishing—parallel the mainline of the Montana Rail Link (formerly the Northern Pacific Railroad [the very railroad whose surveying crews Custer was sent to guard in 1873]), power lines, telephone lines and signs indicating an underground gas pipeline. But such is the layering of people, events and structures on the Montana landscape." The thousands of people who travel the interstate every day have no way of knowing this grave exists. You can approach it only from the frontage road, where a roadside historical marker tells you what this insignificant mound between two tiny Montana towns means.

As Paul, Dan, and I looked down at the grave (oddly surrounded by wintering irises), we had a difficult time absorbing the meaning of a single grave of three bodies, killed in 1866, in the vast Yellowstone country. Even as we stood there, cars, semis, pickups, and campers roared by on their way to somewhere. The people in them, warmed by their heaters, must have thought it odd to see three men standing out in the cold between the freeway and the frontage road. But Paul and I had seen, at the state historical society, the arrows, the stick markers, the diary, and one of little Charley's black boots. In these items we saw hope, misunderstanding, conflict—and finally, nothing more than a moment in history that does whiz by like cars on the interstate. And we were late.

We got to Billings just in time to pick up the cinematographer at the airport. Jon Else was coming up from California, where he lives when he's not hopping around the globe shooting film for various productions. He is much in demand, and Paul felt incredibly lucky to get him for our project.

We loaded Jon's dozen aluminum cases of all sizes and shapes into a carryall that we had rented earlier that afternoon and sped off to the battlefield.

The next few days of filming involved a lot of riding around, looking for snow. The winter after the battle had been particularly harsh—cold, windy, blizzardy. Although it was cold now, it wasn't harsh. Jon and Paul were reduced to filming snowflakes and frost-

The production crew for *Last Stand at Little Bighorn*. From left to right: front—Joseph Medicine Crow (Crow), project adviser; Dan Hart, assistant cameraman; Maia Harris and Anne Craig, associate producers; Frederica Lefthand (Crow), sound assistant; and J.T. Takagi, sound recordist; standing—Roy Big Crane (Salish), camera assistant; Jon Else, cinematographer; James Welch; Paul Stekler. *Maia Harris*

rimed weeds around the battlefield. They went farther into the Big-horn Mountains to get real snow, drifts several feet deep, white mead-ows, snow-covered lakes, but no falling snow.

Meanwhile, Maia Harris and the sound person, J. T. Takagi, went off each day to collect sounds—birds, water, wind, stillness. Anything but airplanes and cars. It is surprising to find that even in remote areas of Montana, cars and airplanes, trains and tractors could be such a problem. Jon had to shoot around barbed-wire fences, power lines, dwellings, paved roads, and signs.

The film crew conducted two interviews on that trip. The first one, with Joe Medicine Crow, went very well. Joe's ability to tell sto-ries and his animated expressions and gestures were perfect for the camera. He had been interviewed several times before and knew his stories by heart. He even managed to convey some humor about the coming of the "white eyes" and the battle itself.

Ted Rising Sun was going to be more problematical—he is natu-rally shy, he doesn't tell stories easily (we found that out during our pre-interview), and he wasn't absolutely sure he trusted us. But he met us in his car at the turnoff for Busby, his hometown on the Northern Cheyenne Reservation. He led us down into town to the small office building of the Mennonite church. It was a crisp sunny afternoon, and Ted watched warily as the crew unloaded the equip-ment. Paul and I talked with Ted as the crew set up in the office, moving furniture, taking down a couple of window shades, putting up sheets of colored plastic over the windows, moving more furni-ture, setting up the camera, the lights. Nothing we said could distract Ted from seeing his familiar world suddenly transformed into what looked like a technological torture chamber. When one of the crew came over and asked him where the heat source was for the small building, he looked downright startled. Even when the crew member explained that they were going to have to turn off the forced-air blower because it would make a distracting noise during the quiet of the interview, Ted looked as though he wanted to bolt.

But the interview, after the first several minutes, during which Ted sat rigidly in the corner of a couch and answered Paul's ques-tions with some hesitation, was wonderful. To me, it was the best interview in the whole film, partly because Ted was not used to being interviewed and occasionally had to struggle to find the right word or thought, and partly because he seemed to be seeing and hearing those "early times" just as his grandparents had described them to him. When he spoke of the burning of his grandparents' village by the soldiers, his voice became dark with emotion. You could have heard the proverbial pin drop in that room on that cold sunny afternoon.

On our last day we invited Barbara Booher and Kitty Deer Nose to dinner at the Elks Club just outside Hardin. It was to be the first real dinner we had during that trip—the other nights we just ate fried stuff at the Husky Truck Stop—and we were feeling just a bit giddy as we left our motel to drive the few miles out to the Elks Club. We were happy the winter filming was done (although Paul was very concerned by the lack of snow), and we were looking forward to a good meal.

Barbara had called Paul earlier at the motel and asked if she could bring a last-minute guest. And so we speculated on the identity of the mystery guest—perhaps one of her Park Service superiors, or a local Crow tribal official, or the mayor of Hardin. Paul seemed to know, but he wasn't saying.

We sat at a large table and ordered drinks, relaxing, unwinding, again giddy with something approaching exhaustion. We were a jolly bunch. Then I saw Barbara and Kitty and the mystery guest walk into the dining room. I recognized the guest immediately. I had met him a couple of times, once several years ago in Oklahoma and once in Missoula, where he had come to give a talk. I recognized the potential for trouble, but I also felt a kind of excitement that the evening might turn out to be unforgettable. That's the kind of reaction that Russell Means inspires when he walks into a room.

Barbara introduced him around. He looked us over, then sat next to Paul, across the table from me, a triumphant, tight smile on his face. It was an imposing look, the kind of look he had given to federal agents, marshals, Indian goons at Wounded Knee, white bigots, high government officials across America. And now to a small film crew at the Elks Club just outside of Hardin.

Russell Means is a handsome man, well-built, with hair parted in the middle, braids hanging to his shoulders. He wears Indian-style clothes, the kind AIM members wear as a uniform: ribbon shirts or nineteenth-century-style print cotton blouses, blue jeans, denim jackets, ornate belt buckles, adornments ranging from turquoise and silver rings, watchbands, and bracelets to red cloth woven into the braids, sometimes a bone-and-bead choker around the neck. Means was not as flamboyant in appearance that night in the Elks Club as I remembered him on the two previous occasions. Nevertheless, he turned the heads of the other diners. Even if they didn't recognize him—and they probably didn't—they knew that he was not an Elks Club habitué.

I was interested in Barbara's motive in bringing Means to dinner. And wasn't it a bit risky for her, as an important official of a government agency, to be seen with Means? Had he just shown up, leaving her with no choice but to invite him? As usual, she was cool and unreadable, attractive in her civilian duds, smiling.

At first, Means was hostile and abrupt. Barbara had introduced Paul as the producer and director of the film, and so Means directed his questions to Paul: What kind of film did he think he was making? Why did he think he had the right to make a film about Indians? Was he going to be another one of those whites who came out to exploit Indians, then went home to their comfortable lives?

If Paul hadn't decided to be a filmmaker, he could have been a very successful diplomat. I had been around him enough now and had heard him answer enough similar questions to know from the tone of his voice that he was irritated with Means's imperiousness. He was also exhausted, strung out, and worried about the winter shots, but he managed a calm dignity. After a few more aggressive questions, Means allowed himself a thin smile and looked over the rest of us. The tension was heavy in the air. Nobody wanted particularly to be singled out for God knew what.

Barbara was not exactly worried about the atmosphere, but I imagine she too wondered how we could get out of this charged impasse. She and Means have a friendly but wary relationship. They have had a couple of confrontations concerning Means-planned demonstrations at the battlefield. He is the activist, she the establishment, the adversary. His position is relatively simple—to promote controversy, to call attention to Indian causes. Her position is more complex—to be a part of an establishment, complete with a Smokey the Bear hat, and to effect subtle change within that establishment. And so Barbara had to learn to talk to a Lions Club group in the morning and meet with a Russell Means at night. Hers is a tricky terrain, but she negotiates it.

Finally, the waitress saved us by announcing the specials. We all ordered steaks and another round of drinks, except for Means, who ordered the chicken breast teriyaki. He was on a diet, he told us, and somehow the tension melted away. The rest of the dinner was pleasant. Means was right in there among us now, telling stories, laughing, teasing. He was still the center of attention, but more in the manner of a raconteur than an activist who had stirred more than one audience to action. He was Russell Means and he could not forget that, but he gave his image a rest for this one night.

A week later, Barbara Booher called me from the battlefield. Means had called her from the Navajo Reservation in Arizona. He wanted to know if I wanted to write his biography. She gave me his number, but I never called it. I don't even know why. Or maybe I do. I do know that the Battle of the Little Bighorn, that relatively small event in this country's war history, continues to create division among Indian people, as well as tensions between Indians and whites, over a century later. Custer seems to be alive and well and riding in our midst.

9

My mother worked for many years as a stenographer/secretary for the old Indian Service and later for the Bureau of Indian Affairs. Like many young Indian women (and men), she had gone to school at Haskell Indian School in Lawrence, Kansas, to "learn a skill." It was thought back in those days—in her case, the early thirties—that it was better for an Indian to learn a trade rather than go off to college to learn God knew what. Although my mother, a Gros Ventre, hadn't been raised in the traditional Indian ways, many of her friends at Haskell had their first white man's haircut and wore stylish Anglo clothing for the first time. One picture from this era shows my mother lounging on a lawn with a group of other girls, all in lovely flowing dresses and smart shoes. In contrast to many pictures from this boarding-school era, all the girls are smiling and seem genuinely happy, at least for the moment.

Of course, these boarding schools had another purpose that ran hand in hand with education. That was to cut this generation of Indians off from their traditional upbringing. It was felt by governmental and Christian authorities that if they could break the chain of traditional beliefs and lifeways, they could create new citizens who would take their education (which included table manners, grooming, hygiene, housekeeping skills, and obedience) and melt away into the mainstream of America. Eventually, they would forget that they were once Indians.

Unfortunately, this policy worked in many cases, especially among those young people who were sent off to boarding school as children and didn't return to the reservation until early adulthood. Some of these young people came to loathe the primitive ways and beliefs of their parents. They couldn't stand the way their people lived.

In *The Surrounded,* a wonderful novel written by D'Arcy McNickle in 1936, Archilde, who has been away at boarding school and later worked as a musician in Portland, thinks:

> Actually, in the way he was learning the world, neither Modeste nor his mother was important. They were not real people. . . . After living in Portland, playing the violin, living in a boarding house, reading baseball scores—it was funny to come home and sit at his mother's feast. His eyes saw the old faces, faces he had forgotten about, never thought to see again; and now to be sitting in the circle of firelight and looking at them—but it wasn't really funny, not deeply funny. The deeper feeling was impatience, irritation, an uneasy feeling in the stomach. Why could he not endure them for just these few hours? Why did they make him feel sick? It was not to be reasoned with. It did no good to remind himself that the old faces were not at fault; that his mother, who had never struck him, scarcely even spoken angrily to him, was in no way to blame for what he felt; and neither were the buffalo to blame for being no longer free. Reason wouldn't quite do the trick, but he would try it. He would sit quietly and try not to see or hear or smell too much. He would try not to speak, lest he say more than was necessary. And in a few hours, days—He had come home this time because it would be the last time. When he went away again—this he knew—he would not return.

But for many young Indians who went away to boarding school the feelings were simply resignation, defeat, loss of spirit. They endured the many years of forced exile from their parents, their grandparents, their people, their country. And when they finally went home, they discovered that they knew almost nothing of their culture. They were strangers in their own country—strangers to the white culture, strangers to their people. To make matters worse, when they tried to pick up their lives by marrying and raising a family, they discovered they didn't know how to do it. They discovered they didn't know how to be parents. They had been taken away from their own parents at such an early age, they didn't know what it was like to be raised in a family; consequently, they didn't know how to raise their own families. This led to broken families, which in turn led to a breakdown in culture and pride. Even today, many of the social ills that plague Indian communities can be directly linked to this boarding-school period.

So the grand experiment of taking Indian children away from their parents to be raised by the white men's institutions in a way worked: It broke the vital link to Indian traditions and created a few generations of Indians who learned how to add, subtract, write, cook, sew, use typewriters, fix cars, run machines, play football and bad-minton, ride streetcars, keep house, and set a table. But when they got back to the reservation—and most of them went back in spite of their keepers' efforts—they found disease, poverty, drinking, and dying traditions. And many of them blamed themselves and their parents.

But many survived, and some thrived—including my mother. She immediately went to work at the agency on the Fort Belknap Reservation, her home reservation. Here she met my father, himself a product of a boarding school, and they moved to his reservation, the Blackfeet Reservation, near the Rocky Mountains. My older brother and I were born there at the Public Health Service hospital in Browning.

Although my father did many things in his life, including ranch-ing, welding, and administering Indian community hospitals, my mother stuck with her jobs as a stenographer. Their work for the Indian Service took them to such places as an Indian boarding school in Chemawa, Oregon; an Indian boarding school and hospital in Mount Edgecumbe, Alaska; then back to Browning and finally Fort Belknap, where my father was the hospital administrator and my mother once again was a stenographer.

One day, while she was digging around in the basement of the agency office for some records, she came across some documents that she thought I might be interested in. I was a young man, having just graduated from college, and I was determined to see if I could become a writer. At the time, I had almost no interest in history and very little interest in writing about my Indian people. This was in 1965, and I thought people would not be interested in reading about Indi-ans, especially northern Montana Indians. The area was so remote and the tribes so unheard-of that I thought the people and landscape unworthy of my heroic efforts. In fact, I was thinking about moving to a city, maybe even New York. I had read stories of writers, famous writers such as Thomas Wolfe and Truman Capote, who had left their small hamlets to take New York by storm. Why couldn't I? The idea was so romantic that I damn near wept every time I thought about it.

My mother brought home copies of three documents, only a small sampling of the many such documents in the agency basement. They were annual reports from Fort Belknap Indian agents to the Commissioner of Indian Affairs submitted to the Secretary of the Interior for the years 1880, 1887, and 1897. One of the first things I noticed was the declining numbers of Indians: In 1880, there were 2,112 Gros Ventres and Assiniboins; in 1887, there were 1,720; in 1897, there were 1,305. In the early days of reservations, many people would go from reservation to reservation (without permission) to seek rations, to visit relatives, sometimes to live. This would account for some of the declining population on the Fort Belknap Reservation. But I believe that many Indian young people were already being sent to boarding schools as far away as Carlyle, Pennsylvania, and Haskell, Kansas, and urged never to return.

The reports note that the Indian morals are generally satisfactory. The 1880 report does state that "their morals, from a Christian, or civilized standpoint, are as bad as need be, but from their own standpoint are perhaps not as bad as might be expected."

Things are not much better agriculturally: "The season was cold and backward and generally unfavorable for the fore part of the season. We however managed to plow and plant nearly 50 acres, all of which was fenced; 10 acres of sod was sown to oats, 1 acre to wheat, 5 acres to pumpkins and squashes, 15 acres new-breaking sowed to turnips and the balance planted to corn and potatoes. The crops mentioned started off fairly, but the latter part of the month of June and all of July up to the 25th was entirely without rain and very hot, and consequently so dry that the crops suffered severely, more especially on sod."

The 1880 report also speaks to the problem of illicit trading, especially whiskey trading, and the presence of bad white men who have a habit of hanging around reservations and preying on the Indians: "In any event they [the white men] take advantage of their [the Indians'] loose ideas to dishonor and debauch their [the Indians'] women...."

The 1887 and 1897 reports are more optimistic in the way that only bureaucrats who want to keep their jobs can make them. The 1887 report does indicate that Indians are still stealing horses from each other; in fact, it mentions that the agency Indians made a peace treaty that year with the Blood Indians.

The 1897 report states, "The larger boys and girls have been kept at the [industrial] school [at the agency] during vacation, and for the month of July there was an attendance of 30 pupils. This plan was inaugurated mainly to protect the larger girls from the evil associations of the camps and temptations they would naturally be subjected to. I am pleased to say the plan is working satisfactorily." One is tempted to think that the larger boys and girls would have learned more about their culture had they been allowed to go home after the school year. But such thoughts did not occur to a young man wanting to become a writer back in 1965.

What did strike the young man's curiosity was a short passage from the 1880 report. The agent then was a W. L. Lincoln, and he writes:

In a communication dated February 4, 1880, I had the honor to call the attention of the Commissioner to certain information which I was in receipt of, indicating a disposition on the part of Sitting Bull and his followers to come to an amicable arrangement with the United States Government, and also asking permission to visit him by authority. In reply thereto I was ordered to abstain from any communication with him, as the government did not wish to make any terms. Of course that ended the matter; but I am convinced that at that time a lasting treaty could have been made. Subsequently Sitting Bull sent me, in token of friendship, a pipe and hatchet, which were to be given me in case terms could be made, otherwise to be returned. Under the circumstances I had to reject the peace offering, since which time I have heard nothing from them directly, although I see by the public journals that bands of them are delivering themselves up at the different military posts and I learn that Sitting Bull and a few of his followers are somewhere in the vicinity of Milk River.

Sitting Bull—in the vicinity of the Milk River! Within miles of where I sat in our government house, reading the agents' reports. At the time, I had no idea that Sitting Bull had come anywhere near the Fort Belknap Reservation in northern Montana, just thirty miles south of Canada. Wasn't Sitting Bull a famous chief? Hadn't he attracted the attention of all America back in those days? Suddenly, the area did not seem so remote. Suddenly, my part of the country had history, a connection with the rest of the country—at least the west.

And it was true that Sitting Bull had crossed the Medicine Line into Canada several months after the Battle of the Little Big Horn. It is a common fallacy, though, that Sitting Bull immediately fled to Canada after the battle to seek sanctuary in "the Grandmother's"— Queen Victoria's—country. In fact, Sitting Bull's Hunkpapas stayed in Montana all that summer and winter, hunting buffalo, fighting soldiers. He even had time to write the following letter (with the help of a breed named Big Leggins Brughière) to a Colonel E. S. Otis, whose troops had escorted a wagon train into the Yellowstone country: "I want to know what you are doing on this road. You scare all the buffalo away. I want to hunt in this place. I want you to turn back from here. If you don't, I will fight you again. I want you to leave what you have got here and turn back from here. I am your friend, Sitting Bull." As a postscript, he wrote: "I mean all the rations you have got and some powder. Wish you would write as soon as you can."

Generals Terry and Crook had spent the summer and fall after the Battle of the Little Bighorn chasing the various bands of Lakotas and Cheyennes, without much success. In the vastness of the Montana plains, they very seldom encountered Indians. Most of the Indians were either back on the reservation or scattered in smaller bands in the hunting country. When they did find Indians, the skirmishes were small and inconclusive. Crook finally gave up the chase and led his men from the Yellowstone country to Deadwood in the Black Hills. It was September and the way was long, muddy and cold; the men had run out of rations and were near starvation. As luck would have it, Crook's battalion practically stumbled on to the small camp of Iron Shield—called American Horse by the whites—at Slim Buttes, about ninety miles north of Crook's destination in the Black Hills. The two thousand troopers pitched into the thirty-lodge camp with enthusiasm and killed many of the people, including Iron Shield and a mother with a still-suckling baby. Many of the soldiers did not pursue the survivors, who had run into ravines to hide. The soldiers instead ate meat off the drying racks.

Crazy Horse and his Oglalas were camped nearby on the Little Missouri. Upon hearing of the disaster, he and two hundred warriors galloped off to fight the soldiers. They caught the troops napping and looking for food in the village, and a hot fight ensued. Finally Crook and his two thousand men managed to retreat down the trail toward the Black Hills.

Lakota prisoners, captured at the Battle of Slim Buttes, 1876, posed in front of their tipi and holding a 7th Cavalry flag taken at Little Bighorn. *W.H. Over Museum*

The sight of the troops, exhausted, starving, demoralized, strung out over several miles, riding starving, exhausted horses, being picked off by sharpshooters, presented a pathetic image of the United States Army. Although Crook would have success later against the Apaches in the southwest, his 1876 campaign on the northern plains was one of incompetence, repeated humiliation, and, finally, defeat.

After Crook and Terry's failed summer campaign, the command was turned over to Colonel Nelson A. Miles, another Civil War veteran who had had great success against the Indians on the southern plains. He arrived in October of 1876 and established headquarters at the mouth of the Tongue River, where it empties into the Yellowstone. Later, this fort would become a cow town by the name of Miles City.

Miles was a no-nonsense military man, and he immediately set about planning a winter campaign. He knew that the Indians were hungry—the white buffalo hunters had already decimated the vast herds on the southern plains and most of the northern plains; in fact, the only large herds left in America were in the Yellowstone and Power River country of Montana. Their horses were used up and their ammunition and powder were almost gone. In other words, they were vulnerable—and would be more so by the time the snows and cold came.

But even before winter, on October 20, 1876, Miles set up a council with Sitting Bull. The soldiers and Indians were only four miles apart on this particular day, and so Miles sent word with some agency Hunkpapas that he would like to treat with Sitting Bull. The chief, thinking that maybe he could get some supplies and ammunition out of the deal, agreed, and he and his warriors accompanied the emissaries in the direction of Miles's camp.

But Sitting Bull, being the wily old white fighter that he was, insisted that the meeting take place at a neutral site between the camps. The Indians set out buffalo robes on the prairie, and the two sides sat down to talk. It was a cold day, and Miles wore a coat trimmed with bear fur. The Indians, who had not met him before, named him Bear Coat. They must have wondered what he would be like to deal with. They had dealt with Long Hair (Custer) and Three Stars (Crook) and One Star (Terry), and the results had not been good. Now this man, Bear Coat, had come into their country, representing the Grandfather to the east. Would he be any different from the others?

The meeting started out calmly but curiously. Miles kept insisting that Sitting Bull had always hated the whites, while Sitting Bull insisted that Miles had bad information. According to several Indians who were there and were interviewed by Stanley Vestal for his biography of Sitting Bull, the following exchange took place:

BEAR COAT: You are against white people, ready to fight white people, and you like to fight all the time.

SITTING BULL: I never had any such idea.

BEAR COAT: Then why is it that everybody keeps saying you are so strong against the whites?

SITTING BULL: They are all wrong. I have always been glad to see white men. I like to be friendly. I don't want to fight, if I don't have to.

BEAR COAT: All the same, that is what I've heard. They say you are well known to be hostile to the white man.

SITTING BULL: That's all wrong. All I am looking out for is to see how and where I can find more meat for my people, more game animals for my people, and to find what God has given me to eat.

BEAR COAT: Nevertheless, that is what they are saying about you all the time.

Things went a little better after this initial exchange, but the council ended for the day with little being agreed on. In fact, Sitting Bull wanted to go on another hunt before winter set in, and Miles wanted to go along with him. Miles even agreed to supply the Indians with ammunition, provided Sitting Bull would agree to go, under Miles's escort, to the Great Sioux Reservation after the hunt. Both sides retired for the day to discuss the proceedings among themselves.

When they got together the next day, things were not so rosy—apparently a good night's sleep had not had a salutary effect on either side. Part of the reason for growing hostility and tension is that both sides realized that they were all armed, in spite of an agreement to come together empty-handed.

Miles had come to the meeting expecting to persuade Sitting Bull to give up his arms and horses, after which the chief would lead his Hunkpapas to an agency on the reservation in South Dakota. Even though Sitting Bull had declared many times in his life that he would never surrender to the whites, that he would fight them to the death, if necessary, Miles apparently thought he could "talk Sitting

Bull out of a lifelong policy in fifteen minutes."

Sitting Bull, the victorious chief at the Little Bighorn, wanted the military posts out of his territory and the Black Hills cleared of the whites. He was somewhat thunderstruck when Miles asked him to surrender his arms and ponies. Clearly the two sides could not have been farther apart.

Miles, who had earlier described Sitting Bull as "a fine, powerful, intelligent, determined-looking man" whose manner was "cold, but dignified and courteous," now saw him as a savage who "finally gave an exhibition of wild frenzy. His whole manner seemed more like that of a wild beast than a human being. His face assumed a furious expression. His jaws were tightly closed, his lips compressed, and you could see his eyes glisten with the fire of savage hatred."

It is doubtful that Sitting Bull was out of control. In his few encounters with the whites, he had never displayed such "wild frenzy." After all, a chief could not afford such emotions. He had to be rational, thoughtful, the leader always.

But Sitting Bull was angry. After reaching the beginning of a settlement the day before, now Miles wanted nothing less than unconditional surrender Furthermore, it was brought to Sitting Bull's attention by his nephew, White Bull, that all the time the council was taking place, the soldiers had a hidden Gatling gun trained on the Indian negotiators.

Miles was angry too. He couldn't understand the reluctance of the Indian leaders to give up a lifetime of free passage over the plains, hunting buffalo, living and camping where they chose, for an existence on a reservation, where rations were normally short or nonexistent, where the buffalo had long since disappeared, where they would have to give up their weapons and horses and live by the white man's rules. Or maybe he did understand it but chose to ignore the reality of what he was asking.

At any rate, the council broke up, each side warily retreating back to its own lines. But Miles wasn't through. He told Big Leggins Brughière to tell Sitting Bull that he had fifteen minutes before the soldiers would open fire. That such a time concept was untranslatable apparently did not occur to Miles. He said, "If Sitting Bull wants to fight, I'll give him a fight!" Apparently he also missed the whole point of the council: Sitting Bull did not want to fight and that is why he had sat down with the white men.

Nevertheless, the soldiers opened fire, and miraculously, not an Indian was hit. In eloquent testimony to frontier marksmanship, the battle lasted two days and only one Indian was killed, an unlucky young man named Iron Ribs. But the Hunkpapas were forced to run away, leaving much of their winter meat.

After that, Sitting Bull's band roamed the unceded territory in pursuit of the increasingly scarce buffalo, but the people were growing weary of hunger and cold and the harassment of the soldiers. They lasted through the winter, but in May of 1877, they slipped across the border into the Queen's country, where they would remain for the next four years.

Meanwhile, in America, Colonel Miles went about his job with great efficiency. During the winter of 1876–77, he and his foot soldiers fought several skirmishes with various bands of Sioux and sent the survivors off to the reservation. Other times, he persuaded band chiefs to negotiate peace with the government, which the government in official documents called "surrenders."

Three Stars—Crook—even managed to get back into the act, although not in person. His army, under Colonel Ranald S. Mackenzie, on November 25, 1876, surprised a Cheyenne camp, under the leadership of Chief Dull Knife, on the Red Forks of the Powder River. Although a blind medicine man, Box Elder, who could predict the future, had warned the Cheyennes that the soldiers were coming, something akin to mutiny occurred in the village that prevented the Indians from acting.

According to Ted Rising Sun, whose grandparents were in the village, and whose account is documented by other sources, the disaster could have been averted:

. . . the day before, a man had gone out to hobble his horses on some grass. And after he hobbled his horses on this grass he went up a little ways on the side of the hill to watch his horses for a while to note what direction that they would be grazing. So that the next morning when he came looking for them he would have a good idea where they were, where they would be. And while he was sitting there watching his horses he heard the earth tremble and kind of rumble and he thought that there was a great herd of animals nearby. It could be buffalo and then he thought, it could also be soldiers. And so he hid. He hid himself on the side of the hill. He no [sooner] got under cover when the horsemen appeared on the ridgeline near him.

And they saw his horses, and they rode down to his horses, unhobbled the horses and drove them away. He recognized who they were. They were Pawnee scouts.

In those days they could, each Indian, or all the Plains tribes could recognize each other by the way he dressed. And when the Pawnee scouts had driven his horses out of sight, he immediately went back down and reported this to the camp. The headmen got together and they planned that the women, children, old men should begin to move out of the camp. "Make preparations to move out and move out one by one, two by two, don't be obvious," they said. "In case there [are] some observers in the hills. Make it, try to make it so natural. But we start moving the children and old women and old men out so that in the morning when the attack comes only the fighting men will be here to meet the attack."

About that time, some Kit Fox Warrior Society members came in and they had some scalps that they had taken somewhere. And they noticed what was going on. "What's going on?" they said. And they [the headmen] told them that Pawnee scouts had been sighted and there were no doubt troops in the area. And that they would no doubt attack the village early the next morning. And that they were getting the old men, women, and children out and onto the high places, and only the fighting men would stay in the camp and meet the attack.

But the head of the Kit Fox Warrior Society [Last Bull] said, "Who brought the report?" And they named the man, and [Last Bull] began to discredit this man, and says, "Aw, he tells tall tales; he tells lies and this is no doubt one of his, just one of his tales." He [Last Bull] was a society chief, and in those days, the societies wielded power. So they went around and he ordered his young men ... to go around and unsaddle ... the horses that were gonna take these noncombatants out of the area, and [he] said, "We're gonna have a victory dance tonight." [Last Bull and his warriors had returned with thirty Shoshone scalps and they wanted the people to honor them.]

And so they had a victory dance. They danced all night. And early the next morning when the attack came, most of them were still in bed. And of course their village, they were driven out of the village, and they watched their tipis burn and their horses slaughtered, and they had to get away from the soldiers on foot with very few horses.

And so the Cheyennes danced all night, and when they went to bed at dawn, Mackenzie's eleven hundred horsemen attacked the 183 lodges of the people. In addition to his army, Mackenzie had four hundred enlisted Indian scouts. Many of these scout were old ene- mies—Pawnees and Shoshones—but some were Cheyennes and Sioux who had given themselves up after Little Bighorn.

This turncoat behavior became a pattern for the rest of the win- ter campaign. Some agency Indians were sent out to try to talk the "hostiles" into giving up. They were sent with gifts of meat, sugar, coffee, blankets, and tobacco. To most of the starving "free" Indians, these gifts and the promises that went with them were enough. They gave up their ponies and weapons and turned themselves in at the agencies. The agency Indians who brought them in often got the ponies, and sometimes some of the guns so they could hunt small game (the buffalo were gone) around the agencies.

But not all the agency Indians took so benign an approach as the "peace talkers" in helping the authorities bring in the "hostiles." Many of the Sioux and Cheyennes, friends and relatives, turned to scouting and led the soldiers directly to the free camps. Such was the case at the Red Forks battle. Cheyennes fought Cheyennes.

After driving the half-naked people from their village, the sol- diers and scouts set the tipis afire. Inside the tipis were all the stores of meat, robes, and clothing. The survivors stood in the intense cold on the ridgetop and watched their winter gear burn up. They also watched their six hundred ponies being driven away.

After the soldiers left, the Cheyennes started walking north, first along the slope of the Bighorns, then down the Powder River, cutting across to the Tongue, where they found Crazy Horse's camp of Oglalas. The journey took eleven sleeps. Most of them had no robes or blan- kets and little clothing on their backs and hardly any food—many of the babies, old ones, and wounded ones died of cold and hunger along the way.

The Oglalas took them in and fed them, sheltered and clothed them as best they could. But the Oglalas themselves had very little meat and supplies by this time and could not offer the demoralized Cheyennes much more than necessities. In fact, many of the Oglalas were downright cool to the newcomers. The Cheyennes must have contrasted this welcome with the one that they had received earlier in the year—after Crook's attack on March 17—when the Oglalas took them in and gave them new lodges, furniture, weapons, and hope. That earlier attack had led to the largest gathering of Indians on the plains and eventual victory at the Little Bighorn. All that time the Oglalas and Cheyennes, these very same Oglalas and Cheyennes, camped together at the head of the procession.

Now Sitting Bull was on his way to Canada, most of the other Indians had given themselves up, and Crazy Horse's band was laid low with winter sickness and hunger. There was no real hope for Dull Knife's people, just a lot of suffering until the inevitable surrender occurred. Nevertheless, the Cheyennes stayed with the Oglalas for the rest of the winter.

Crazy Horse, always queer, had been acting stranger than ever during this period. He went out by himself for days—sometimes he had a destination, sometimes he brought back meat or news, but most of the time he wandered. Several times hunters found him sitting alone on the snow-covered prairie, wrapped in his robe, looking off to the distance. Once, Black Elk's father found him like that and encouraged him to come back to camp, but Crazy Horse instead comforted the warrior: "Uncle, you have noticed me the way I act. But do not worry; there are caves and holes for me to live in, and out here the spirits may help me. I am making plans for the good of my people." Black Elk thought that maybe Crazy Horse carried with him a vision of his own death and was thinking how he could help the people when he was gone.

Such behavior in their indomitable leader troubled the people. They had counted on him to lead them through bad times as well as good, and now he seemed to be losing it. Even in camp he walked, like the man in his vision, with his eyes straight ahead, seemingly indifferent to the desperation of his people. But unlike the man in the vision, his feet did touch the ground, he wore no lightning-and-hailstone paint, and he seemed incapable of making the grand decision which would make his people's lives better.

Finally, on January 8, 1877, Colonel Miles and his foot soldiers caught up with Crazy Horse's camp at the mouth of Hanging Woman's Fork on the Tongue. With their big wagon guns, the soldiers drove the Oglalas and Cheyennes from their warm camp under a bluff into a raging blizzard. From a ridge, the Indians fought back with bows and arrows. Most of their ammunition had run out. But the warriors managed to hold the soldiers off until the women and children had disappeared into the swirling whiteness. Then they too turned and vanished.

After this encounter with Miles, Crazy Horse realized that his cold, hungry, ragged people were no match for the well-supplied, well-armed troops of the United States Army. It is interesting to note that soon after this battle, Miles and his troops retired to their fort on

Nelson Miles and his staff, dressed in buffalo coats against the bitter cold, on the eve of their attack on Crazy Horse's camp at the mouth of Hanging Woman's Fork in January 1877. *National Archives*

A Lakota woman and her two children, taken captive during the army's campaign to avenge Custer, 1877. *South Dakota Historical Society* the Yellowstone. Crook, shortly after the attack on Dull Knife's village, went back to sit out the winter at Fort Robinson in Nebraska. From these comfortable quarters, they kept sending out agency runners to talk Crazy Horse into surrendering. Both officers vied for the honor of capturing the renowned war leader.

The Oglalas stayed out in the unceded territory through the rest of the winter, battling weather, famine, and sickness. Crazy Horse's own wife, Black Shawl, had tuberculosis. Others had frozen hands and feet. And they were killing their ponies for meat. Desperate families left in the middle of the night for the agencies, leaving bare circles on the earth where their lodges had been. At first, Crazy Horse sent the *akecita* to bring them back, taking away their horses, but gradually he began to let them go, because he could see no reason to keep them in the village against their will. To maintain such a large village as a show of force was futile now.

Red Cloud Agency, close to Fort Robinson, Nebraska, where Crazy Horse and his band surrendered—and where he was later killed. *Nebraska Historical Society*

Meanwhile, the "peace talkers" kept coming, bringing gifts, promising the people that life on the reservation would be good, that the whites would welcome them, feed them. To sweeten the pot, the agency Indians said that the Oglalas would be given an agency right out here in the unceded territory if they would come in to Fort Robinson to surrender. The Oglala people were greatly heartened by this news, and Crazy Horse knew he had lost them. But he knew too that his people must surrender to survive.

On the 6th of May, the Moon of Shedding Ponies, 1877, less than a year after Little Bighorn, Crazy Horse led eleven hundred Oglalas and Cheyennes into Red Cloud Agency, a mile east of Fort Robinson.

Red Cloud himself and the agency chief, White Hat Clark, rode at the head of the column. Behind them, Crazy Horse, flanked by his subchiefs, Little Hawk, Big Road, He Dog, and Little Big Man, rode quietly, looking straight ahead. Many of the thousands of turned-out

agency Indians had never seen Crazy Horse, and they were surprised at his appearance. They had not expected that he would be so slight, so much smaller than the other warriors. His light hair was braided and wrapped in fur. A single eagle feather stood upright from the back of his head. He wore a buckskin shirt and carried a Winchester across his lap. Unlike his subchiefs, in their feathered bonnets, fringed, beaded buckskin, face paint, and the accouterments of war and power, Crazy Horse wore no adornment. The strange man of the Oglalas did not disappoint the agency Indians.

As the chiefs passed by Fort Robinson, they began to sing; then the warriors behind them sang; then the women on the pony-drags sang; then the thousands of reservation Indians joined in. They sang a peace song that filled the White Earth River valley with power and caused much consternation among the white men. As one army officer said, "By God, this is a triumphal march, not a surrender!"

In a simple ceremony, Crazy Horse surrendered 889 Oglalas, 1,700 ponies, 117 firearms, and himself. If Crazy Horse had wondered why the agency Indians had come to his camp so often to urge him to surrender, he now saw the reason: As the soldiers counted the horses, they gave them, buffalo runners and pack animals, to the very Indians who had seemed so selfless in riding the hundreds of miles to his camp. Even his childhood friend Young Man Afraid led some horses off to his lodge.

Because Crazy Horse had been promised that he could establish his agency back out in the unceded territory, he told White Hat Clark, in a meeting with an interpreter, Billy Garnett, present, that he had a site in mind, where Beaver Creek enters the Powder River. If that wasn't feasible, he knew of another place near the Bighorn Mountains. After his people rested, he wanted to go right back out to his chosen (and promised) country.

But White Hat told him that first he must go to Washington. He was to present himself to the Great Father as living proof (a trophy) that the Indian wars were over. Crazy Horse did not want to do this and reminded the soldier chief that he had been promised an agency at a location of his choosing. White Hat said that was the case, but first he must go to Washington.

Because Crazy Horse had lived away from the whites all of his adult life, he didn't know that he was a prisoner without rights. He had been promised certain things and he expected the whites to honor the promises. But White Hat was unrelenting—first Washington, then his agency. Crazy Horse was equally obstinate, and so the meeting ended without resolution. Clark did remind Crazy Horse that Red Cloud was the head chief of the agency and that Crazy Horse must obey him in tribal matters.

As it happened, the day before Crazy Horse surrendered, Sitting Bull and his Hunkpapas crossed the Medicine Line into Canada. The day after his surrender, a small band of Minneconjous, the last hold-outs in the Yellowstone country, was whipped by Colonel Miles on the Tongue River. The Great Sioux War was over.

Crazy Horse became an immediate celebrity in camp. Gifts were sent to him by both the agency Indians and the whites. Red Cloud even presented him with a young half-breed girl, the daughter of a trader named Larrabee, to be his second wife. Every day his lodge was filled with visitors. Officers came to gaze upon the man who had defeated Fetterman, Crook, and Custer. They came away with mixed feelings—some found him dignified, generous, brave, "a pillar of strength for good or evil"; others found him morose, dogged, tenacious, melancholy, gloomy, and reserved; still others found him to be all of these. The truth was that Crazy Horse was naturally reticent, not given to hearty handclasps or swapping war stories with his enemies. He was polite but always on guard (as well he should have been).

Also, he was a reservation Indian now, dependent upon the white men for his meat, clothing, and shelter. He could not forget this—even while he was being feasted. He saw the old skin tipis replaced with canvas ones; he saw his people wearing pants and shirts and cotton dresses; he had no weapons or horses. He had not imagined it would be like this—thousands of Indians camped within three miles of Red Cloud Agency without sanitary facilities, most without horses or guns, most without purpose. Nothing to do but sit around all day waiting for rations.

Things had to go bad. And Red Cloud and his cohorts made sure they did. Red Cloud had imagined himself covered with glory for bringing in Crazy Horse. He had been given the honor of accompanying White Hat Clark out to meet the Oglalas and lead the prisoners into the agency, but when he heard the peace song and saw his own agency Indians singing and cheering Crazy Horse, he began to think things were not right. And when he saw the soldier chiefs presenting themselves at the lodge of Crazy Horse, he knew he was losing some of his power as principal chief of the agency named after him. In fact, the rumor was going around that when Crazy Horse went to Washington, the Great Father was going to make him chief of all the Lakotas.

So the jealous Red Cloud engaged in a bit of reservation politics himself. He and his loyalists leaked word to the soldier chiefs that Crazy Horse was planning to break out, leave the reservation, and make more war on the whites. Most of the military men did not believe this—Crazy Horse and the Oglalas had no weapons or horses; how could they do this?

One white man who did believe Red Cloud was the Indian agent, James Irwin. In a letter to the Commissioner of Indian Affairs, he wrote: "Crazy Horse manifests a sullen, morose disposition; evidently a man of small capacity, brought into notoriety by his stubborn will and brute courage. His dictatorial manners, and disregard for the comfort of his people, have caused dissatisfaction among them and his want of truthfulness with the military department has rendered him unpopular with the leading men of his band, who have drawn off from him, and say that they are determined to carry out their promise to General Crook, and their original intention to obey orders and keep the peace."

But Irwin and the military men kept working on Crazy Horse to go to Washington. They promised repeatedly that if he went, he could have his reservation out in the Powder River country, they would give back his people's guns and horses and allow them to conduct a big hunt, they would increase the Oglala rations. Crazy Horse refused. In late May, General Crook came to the agency to meet with the chiefs about the trip, but Crazy Horse refused to attend. This irritated Crook no end—he wanted to show off his prize to the Great Father. Crook departed in a huff, but left orders that Crazy Horse must be made to go to Washington.

The only people who did not want Crazy Horse to make the trip were the reservation leaders, Red Cloud and Spotted Tail, and their cronies. Spotted Tail, a Brulé, had his own agency several miles away and had been made principal chief of all the Lakotas by General Crook. Spotted Tail was also Crazy Horse's uncle, but familial feelings had no place in this power struggle. Spotted Tail had usurped Red Cloud's authority over all the Lakotas, and he wasn't about to let Crazy Horse usurp him. He branded the Oglala leader a troublemaker and let his feeling be known to the soldiers.

By now Crazy Horse was bored with reservation life. He wanted to make something happen, so he finally consented to go to Washington. His only real white friend, Major V. T. McGillicuddy, the post surgeon, who had successfully treated Black Shawl for her tuberculosis, was instrumental in talking Crazy Horse into action. But the Oglala had one more little dig at those who were so anxious for him to go. McGillicuddy reports him saying that he "was not hunting for any Great Father; his father [Worm] was with him, and there was no Great Father between him and the Great Spirit."

Part of Crazy Horse's reluctance to go to Washington was that he had never ridden on a train. While the reservation chiefs were commuting back and forth, he was out on the plains with his people, trying to avoid the whites. He had questions. How do you ride on a train? How long does it take? How do you eat and relieve yourself? How do you sleep? What happens once you get to Washington? He even had Billy Garnett teach him how to use a fork.

Nevertheless, he decided to go, and a great feast was planned by the officers as a sendoff. Again Red Cloud, fearing that the Oglala chief would be wined and dined and made the big chief while he was in Washington, stepped in and told Crazy Horse that it was a trap, that once he got to the big white man's town he would be clapped in chains and sent off to prison. Even Crazy Horse's new young wife, apparently planted by Red Cloud as a kind of "mole," discouraged him from making the trip. The white men were not to be trusted. Something bad would happen. And in fact the naysayers were right: Crook had planned all along to send Crazy Horse off to the Dry Tortugas, a notorious, desolate island prison off the Florida Keys, after the chief's presentation to the Great Father. Crazy Horse changed his mind—he would not go.

While all of this was happening, word came that the Nez Perce had left their reservation in Idaho and were in Montana, whipping the local soldiers right and left. Crook was to take his troops into Montana and head them off. Accordingly, he began to recruit scouts among the Oglalas, since they had been free Indians and knew the country well. White Hat Clark tried to get Crazy Horse to go, promising him a horse, a uniform, and a repeating rifle, but again Crazy Horse refused to go where he did not want to go. He said he had untied his horse's tail and would not fight again. But the officers pestered him until he finally said with annoyance that he would go and would fight until not a Nez Perce was left standing. Frank Grouard, Crook's sly old scout, was the translator, and for reasons not known to this day he mistranslated the Oglala leader's statement into something quite different—that Crazy Horse would fight until not a *white man* was left.

The reason Crazy Horse did not want to go in the first place was that he became convinced that Crook's forces were really going after his comrade Sitting Bull. His recalcitrance and Grouard's mistranslation frightened the officers. The commanding officer at Fort Robinson telegraphed Sheridan, "There is a good chance of trouble here and there is plenty of bad blood. I think the departure of the scouts will bring on a collision here." Sheridan immediately wired Crook to go to Fort Robinson and straighten out the situation.

Crook arrived at the agency on September 2, 1877. He ordered all the chiefs to come to him for a council. Crazy Horse refused. Of all the officers on the plains, he probably hated Crook the most. But by then, the Oglalas were getting tired of all the pressure brought about by their leader's refusals to cooperate with the whites. They had had a hard year and they just wanted to be at peace and live the best they could. The village began to split up, most of the people following He Dog, Crazy Horse's friend and subchief, to Crook's council site across the White River.

But as Crook was riding to the council, Woman's Dress, an informer, told him that Crazy Horse was planning to kill him there. Crook blustered around before hurrying back to the fort, then summoned the chiefs to come to him. When they assembled, Crook told them that Crazy Horse was big trouble and he wanted him arrested. Red Cloud and Spotted Tail went him one better—they proposed that Crazy Horse be killed at once. Crook thought about it for a moment, but he knew that such a drastic action would take some explaining. Again, he ordered the Oglala's arrest.

On the 4th of September, the Moon of the Black Calf, four hundred agency warriors, backed up by eight companies of the 3rd Cavalry, set out to arrest Crazy Horse. This force, twice as large as Custer's command on the Little Bighorn, rode the six miles from the fort to Crazy Horse's camp only to find that he wasn't there. He had been tipped off. With Black Shawl (but without his young wife) and two young warriors who had vowed to protect him, he had fled to his uncle Spotted Tail's agency, some forty-five miles distant. Although Crazy Horse did not have much of a start on the large army, they gave up the chase. Instead, White Hat sent two groups of armed Indian scouts after him—thirty under No Flesh, twenty-five under No Water (the man whose wife Crazy Horse had enticed away many years ago and who shot him in the face in revenge). He promised two hundred white man's dollars to the group that caught him. No Water was in such a lather to get at his detested enemy that he burned up two horses in the chase.

The scouts did not catch Crazy Horse on the plain, but they arrived at Spotted Tail Agency a short time after him. A confrontation ensued which also involved Minneconjous and Brulés. The Brulés wanted to give Crazy Horse to the scouts, while the Minneconjous, under Touch the Clouds, their seven-foot leader, protected him. Finally, the Minneconjous won out, and the scouts left, angry and empty-handed.

That night, in a council with Spotted Tail, his good friend Touch the Clouds, and the agent, Lieutenant Jesse Lee, Crazy Horse said that he was a man of peace, that he only wanted a safe place for his people, that he was not a troublemaker but that others around him were causing trouble with their jealous rumors. He then asked his uncle if his Oglalas could live at Spotted Tail Agency. Spotted Tail, in a short but triumphant speech, said, "At my agency the sky is clear and the air still and free from dust. I am chief here. Every Indian must obey me. You say you want to come here to live in peace. If you stay you must listen to me in all things. That is what I have to say."

The agent, in a more conciliatory tone, said that Crazy Horse must go back to Fort Robinson in the morning and tell the officers there what he had just said. He said they were men of goodwill and would listen to reason. They would clear the charges against Crazy Horse and grant him his request to live at Spotted Tail Agency for the interim.

That night he stayed with the Minneconjous. He was worn out from the day's chase and confrontation, and he was clearly nervous, agitated. He knew that he was a wanted man, wanted not only by the white soldiers but by some of his own Lakotas. He was discouraged by the large party of Indians that had come to arrest him at his camp. He felt that he and Black Shawl were alone in the world.

In the morning, he went to agent Lee and asked that he not have to go back to Fort Robinson. "Something bad will happen," he said. But the agent talked him out of his fear, and presently a small party, including Lee and Touch the Clouds, left Spotted Tail Agency. Within a few miles, several of Spotted Tail's warriors joined the party, and Crazy Horse knew he was a prisoner.

When the party came to Crow Butte, which overlooked both Red Cloud Agency and Fort Robinson, Lee sent a messenger ahead to ask whether they should come to the agency or the fort. He also told of the promises that he had made to Crazy Horse. The response from White Hat Clark was that they should come to the fort, but he made no mention of the promises.

As the party rode down to the fort at dusk, they were surrounded by mounted Indians. Other Indians lined the way, silent and dark.

Crazy Horse must have wondered that only four months ago these people had sung and cheered as he led his people into the agency. But he noticed that more Indians, friends and foes, were falling in behind him.

When they reached the fort and dismounted, Little Big Man, the warrior who had once threatened the whole Black Hills Peace Commission, who was once one of Crazy Horse's trusted warriors but now had become a reservation Indian, grabbed Crazy Horse by the arm, calling him a man of no-fight, a coward, and led him toward the adjutant's office. Soldiers and Indians fell in beside and behind them.

Lee went in to talk with the officer of the day, telling him that he thought Crazy Horse was the victim of malicious rumors and misinterpretation, but the officer would have none of it. He said that at first light Crazy Horse was to be taken to Omaha, then shipped on to the Dry Tortugas.

And so Crazy Horse, knowing nothing of this exchange, was led

The killing of Crazy Horse, drawn by Amos Bad Heart Bull.
University of Nebraska Press

to the stockade, a small building next to the adjutant's. When he entered, he saw bars, a small high window. He smelled the stench of urine. He knew it was an iron house.

With all his strength he pulled free of Little Big Man, pulled a concealed knife from his belt, and slashed his way out. But Little Big Man again grabbed his arms, and the officer of the day yelled, "Stab him! Kill the son of a bitch!" A guard ran up and thrust at Crazy Horse with his bayonet again and again, deep in the side, then in the back, until the Oglala leader slumped to the floor, his clothes red with blood. At another attempt, Crazy Horse stopped the guard, saying "Let me go, my friends, you have got me hurt enough."

The guards tried to drag Crazy Horse into the iron house, but Touch the Clouds stopped them. He carried Crazy Horse in his arms to a bed in the adjutant's office, but the wounded Oglala indicated that he wanted to lie on the floor, close to the earth. Then Touch the Clouds cleared the room of everyone except Crazy Horse's father, Worm, and himself. As the dusk turned to dark, many of the reservation Indians turned back to their camps. Crazy Horse's Oglala men and women stood vigil on the parade ground. Inside the room it was quiet for a long time. Finally Crazy Horse opened his eyes. Worm leaned close. "Ah, my father, I am hurt bad—tell the people it is no use to depend on me anymore." Then it was quiet again. An hour later, Crazy Horse died.

Touch the Clouds, sensing that the death of this great leader might trigger a new round of hostility, a senseless, futile violence when survival was all that mattered, walked outside and addressed the dark assemblage: "It is well," he said quietly. "He has looked for death and it has come."

10

Sitting Bull and his Hunkpapa band stayed in Canada, the Grandmother's country, for four years, from May 1877 to July 1881. The first year was good—for the first time in over two years the Hunkapapas were not fighting or fleeing the U.S. Army. The "Red Coats" treated them firmly and well, leaving them alone except for the occasional policing action when nearby horses were stolen or word came that some young Hunkpapas had raided south of the border. Such violations were rare, and Sitting Bull gave his word that violators would be severely punished.

That first year was idyllic for Sitting Bull. He had enough meat for his people, he could rest as much as he wanted, and he could play with his children and make friends with neighboring tribes (Sitting Bull was always a fine politician when he wanted to be). He even had time to compose songs—one honoring his mother, Her Holy Door, for having given him birth, and another to a young daughter who was afraid of owls. He truly was a man of peace in the Grandmother's country.

But reality has a way of creeping in, even during the most idyllic of times. The reality was that the young warriors became quickly bored with their semi-sedentary life. Sitting Bull had formed a society of hunters who would keep the young and old, the infirm, and the widows supplied with meat. That was their sole responsibility—unless trouble came. In that case these one hundred chosen warriors would act as a kind of palace guard around their chief. But trouble was almost nonexistent then, and the young men were impatient to prove themselves as warriors—and the only way to do this now was by stealing horses.

Sitting Bull held a Sun Dance that summer on the slopes of Wood Mountain, near a village of French Indians. Although the Sun Dance was a solemn occasion, many other events took place during this ceremony, among them horse races. The French Indians, or Slotas, had a horse that was faster than anything the Hunkpapas could throw at him. He won race after race and brought his owner much glory and the Slotas who bet on him much booty.

One night, as the two villages slept, the racehorse and a hundred others disappeared. The Slotas complained to the Red Coats, and shortly the Mounties came to Sitting Bull's lodge. Sitting Bull became angry with the young thieves, because he had been content to keep the peace and now they were causing him trouble. He told the Red Coats that he would punish them, and he did, devising a kind of rack that spread-eagled the men vertically for a week. The punishment was severe, but Sitting Bull could not take a chance that his people would be sent back to the United States and Bear Coat's soldiers.

After this incident, the dominion government began to ask the U.S. government to arrange for the Hunkpapas to return to American soil. Sitting Bull did not seem to be aware of this backstage betrayal, for he kept referring to the Canadian government as honorable, just, and fair, as opposed to the corrupt, cruel, grasping government of the United States.

Finally, on October 17, 1877, a U.S. commission led by General Terry (One Star), who had chased Sitting Bull all over Montana after the Little Bighorn, arrived to offer terms to Sitting Bull. Basically, these terms were peace with the Sioux, a full pardon to those who surrendered, and the same treatment as that given the other surrendered Sioux. As frosting, Terry said the Hunkpapas would get rations and cows to replace the surrendered guns and horses.

Sitting Bull was outraged that these men who had taken his sacred Black Hills and all the Lakota territory, who had never given him and his people a day of peace, would offer such meager terms. He was particularly incensed that the soldier chief wanted to take away their horses and walk them to the reservation—over a thousand miles away. In reply to Terry, Sitting Bull said, "Look at me. I have ears, I have eyes to see with. If you think me a fool, you are a bigger fool than I am. This house is a medicine house. You come here to tell us lies, but we do not want to listen to them. I don't wish such language used to me, nor any such lies told to me in my Grandmother's house. Don't say two more words. Go back where you came from. This country is my country now, and I intend to stay here and raise people up to fill it. I shake hands with these people [he shook hands with the Red Coats]. You see me; that's enough. The country that belonged to us, you ran me out of it. I have come here, and here I intend to stay."

Sitting Bull may have been influenced in his stubbornness (and fear) by the arrival in his camp a few days earlier of hungry, exhausted Nez Perce Indians who had escaped the Battle of the Bear Paws, some forty miles south of the Canadian border. It is commonly thought that all of the Nez Perces, following their leader, Chief Joseph, had surrendered to Bear Coat Miles on October 5, 1877, but over a hundred, under the leadership of White Bird, had escaped and made it to Canada. The Nez Perces were in desperate shape, many of the men, women, and children wounded, some dying. The generous Sitting Bull took them in and offered them sanctuary with his Hunkpapas. But the arrival of the pitiful people must have reinforced his belief that the U.S. Army was as ruthless as ever. What he didn't know was that the Northern Cheyennes, his old allies, were scouting for Miles. There were even a few Lakotas.

After the peace commission left for the day, Colonel James F. McLeod of the Mounted Police held a meeting with the Hunkpapas. He asked Sitting Bull to reconsider his answer to Terry. The Hunkpapas could never become British citizens. The buffalo would not last forever. The government would never feed them. They must behave themselves. There could be no raiding across the border. The young men must be controlled—if some got into trouble, there would be trouble for all.

Sitting Bull, still angry at the U.S. commissioners, itemized for McLeod all the injustices done to his people by the Americans. Why would they want him to return now if not to kill him? He had heard stories of how the reservation Indians were treated, how they were turned on one another. He was particularly concerned that his friend and fellow leader Crazy Horse had been killed by *wasichus* and Indians alike. Sitting Bull knew that the same fate probably awaited him on American soil.

McLeod was a reasonable man—it seems that all Canadian authorities were more reasonable than their American counterparts—and he said Sitting Bull could stay if his Hunkpapas abided by the rules of the Grandmother's country. He even said that the traders could sell ammunition and supplies to the Indians to help them in the hunt.

Sitting Bull was happy with this arrangement. He was happy that the U.S. commissioners would return to their country empty-handed. He did not know how his harsh words had affected them. He had called them liars and treated them brusquely in the presence of Canadian officials. He had embarrassed the United States, and the frontier officers and their agents would not forget. They had suffered one humiliating defeat at the hands of this "hostile" at Little Bighorn. It would not happen again.

Things deteriorated for the Hunkpapas after this meeting. The buffalo became scarce on the surrounding plains, and so Sitting Bull and his warriors began to cross the Medicine Line into the Milk River valley of Montana, which was about as far north as the larger herds of buffalo roamed. Settlers became frightened and reported them. Peaceful Indians, the Gros Ventres and Assiniboins, were afraid of them and joined the protest. Sitting Bull himself was afraid that Bear Coat's soldiers would find them and attack them. His hunting forays were swift and efficient and did not include harassment of the locals.

But finally *pte,* the buffalo, began to disappear from the Milk River valley, killed by settlers and Indians and the few hide hunters left. The Hunkapapas were in serious trouble without meat. Other problems arose. The cold Canadian winter began to take its toll on the people, as well as the horse herds. It was the winters that had decided things for Crazy Horse before he surrendered at Fort Robinson. Sitting Bull had invited him to come up and live with the Hunkpapas, but Crazy Horse knew that his people, with their meager shelters and lack of weapons, could not survive the winters. He declined Sitting Bull's offer and that spring led his people into Fort Robinson.

But after Crazy Horse's death, it was decided by the *wasichus* that his Oglalas were to be removed from Red Cloud Agency in Nebraska to newly created Pine Ridge Agency in South Dakota. As the troubled Oglalas were being moved, many of them drifted north into the unceded territory—and gradually made their way into Canada. The reality of reservation life—short rations, soldiers everywhere, no freedom—had finally sunk in, and the Oglalas wanted to return to the old way of life. They had heard that Sitting Bull was leading the good life in Canada—the buffalo were numerous, there were no soldiers up there, and the Grandmother was benevolent.

By the spring of 1878, Sitting Bull's bands of Hunkpapas, Oglalas, and Nez Perces numbered around five thousand people. In 1876, before the Little Bighorn, this large a gathering would have been cause for great rejoicing. But now, scarcely two years later, it presented insurmountable problems. Contrary to what the Oglalas thought, the buffalo were fast disappearing, the people were growing hungry, the Canadian government was nervous, and Bear Coat waited just south of the border.

But Sitting Bull was determined to live in the Grandmother's country, even if he was forced to ask the dominion for rations because his people had no buffalo robes left to sell to the traders. As a "free" Indian, Sitting Bull had moved where he chose, lived off the buffalo, and provided his followers with a life of independence. He had scorned those who lived on the reservation and depended on the government for handouts. He had often told his people to avoid *wasichu* things, for once they became accustomed to these things they would not be able to live without them. And now he was forced to ask the Grandmother for such things.

But even as he was asking for handouts, emissaries of the U. S. government were coming into his camp—scouts, "black robes" (Catholic missionaries), agency Indians—to entice him to surrender. These sweet-talkers persuaded many small bands to return south with them. The great camp was beginning to break up. At first Sitting Bull sent the *akecita* after them to take away their horses, break their lodgepoles, and bring them back. But he soon realized that he was acting not like a chief but like one of the very soldiers he despised.

Perhaps the biggest blow to Sitting Bull's ego was the Canadian authorities' growing refusal to treat him as the leader of his dwindling gathering. They treated him as just another refugee, which severely undermined his authority with his own people. (This was a tactic that would later work for the American officials at the Standing Rock Reservation, where Sitting Bull would end up.) Sitting Bull was a proud man to the extreme, and he insisted on being recognized as the chief representative of his people. Time after time in his later years in Canada and Standing Rock, the whites ignored him, and time after time, Sitting Bull declared that he was still head chief of all the Lakotas. To Sitting Bull's credit, he was never beaten down.

By early 1881, Sitting Bull had lost most of his followers to the promises of U. S. authorities and was left with a small band of mostly old people. Still, he refused to surrender, although the old people did not have enough to eat and were living under deplorable conditions. They were homesick and desperate, but they stayed because of loyalty to their chief. For his part, Sitting Bull loved these old people. They were relatives and friends, and they had traveled together for many years. Sitting Bull had made sacrifices for them, had advised and led them to the best of his ability. Responsibility for them lay heavy and real in his heart.

Out of desperation, Sitting Bull and some of his followers went to Fort Qu'-Appelle to plead one last time with the superintendent of the Red Coats to allow them a reserve in Canada. The superintendent's response was that the Hunkpapas already had a reservation in America. Why did they not go there? They had made too much trouble in their Grandmother's country. At the end of the meeting, the interpreter, a French Indian, told Sitting Bull, "When you return to the Grandfather's country, you will be killed." The interpreter wept.

Sitting Bull returned to his camp to find that more of his followers had deserted him and crossed the border. Now, the leader of the small impoverished band of Hunkpapas, the once great leader of all the Lakotas during their glory time on the plains, had to confront the inevitable. He sought out the principal trader of the district, a Jean Louis LeGare, and told him he wanted to think about surrendering. LeGare, who had been carting off the Hunkpapas to the United States as a kind of enterprise, gave Sitting Bull seven days to think about it. Sitting Bull thought about it for seven days. He was always a thoughtful man, weighing all consequences of his actions, what effect they would have on his people, the pros and cons of going or not going. He smoked his pipe and he thought.

On July 10, 1881, some five years after Little Bighorn, Sitting Bull and the remaining 187 Hunkpapas (out of his original camp of five thousand, about fifteen hundred of them warriors) trailed south with the wagons and Red River carts of LeGare. As Sitting Bull passed through the country, he must have looked at it with fresh eyes. He must have seen every hill, every bird, every buffalo skeleton that marked the journey. He must have thought of past triumphs, of his childhood, of the many times he had sacrificed before the medicine pole, of the gathering of the people at the Little Bighorn—and he must have known that that way of life was irretrievably over. What he thought of the future, especially the near future at the end of the road, must have made him tremble.

At noon of July 19, Sitting Bull and his people rode into Fort Buford at the confluence of the Yellowstone and Missouri rivers. William Bowen, a young officer, wrote that the chief "did not appear to be a well man, showing in his face and figure the ravages of worry and hunger he had gone through. He was getting old. Since the sixties he had been the hero of his race. Giving in to the hated whites and the final surrender of his cherished independence was a hard blow to his pride, and he took it hard. He was much broken."

Sitting Bull certainly did not look well. He and his people had not eaten properly for three years. He was dressed in rags. He had a severe eye infection. He was demoralized.

Sitting Bull and his Hunkpapas surrendered their guns and horses, but Sitting Bull told the soldier chiefs that he had never given up his land and now that he had returned, it was his again. The usual promises were made: full pardon, rations, his own agency. In fact, his agency had already been "given" to him. The Hunkpapas who had left Canada earlier had been sent to Standing Rock Agency on the Missouri. Sitting Bull was to go join them. Although he had preferred an agency along the Little Missouri River, a beautiful river in a fertile valley, he had no choice in the matter. Again, he was not being treated as a chief, but as just another prisoner.

He and his people boarded the steamboat *General Sherman* for the journey. Sitting Bull must have thought that at least he could have his own place on the reservation and assume his leadership role among the Hunkpapas.

But that was not the case. Instead, he was taken to Fort Randall, several miles farther down the river, and there he remained as a prisoner of war for the next two years.

But even before he got to Fort Randall, Sitting Bull experienced something that would dog him for the rest of his life—not that he minded it: celebrity. He had been interviewed several times in Canada by American journalists, most of whom contrived to misquote him or portray him as a fiendish savage, or both, but now he was about to meet with the masses face to face. The *General Sherman* docked in Bismarck, and Sitting Bull saw hundreds of *wasichus,* dressed in their finest Sunday clothes, and they were there to see him. They had read about this most famous of all Indians, and they turned out as though the circus had come to town. It is difficult to imagine what they thought of this great leader in his dirty pants and shirt, red paint on his face and a pair of smoked goggles shielding his infected eye. A reporter wrote that Sitting Bull's appearance "is for the purpose of impressing the sentimental white man with his poverty."

It is even more difficult to imagine what Sitting Bull thought of them. He had never been in a white man's town. He had never seen a train. And he had never seen such a large group of civilians. Nevertheless, he greeted them, signed autographs (he had been taught to sign his name by a Canadian trader), and attended a dinner in his honor at the fanciest hotel in town. He endured such attention with dignity and patience.

At Fort Randall, Sitting Bull entertained visiting chiefs, military officers, reporters, and lucky civilians who managed to get close to him. An artist came to sketch him and others of his band. Such lifelike portraits excited the Indians and gave them small moments of pleasure in the long tedium. But mostly Sitting Bull sat and waited and thought. He now understood that he no longer had any freedom, that his and his people's future depended on his old enemies. Finally, in the late summer of 1882, Sitting Bull dictated a letter to the Commissioner of Indian Affairs stating that although he had never signed a treaty and therefore had never violated a treaty, he and his people were ready to accept the terms of the 1868 treaty. He begged to be sent to Standing Rock Agency.

After several months of bureaucratic maneuvering between the military and civilian agencies (perhaps motivated by a desire to let the chief stew in his own juices), Sitting Bull and his 187 followers were allowed to go to their new home. On May 10, 1883, the small band stepped from a steamboat onto the soil of Standing Rock, where they would remain for the rest of their lives, and where their descendants live today.

It is clear that Sitting Bull expected to return to his position as head chief of the Hunkpapas, and for that matter, of all the Lakotas. But when he stepped from the steamboat, he stepped into an alien world of reservation politics, jealousies, intrigue, favoritism, and power-grabbing.

Sitting Bull, the innocent in agency ways, went to the Indian agent's office and presented his demands—he would handle the distribution of rations for his people, he had a set of handpicked subchiefs (a cabinet) he wanted recognized, he would not plant a crop this year but maybe next year, he wanted a house built for himself, a horse and buggy, etc.

The agent, James McLaughlin, heard this "inflated nonsense" to the end, then apprised Sitting Bull of the situation. Sitting Bull was not a chief on the agency, he would receive his own rations just like any other Indian, he would follow the regulations laid down by McLaughlin. And he would start to farm immediately.

McLaughlin was a no-nonsense agent. He had been around Indi-

Sitting Bull as a captive at Fort Randall with his family. *Smithsonian Institution*

Sitting Bull posing with his family. *North Dakota Historical Society*

ans for many years, and he felt he knew them. He didn't think they were much different from anybody else—they could be civilized, Christianized, turned into God-fearing farmers just like the whites in the west. McLaughlin was only half right. He continually underestimated the power of tribalism, the fealty of families and bands and societies, although he fought against it constantly. True, many of the Indians did try to do it his way, but at least economically, his policies were a failure. The plains of North Dakota do not invite farming on a small scale. Most of the white settlers discovered this, abandoned their small homesteads, and headed back east. Today, farms on the northern plains of the Dakotas and Montana commonly consist of ten thousand acres, and too often that is not enough.

Sitting Bull and his family did scratch out a garden, and he lived quietly for the most part. But he was the center of a maelstrom of rumors and stories. Some of his old comrades in arms—men such as Gall and Crow King—were encouraged by McLaughlin to spread untruths about the chief. Gall, in particular, relished this role. With McLaughlin's backing, he spread the story that Sitting Bull had been a coward at Little Bighorn, that he had not led the Lakotas but hidden behind the skirts of women along with the children, that Gall and the other warriors had only ridicule and scorn for Sitting Bull. Poor Gall, in his anxiety to please his agent, had fallen into the precise trap that McLaughlin had set. By spreading vicious rumors about Sitting Bull, Gall had made a huge contribution to the policy of divide and conquer—an old *wasichu* trick.

McLaughlin also controlled two chiefs of the Yanktonais—Mad Bear and Two Bears—as well as the chief of the Blackfeet Lakotas— John Grass. With these subservient leaders, along with Gall and Crow King of the Hunkpapas, McLaughlin felt he had enough powerful allies to run the agency the way he wanted.

And finally, McLaughlin controlled the tribal court and tribal police. Many warriors who had been members of the old *akecita* had become policemen, and they took their work seriously. Perhaps it was the only job on the reservation that reminded them of their old warrior ways. In any event, these new-age warriors were quite willing to bully and arrest their own people if they got out of line.

In the spring of 1884, Sitting Bull and most of his Hunkpapas moved down to the Grand River, south of the agency, where they again took up farming. Sitting Bull's cabin was just across the river from his birthplace, where he had first seen the light of day fifty-three years before.

Sitting Bull did pretty well as a farmer, raising oats, potatoes, and corn. In addition, he kept horses, cattle and chickens. And he sent his children to the Congregational day school. A model citizen.

But McLaughlin continued to see him as an obstacle to progress. Sitting Bull was a never-ending stimulus for the imperious agent's paranoia. He accused the chief of speaking out against the white man's school, somehow ignoring the fact that Sitting Bull's own children were in school. He thought that Sitting Bull was keeping the Indians from joining the Christian church, but in this the Indians did not need Sitting Bull's views on religion—they felt that the white man's religion was inappropriate for a people who had developed their own religion over the centuries. And finally, McLaughlin thought that any Indian resistance to his policies was led by Sitting Bull. He even accused the Hunkpapa of thwarting his efforts to turn the Indians into farmers, although Sitting Bull was one of the best farmers in the country.

One thing McLaughlin was right about was Sitting Bull's obstinance when it came to the land. In 1883, a commission authorized by Congress and led by Senator Henry L. Dawes of Massachusetts came to Standing Rock to council with the Indians. The year before, another commission had made an agreement with a few tribal chiefs to divide the reservation into tracts of land surrounding each agency. Supposedly, such an agreement would give each Lakota group autonomy from the larger, more unwieldy tribal presence. What the Indians did not understand was that the rest of the Great Sioux Reservation would be thrown open for settlement by whites. Fortunately, because the Treaty of 1868 stated clearly that any cession of land had to be approved by three-quarters of the male voters, Congress refused to ratify the agreement.

The Dawes Commission had come to Standing Rock to listen to Indian grievances about the previous commission and about the way the people were treated by the government, but it seems clear that the current commission was not interested in doing anything constructive. It was simply fulfilling an obligation. Sitting Bull took it on, once again declaring that he was chief of all the Lakotas and that any agreement would have to go though him. Sitting Bull did not lack for ego, and this time his ego almost got him into serious trouble. He angered the commissioners, who viewed themselves as a benevolent presence, there to listen to all the Indians. After Sitting Bull had dressed down the commissioners, one of them, Senator John Logan of Illinois, spoke to Sitting Bull in a like manner, declaring that he was not a chief, that he had no following, that he was a troublemaker who would be thrown into the guardhouse if he didn't shut up. Sitting Bull left the meeting, and the meeting adjourned. some of the Indians present looked at the Hunkpapa chief with new eyes—maybe he was a troublemaker—but most of them thought he was right to confront these white men. In truth, by white standards, Sitting Bull *was* a troublemaker.

Not long after the meeting, Sitting Bull was approached by McLaughlin (ever the opportunist) to go to Bismarck to celebrate its choice as the new capital of Dakota Territory. Sitting Bull agreed to do it and found himself riding in a parade with former President Ulysses S. Grant and other white dignitaries. He liked it. He signed autographs for money and received gifts from the grateful city fathers. This was to begin a year-and-a-half period of hands-on celebrity that took him to New York and Washington and Canada. He rode on trains, he visited museums, he met people, but mostly he appeared on stages in American cities. Perhaps his most well-known tour was as a member of Buffalo Bill Cody's Wild West.

Sitting Bull's appearances had nothing to do with acting. Most of the time, he simply sat on the stage or on a horse, dressed in Indian finery, and watched the show going on around him. When he was invited to speak, he spoke of peace, of his people's lives, of his desire to get along with America. But what came out of the "translator's" mouth was a blood-curdling account of savagery at the Little Bighorn.

Sitting Bull liked Buffalo Bill, and apparently the feeling was mutual. Buffalo Bill, for all his showmanship, had earned his name supplying buffalo meat for railroad crews in the early days, and he seemed to sympathize with the Indians' current plight. Another member of the cast that caught Sitting Bull's eye was Annie Oakley. He called her "Little Sharpshooter," and adopted her.

But after four months of such display it was time to go home. During the shows and parades, Sitting Bull had ridden a circus pony, a pony that could do tricks, and he become fond of the animal. As a token of friendship, Buffalo Bill gave the horse to Sitting Bull, along with a white ten-gallon hat.

Sitting Bull had made lots of money from appearing in the shows and from selling his autograph and pictures of himself, but he had given it away to poor people in the cities of the east. Agent McLaughlin chastized the chief for "squandering" his money. And he forbade Sitting Bull from making any more appearances in the big

Sitting Bull and Buffalo Bill on tour with the Wild West show in Montreal, 1885. *Buffalo Bill Historical Center*

cities because he came back with "the most astounding falsehoods." Sitting Bull's show-business career had come to an end.

What a contrast between life in the United States and life on the reservation! Once again, Sitting Bull took up the sedentary life of farming, of being a good husband to his two wives, Seen-by-the-Nation and Four Robes, and a good father to his five children, especially his favorite young son, Crow Foot, who had actually handed over Sitting Bull's gun at the surrender at Fort Buford. Crow Foot would become wise beyond his years, what years he had left, from his councils with his father.

Once every two weeks, Sitting Bull and his family would join the other Grand River families for the trip to the agency to collect their beef rations. The animals were slaughtered on the spot and divided up. Because the gathering was a great social event, friends greeting friends, relatives joining together, great feasts would ensue at the agency. McLaughlin did not look favorably on this event, because it reminded him of the old buffalo-hunting days. But he had another reason for disapproval—he wanted the Indians off rations because such government "largess" kept the Indian farmers from becoming totally self-sufficient. McLaughlin, in spite of the bitter winters and drought-plagued summers, still felt that farming was the future of his charges.

McLaughlin was not alone in this belief. In 1887, Congress passed the Dawes Severalty Act, which in essence said that each Indian head of household would be allotted 180 acres and other Indians would receive a smaller acreage. After this distribution, the rest of Indian country would be thrown open to white settlement. While this was bad enough, Congress, seeking to speed up the process on the Great Sioux Reservation, passed another bill which opened up the land even before allotments were made to the Indians. The Sioux Act of 1888 created six smaller reservations, each around the current six agencies: Standing Rock, Crow Creek, Cheyenne River, Lower Brulé, Rosebud, and Pine Ridge. The rest of the great reservation would be sold off at 50 cents an acre.

Sitting Bull, of course, strenuously objected to the act. He had never in his life surrendered any land, and he wasn't about to start selling it. He wanted all the bands of the Lakotas to have access to each other. He knew that if they were to survive as a tribe, they needed to have freedom of passage from one reservation to another. He said, "I would rather die an Indian than live [as] a white man," separated from his people.

Even Red Cloud, on the Pine Ridge Reservation, objected to such an agreement. Like Sitting Bull and the other important chiefs, he was left out of the negotiations for the land. But he complained bitterly, through his subordinates, that the treaties of 1868 and 1875 had not been honored, that the Great Sioux Reservation had never really been marked out, and that 50 cents an acre was absurd in the face of the going price for land around the reservation—$1.25 per acre.

In the end, the Pratt Commission which had been sent from Washington to secure the necessary agreement, collected only twenty-two votes for the government plan out of the thousands of males on Standing Rock land. The commission did not even visit the other reservations. The report by the commission denounced the Indians for not recognizing that the Great Father was doing a favor for his children.

But the government was not through. It brought sixty-one chiefs to Washington to further discuss the land issue. Although Sitting Bull did not speak much at the hearings, he was very busy during the councils at night. In a shocking turnabout from his previous views, he advocated selling the nine million acres for $1.25 an acre. It has been speculated that Sitting Bull finally wanted to be left alone to pursue his farming and raise his children peacefully. Others have said that Sitting Bull knew that the government would never accept such a high price per acre and would summarily discontinue the talks. And the land would be safe again. Whatever his motive, the hearings ended and the Indians went home.

But again, the government was not through. Congress passed the Sioux Act of 1889, which promised $1.25 per acre for the first three years, 75 cents for the next two, and 50 cents thereafter. And again, the government sent a commission out west, this one including redoubtable old Indian fighter General George Crook.

As in the past, John Grass, Gall, Mad Bear, and Big Head spoke for the Standing Rock Indians. And as in the past, they spoke against the new agreement. But this time, the commission was more clever than the past ones. Crook and his cronies sent agent McLaughlin to speak secretly with each of the Indian negotiators. McLaughlin, by turns sweet-talking and menacing, managed to persuade these incipient yes-men that it was in their own best interests to talk their followers into signing the agreement. He met with John Grass in an abandoned building. In *My Friend the Indian,* he recalls, "I had arranged with Grass that the Indians were to talk the next day in the line of asking concessions, then to formulate the concessions, in which I instructed him; and finally we fixed up the speech he was to make receding from his former position gracefully, thus to bring him the active support of the other chiefs [Gall, Mad Bear, and Big Head] and settle the matter." Although Sitting Bull and his followers tried to break up the voting-day turnout by force, they were turned away, and the measure passed with well over 75 percent majority.

Things went the same at other agencies. Although the Indians were initially overwhelmingly against the measure, by the same sort of chicanery used at Standing Rock, the chiefs were brought into line. They, in turn, delivered the votes.

Thus, on February 10, 1890, President Benjamin Harrison announced that the land agreement would go through and the Great Sioux Reservation would be no more. As a postscript, almost none of the concessions and promises made by Crook and McLaughlin were awarded to the Indians.

In the summer of 1889, even while the Lakotas were giving up their land, a curious event was taking place out in Nevada. It was said among the western tribes that a god had come to earth to save his children from the clutches of the *wasichus*. As the rumor persisted and spread, the Lakotas sent emissaries to Nevada to find out the truth of the news. There they met a Paiute holy man named Wovoka, and he told them that by practicing his teachings and dancing a sacred "Ghost Dance" they could make all the white men go away. Furthermore, the tired land would be restored and rejuvenated and all the creatures, including the long-departed ancestors and the buffalo, would return. All tribes would live in abundance and peace.

Soon Ghost Dancers appeared on all six agencies of the Lakotas. The Ghost Dance was a frenzied affair, with much whirling and shrieking and praying, until people would drop from exhaustion and convulse and have visions. Ghost shirts protected the dancers from the bullets of whites who might seek to interfere. The object of the Ghost Dance was to induce a cataclysm which would destroy the unbelievers and prepare the world for a fresh beginning. The dancers would be lifted on high, then set back down on earth after the millennium. Wovoka had adapted a very Christian element into this new religion.

Because the Ghost Dance promised some sort of violence to the *wasichus*, the nervous agents and their superiors immediately banned it on the Lakota reservations. They sent their tribal policemen to break up these gatherings. But the movement was too strong, and the police were hard put to quell this so far benign religion. They did manage to drive it into the hills on some reservations. On the Pine Ridge Reservation, the dancers moved to a table of land in the center of the badlands called the Stronghold.

These efforts to suppress the new religion only made the people more committed to carry out Wovoka's prophecy. None were more committed than the people at Standing Rock. The dances were held on a flat very near Sitting Bull's cabin. Although the chief and holy man did not participate in the dancing, he sat in a lodge at the site and interpreted the stricken dancers' visions. McLaughlin chose to interpret Sitting Bull's presence as incitement to rioting. Once again, the agent's paranoia concerning Sitting Bull had reached a fever pitch. He sent a letter to the Commissioner of Indian Affairs urging the arrest of the "high priest and leading apostle."

In actuality, Sitting Bull did not know whether he believed in this new religion or not. He was definitely skeptical. Furthermore, the people had gone over the head of the chief to seek salvation from a new source. Even if he had wanted to, Sitting Bull could no more have stopped the Ghost Dancing than he could have stopped a tornado. Nor could he have assumed absolute authority over the dancers. So Sitting Bull was forced to go along with the new religion in order to maintain his presence as a leader. But he did no more than fulfill his role as a seer, a holy man who could interpret visions.

The Indians danced throughout the fall and into a very mild winter. The authorities had thought that when the winter winds blew and the snows came down from the north, the Ghost Dance would be history. But the winter came in like a lamb, just as Sitting Bull had predicted, and the dancing continued.

McLaughlin sent several Indian emissaries to talk to Sitting Bull, but he told them that if they wanted to live like the white men that was their business. He wanted to live like an Indian, and that was his business. McLaughlin grew so desperate that he paid a visit, in the company of Bull Head, the district police commander, but his threats and cajolements fell on deaf ears. In McLaughlin's mind, the situation was getting to the point where Sitting Bull had to be arrested and transported to a prison far away or all hell would break loose.

Both the government and the military had sat on their hands so far when it came to Standing Rock. But they had already moved, at the panicked request of local settlers and communities, against the Ghost Dancers of Pine Ridge and Rosebud. Soldiers had entered the two reservations, driving all the Ghost Dancers to the Stronghold. But the butte in the badlands proved an impregnable fortress, and the Indians there were well supplied with food and water and shelter. And so the soldiers were forced to sit and watch and wait.

On November 28, 1890, Buffalo Bill, of all people, arrived at Fort Yates on the Standing Rock Reservation. He had orders signed by Bear Coat, General Miles, who now was the commander of the Division of the Missouri, authorizing the great showman to effect the arrest of Sitting Bull. Needless to say, the local officers were quite amazed. Buffalo Bill had just ended a successful tour of Europe, and here he was on the frontier with an official order (from no-nonsense Miles, no less) to arrest his old friend Sitting Bull.

Fortunately, Buffalo Bill had arrived drunk, and the officers contrived to keep him drunk for the next couple of days while they tried to figure out what to do about this potentially disastrous turn of events. Unfortunately, Buffalo Bill sobered up and hit the road, along with his fellow showman, Pony Bob, heading down to the Grand River settlement to carry out his orders. Along the way, he met Louis Primeau, the agency interpreter, who told him Sitting Bull was not at home but on another road heading for the agency. Primeau probably saved Buffalo Bill's skin with his lie. The Ghost Dancers would have been in no mood to let the flamboyant showman clap hands on their famous chief. Fortunately for all concerned, the President of the United States rescinded Buffalo Bill's orders before he had time to realize the deception.

But Bear Coat felt he had been humiliated by the whole affair, and he ordered Colonel Drum, the commanding officer at Fort Yates, to arrest his old nemesis "using any practical means." In order to avoid the Ghost Dancers, Drum devised a plan to arrest Sitting Bull on the next ration day at the agency. But word leaked out that the Hunkpapa chief had been invited to visit the Ghost Dancers at the Stronghold. And Sitting Bull had accepted the invitation.

Now the army and McLaughlin had to act fast to prevent the chief from escaping. McLaughlin would order his Indian police to arrest Sitting Bull the next day, December 15. Bull Head, who had nursed a grudge against Sitting Bull dating back to their days in the Powder River country, would head the effort, backed up by two companies of cavalry from Fort Yates.

At 6:00 A.M. of a very cold morning, forty-four Indian policemen kicked open the door of Sitting Bull's cabin and jerked him, naked, from his bed. Sitting Bull, with remarkable calm, asked to be able to put on his clothes. While he was doing this the police were jostling him, demanding that he hurry. When he was dressed, Bull Head grasped one arm, Shave Head grasped the other, and Red Tomahawk, a pistol in his hand, shoved the chief forward from behind. They wanted to hustle Sitting Bull outside and onto his circus pony, which had been made ready by other policemen. But Sitting Bull's son, Crow Foot, the youth who had benefited most from his father's wisdom, chided the chief for going so easily with the policemen. Perhaps because he did not want to appear puny in his son's eyes, Sitting Bull resisted the pushing and shoving.

The police had wanted to get Sitting Bull away from the settlement before any of the other people woke up, but the commotion of

An unknown Hunkpapa Lakota artist's rendition of the arrest and killing of Sitting Bull. *North Dakota Historical Society*

the struggle and the wailing and shrieking of the chief's wives and children had brought people running. Soon a crowd had gathered outside the cabin. Some urged Sitting Bull to go with the police, assuring him that they couldn't hurt him, while others became more threatening.

A shot was fired, and Bull Head went down. He turned and shot Sitting Bull in the chest. Red Tomahawk then shot Sitting Bull in the back of the head. Then all hell did break loose, and by the time the cavalry troops arrived, twelve Indians, both police and civilians, were dead, and three policemen were wounded. One of the dead Indians was Crow Foot, who had been murdered by the policemen because he was in the cabin and they wanted revenge for the shooting of their commander, Bull Head.

A wagon took Sitting Bull's corpse to Fort Yates, where he was wrapped in canvas and quietly buried in a far corner of the post cemetery. The dead Indian policemen were also buried—with full honors.

Two weeks later, On December 29, 1890, a band of Minneconjou Ghost Dancers, led by Big Foot, were gunned down by the 7th Cavalry at a place called Wounded Knee. Custer's old outfit had put an end to one of the greatest resistance movements in history.

Epilogue

———————◆———————

The film crew assembled again in the Little Bighorn area in early June. The winter shots had turned out fine, Paul was both relieved and enthusiastic, the rest of us were in high spirits.

For three days the weather was almost perfect for filming. Hot, blue-sky days, dramatic sunsets, interesting clouds once in a while, cirrus over the battlefield, cumulus over the distant Bighorn Mountains, early-morning fog off the river. Again the crew were up before dawn and in bed long after sunset. The difference was that the days were much longer now, only about ten days before the longest day of summer, about two weeks before the Battle of the Little Bighorn. The temperature wasn't quite as hot as the hundred degrees of that day in 1876, but it was hot enough, in the low nineties. The evenings were warm, but nice, leading to almost chilly nights. Charles Windolph, one of the troopers under siege on Reno Hill, wrote, "The sun went down that night [of June 25] like a ball of fire. Pretty soon the quick Montana twilight settled down on us, and then came the chill of the high plains." One hundred and fifteen years later, the weather was pretty much the same.

The fourth and final day of all-day shooting dawned clear and warm, and the crew set out to do more filming of battlefield, river, and sky. The night before, Paul had given me my first major assignment of the filming venture. I had tried to make myself useful during the first three days, driving the associate producers, Maia Harris and Anne Craig, on various errands, driving back to the motel in Hardin to pick up suddenly needed equipment, fetching lunch, doing scut work. In between errands, I made notes, took pictures, sat in the shade, wondered if there were any fish in the Little Bighorn. The runoff was still high, so dry flies were out of the question. The Lakotas and Cheyennes had used grasshoppers.

Maia was actually in charge of the project which would end the filming for the documentary in flamboyant style. Windolph, a couple of paragraphs after his description of the "Montana twilight," wrote, "Across the river and down below in the valley of the Little [Big]horn, where so many of our men lay dead, we could see great fires and hear the steady rhythm of Indian tomtoms beating for their wild victory dances." Although there is some dispute over the celebrating in the Indian camp (Old Sioux warriors told Stanley Vestal, "There were no scalp dances that night.... Too many Sioux warriors had fallen; there were too many mourners in camp." There is no doubt that the Indians were up all night and that great "skunks," or bonfires, had been lit.

And that was Maia's and my job, to light bonfires in the valley just across the river from Reno Hill, where the large village had been. We spent that afternoon gathering materials: charcoal lighter fluid, artificial logs, a foot's worth of fliers from a grocery store advertising specials, and on and on. By the time we returned to the bonfire site to start looking for cottonwood deadfalls to build up the skunks, a battered white three-quarter-ton pickup was parked in the shade of a cottonwood, its bed loaded with wood. Gilbert Birdinground was sitting sideways behind the steering wheel, cap in hand, his feet resting on the running board. A small boy, about four or five, stood on the seat beside him.

When we had first met Mr. Birdinground, during our scouting trip in late October of the previous year, he had not been friendly. We had Joe Medicine Crow with us, who could probably disarm a rattlesnake, but even he could not allay Mr. Birdinground's suspicions that we were yet another ripoff film outfit seeking to use his land, which is right opposite Reno Hill and which was the site of the southern (Hunkpapa) end of the village. At least one feature film and several documentaries, some European, had been filmed on his land, and the filmmakers had apparently not treated him right.

While Joe had talked with him about thirty yards from the car, we stood watching three boys shooting baskets, each of whom looked capable of tipping over our car. Mr. Birdinground, a tall, good-looking

Crow of about eighty winters, kept glancing over Joe's head toward Paul, Maia, and me. His expression was not encouraging. Finally, Joe came back, jumped into the front seat, not smiling, and said, "He'll think about it. Come back when you get ready to film." Then Joe explained that the previous film outfits had paid Mr. Birdinground a pittance for his valuable location. Some had downright reneged on the agreed-upon fee.

When we did get ready to film, Paul negotiated a fair price for the location. And now, Mr. Birdinground was offering his labor and wood gratis. When Maia and I pulled up, he stepped from the pickup and pointed out a couple of places that he thought would be good for bonfires, easily visible from Reno Hill, back a way from the cottonwoods that lined the Little Bighorn, far enough apart so that in the dark they would be distinct fires. Then we began to build the skunks, large and conical, like tipis.

It was still almost four hours until dark when we finished. I brought out the charcoal starter to set on the ground near one of the skunks, and Mr. Birdinground smiled at me. He went over to the white pickup and pulled out a dirty old Purex bleach bottle, which was stopped up with a rag. "Diesel fuel," he said. We were in the company of an expert firemaker.

Mr. Birdinground and his grandson went back to their house for supper, and Maia and I drove the few miles to the Sagebrush Inn, where we met Anne Craig for a leisurely buffaloburger. Anne had already delivered food and soft drinks to the film crew up on the battlefield, so we sat and ate and smoked for a couple of hours.

As we drove back to the location, I could see in my rearview mirror the sun just touching the western horizon. It did look like a ball of fire. In front of us, the thunderheads which had been perched over the Bighorns the past few days were now a lot closer, moving down the Little Bighorn valley. The muscular tops were stark white, but the bottoms were flat and blue-black. They were still far enough away that we couldn't hear the thunder, but we did see a couple of flashes of lightning, which was mildly worrisome.

Mr. Birdinground and his grandson were already at the site, which was a long narrow bench just above the floodplain of the river. Actually, the Lakotas would have been camped on a higher bench a little farther from the river, but that land was now alfalfa fields and too far away to be picked up clearly by the camera.

The little bench was almost idyllic, with stands of cottonwoods marking the river and patches of wild rose with their pink flowers around the perimeter of a grazed-down but grassy flat. It had once been a small campground—even some Germans had camped there—but the only sign was a small white outhouse in the far corner. Mr. Birdinground was going to take it down when he had the time.

It was beginning to get dark down in the river bottom. Maia unhooked the walkie-talkie from her belt and spoke into it: "Paul, can you hear me? Paul?" No answer. She repeated the query. Again, no answer. "I wonder if this thing is working."

Anne came over. "Is it charged up?"

"It says that it is."

"Did you press the right button?"

Just then, Paul's voice came on. "Maia? Is that you?"

"Who did you think it was? Where are you?"

"We just finished the sunset. Wow, it was great from up here. Jon says it was the best one he's ever shot."

"Well, you'd better get over here. It's getting dark down here."

Paul Stekler and Jon Else filming on Last Stand Hill. *Maia Harris*

"My God, did you see the lightning? Right behind you, up the valley."

As if on cue, we heard a low rumble of thunder. Then a gust of wind struck the little bench, rattling the waxy leaves of the cottonwoods over our heads.

"We're loading up the rig now. We'll be there in twenty minutes."

The film crew was going to set up across the river, from the vantage point of the soldiers looking down at the bonfires, listening to the Indian "tomtoms beating for their wild victory dances." This would be one of the few staged shots in the film. The day before, the crew had filmed three young Crows on horses on a hilltop, just sitting quietly with a wide sky as a backdrop. In the film, they would be cut into a journal entry by Lieutenant James Bradley, chief of scouts for General Gibbons. A voice would say, ". . . three men were discovered on the opposite side of the Bighorn, apparently watching our movements, some of the Crow scouts whom I had furnished to General Custer." Bradley would follow them to the battlefield and see the corpses of Custer's men strewn all over the country. It turned out beautifully.

But the bonfires were the *pièce de résistance,* the dramatic culmination of the filming of the Battle of the Little Bighorn, with the Indian women wailing in grief in the darkness, fading into the Christian hymns Libbie Custer and the other wives of the 7th Cavalry officers sang as they waited for news of their men. A big moment.

After half an hour, Maia tried to reach Paul on the walkie-talkie. The wind had really kicked up, and the lightning strikes were getting close, the thunder filling our bodies. But no answer.

It was dark now, and the approaching thunderstorm made it even darker. The leaves were rattling loudly and unceasingly, the trees squeaked and groaned, and the wind blew in our hair and through our clothes. Then a bright streak with a loud crack fading into a long deep rumble made me truly nervous.

I thought of many things as we waited for the film crew and the storm, about our safety, about the odd circumstance of being on Crow land filming a story about their mortal enemies, the Lakotas and Cheyennes, but what I thought about most was the propriety of what we were doing. I had read many accounts of Thunder Chief and Coldmaker punishing those who went against their wishes, those who broke the ancient laws of nature and paid the price. Perhaps we weren't supposed to be out here; perhaps it was not right to disturb the spirits of those Lakotas and Cheyennes who had fought here and died. Perhaps Thunder Chief was going to punish us for raising the spirits of the dead. Moments of such violent weather make one think such thoughts. I wondered what Mr. Birdinground was thinking. His grandson was hanging on to his leg, and the old man was absently stroking the small head.

"Maia? Can you hear me?"

"Paul, where *are* you?"

"You won't believe what happened to us. We'll be there in five minutes."

Later that night, back at the motel, Paul told us that just as they had been loading up the carryall, a young park ranger had driven up and told them they would have to leave the battlefield because of the storm and because rattlesnakes liked to head for the high warmth of the paved road when it got cool. They had had to drive down to the visitor center to call Barbara Booher to get permission to stay and film. He also told us that Roy Big Crane, a member of the crew, had burned sweet grass all around them while they were shooting to protect them. ("I smelled something burning in the dark and I thought a lightning strike had torched the grass, but it was Roy. It was great. And it worked.")

Finally the crew arrived on Reno Hill. They set up in record time, and just as the first large drops of rain stung our heads, Mr. Birdinground poured the diesel fuel onto the skunks and torched them off. Then we hid behind trees. This was minimalist filming, no bodies dancing around the large blazes, only the blazes themselves. And Roy Big Crane's protective smoke.

Now the rain was coming harder, blowing in sheets across the bench, but the fires were not disturbed. Sparks flew up, the rain came down, and we were getting soaked as we stood behind our trees, watching the orange, licking flames illuminate the clacking cottonwood leaves. Of all the hours and days of filming, this was the moment that was most alive for me. Perhaps it was the fire, the thunder, lightning, and rain, but I imagined I could hear the voices of mourning women carried by the wind. I thought if I walked up to the upper bench where the large village really stood I would see a small group of Lakotas and Cheyennes standing silently, watching the fires, watching us, thinking of long-ago fires. Perhaps they would know that their ancestors were safe in the real world behind this one.

When the news of the slaughter of Custer and his whole command swept across the nation, the initial reaction was disbelief—this was impossible, it couldn't have happened, not in 1876. In that centennial year of technological wonders, of great progress, of expanding cities, of steam engines, railroads across the continent, modern factories, it was not easy to understand how a group of savages could defeat the most modern army in the world. What happened to the divine right of Caucasians to conquer, even annihilate, dark people? What happened to Manifest Destiny? Where was God in all this?

Disbelief quickly gave way to sorrow, to anger, to outrage. Congressmen leaped to their feet, demanding that this Indian nuisance be eliminated once and for all. Nits make lice. The relatively new national press spoke of Indians as the scum of the earth, fit only for extermination. Political cartoons showed Indians with bones in their oversized noses, a savage glint in their eyes, holding the scalps of

Newspaper cartoon expressing the national outrage at Custer's defeat. *Montana Historical Society*

Custer and his hapless soldiers. Even some reformers and religious groups, perhaps resigned to the nation's mood, called for a final answer to the "Indian problem."

Not to be outdone, the poets were feverishly composing verse about the golden-haired Custer and his tragic death in a godforsaken country at the hands of Sitting Bull, the demonic chief. Even Walt Whitman was among them; he sold a poem to the *New York Tribune* for $10, urging the paper, "If it comes in time, get it in tonight as earliness is everything." Whitman's poem, "A Death-Sonnet for Custer," which became "From Far Dakota's Canons" in *Leaves of Grass,* while better than the rest, perfectly illustrates the elevation of event to myth:

> *Continues yet the old, old legend of our race,*
> *The loftiest of life upheld by death,*
> *The ancient banner perfectly maintain'd,*
> *O lesson opportune, O how I welcome thee! . . .*
>
> *Thou of the tawny flowing hair in battle,*
> *I erewhile saw, with erect head, pressing ever in front, bearing a*
> *   bright sword in thy hand,*
> *Now ending well in death the splendid fever of thy deeds,*
> *(I bring no dirge for it or thee, I bring a glad triumphal sonnet,)*
> *Desperate and glorious, aye in defeat most desperate, most*
> *   glorious,*
> *After thy many battles in which never yielding up a gun or a*
> *   color,*
> *Leaving behind thee a memory sweet to soldiers,*
> *Thou yieldest up thyself.*

And so as it should have been in an age which honored its poets, these bards, good and bad, began to create the Custer myth. The number of times "glory" and "glorious" appeared in print or in speech next to Custer's name might even outrank his "tawny [or golden or yellow or long] flowing hair." Custer became a martyr, yielding up himself to save—what? Humanity? The white race? No matter. For almost a century, certainly until well after the Second World War, Custer's name was synonymous with glorious mortality, or better yet, glorious immortality. It was inevitable that historians would get into the act and perpetuate the myth—objectivity be damned—that Custer was "brave" and "noble" and Sitting Bull was "clever" and "cunning." In our historical memory the Indians remained savages, redskins, fiendish, bloodthirsty, soulless.

But for all the sentimental verses and the anger of the public and politicians, Custer's legend might have died a lingering but merciful death had it not been for two people: Buffalo Bill Cody and Elizabeth Bacon Custer. Together they managed to keep Custer's memory alive, and furthermore, they were able to make his name a household word in both America and Europe.

Buffalo Bill's Wild West show traveled all through America and Europe, staging fierce fights, hellacious rides, fancy shooting, and, above all, pageantry. The stages or stadiums he played were filled with Indians, Mexican vaqueros, cowboy heroes, soldiers, frontiersmen. One of his most popular acts was the staging of Custer's Last

Cassily Adams's *Custer's Last Fight* became an Anheuser-Busch poster that was hung over the bar in saloons all across the country. *Little Big Horn Battlefield National Monument*

Custer's Last Stand as the featured finale on the poster for Buffalo Bill's Wild West show in 1904. *Buffalo Bill Historical Society*

Black Elk (left) and friend, traveling as part of Buffalo Bill's Wild West show. *Smithsonian Institution*

Battle. Queen Victoria watched it, along with the Prince of Wales, in 1887 in London. Paris society turned out the next year. Although they were properly thrilled by the trick riding, the sight of buffalo, elk, bears, sharpshooting, the famous Deadwood stagecoach at full tilt, and Buffalo Bill himself, they went home with the image of Custer and his troops slaughtered by savages. The Custer myth grew. Elizabeth Custer sent Buffalo Bill a note thanking him for keeping her husband's memory "green." "You have done so much to make him an idol among children and young people."

But it was finally the tenacious Libbie Custer who did the most to keep her husband's name and honor bright and shining. She wrote three books about their lives together, including *"Boots and Saddles,"* a best-seller. She lectured indefatigably at libraries and garden clubs, wherever anybody would have her. She lobbied for a statue of Custer to be placed "at a lovely spot" at West Point. Unfortunately, when it was unveiled she hated it; she shed enough tears that the statue was taken down and another monument was erected, more to her liking.

Libby outlived her husband by fifty-seven years, finally expiring in 1933. By then she was a woman of affluence, living on Park Avenue in New York, a grand dame. She had kept the myth of her husband and the Battle of the Little Bighorn green for more than half a century. The only regret she expressed upon dying was that Custer's detractors would now be free to tarnish his image.

Sixty years after her death, it would seem that her fear has been justified. The Battle of the Little Bighorn, starring George Armstrong Custer, for most of us has been demoted from myth to event, perhaps even an onerous event. Since Vietnam, we have been questioning the need for war, or at least American involvement in wars. It seems that war has become a political game in this country. Presidents have wars—Reagan had Grenada and Panama, Bush had Desert Storm, now Clinton has his Somalia. Wars have become trophies to these leaders, suitable for the mantel along with their other memorabilia. But ordinary Americans are not so enamored of war. They do not like to see innocent bodies pulled from the rubble. And when "our boys" are killed, they wonder what the hell we were doing there in the first place. Even those in the military are more prone to question the need for heroics. On being asked why his ground forces didn't charge into a hot spot during the Desert Storm battle, a commander answered, "I'm no Custer." Custer's Last Stand has become a cautionary tale, and the Custer Myth, unhappily for Libbie's ghost, has turned to tarnished brass.

Elizabeth Custer as a young widow in mourning in 1876. *Little Bighorn Battlefield National Monument*

Elizabeth Custer as the author of best-selling books about her late husband's life. She outlived him by fifty-seven years, living until 1933. *Monroe County Historical Society*

In talking with several Indian people, especially Lakotas and Cheyennes, I was surprised to learn that the Battle of the Little Bighorn was not the major event in their tribal memory that one might assume. Ted Rising Sun and Bill Tall Bull, both Cheyennes, while forthcoming, preferred to talk about MacKenzie's attack on Dull Knife's camp, when the soldiers drove the people out into the cold without food, horses, or proper clothing. Many Lakotas spoke of the Massacre at Wounded Knee or the killing of Crazy Horse and Sitting Bull. Recently a large group of Lakotas retraced the hundred-year-old hoofprints of Big Foot's Minneconjou people to Wounded Knee. The weather was atrocious, far below zero all the way, just as it had been on that day. Yet they persisted.

Why? Why not forget the old defeats and bask in the memory that once their people were victorious in a battle that became one of the most celebrated events in this nation's history?

Perhaps it has to do with the nature of defeat. If Custer had emerged triumphant, he probably would have lived to be a bald old man (his hairline was already receding), writing his memoirs, and the Little Bighorn would have been a paragraph or two in a biographer's temporary best-seller, but in defeat and death, he became, and remains, a name recognized the world over.

Defeat touches people deeply because of the sheer weight of loss. Victory is generally fleeting, a good, often exhilarating feeling, a celebration, but loss lingers long after the event. Loss in battle means the death of loved ones, hardship, and suffering. It often means the death of an ideal, or in the Indian' case, of a way of life too. And so loss stays with a people, often at the fringe of the desperation of getting on with life, but always there. Loss is a hard legacy to pass on to their children and to their children's children.

For the Lakotas and Cheyennes, who all with the exception of Sitting Bull surrendered within a year of Little Bighorn, loss was especially heavy, because they couldn't see what they had done to invite such all-encompassing tragedy into their lives. They had lived in perfect accord with Wakan Tanka, the Great Mystery. They had lived on this earth in harmony with *pte* and the other four-leggeds, with the Mother, with the wings of the air and the green things, with the four directions and the sacred beings. They had tried to live with the *wasichus*. Many of them had signed treaties; others, including Sitting Bull and Crazy Horse, had desired only to live as far away from the white people as possible. And yet, because they responded to this alien aggression, they became a lost people in their own country. All were bewildered, and many blamed themselves. Black Elk, who had been a youth at Little Bighorn and lived to be an old man, was also at Wounded Knee after the massacre:

> And so it was all over.
> I did not know then how much was ended. When I look back now from this high hill of my old age, I can still see the butchered women and children lying heaped and scattered all along the crooked gulch as plain as when I saw them with eyes still young. And I can see that something else died there in the bloody mud, and was buried in the blizzard. A people's dream died there. It was a beautiful dream.
> And I, to whom so great a vision was given in my youth— you see me now a pitiful old man who has done nothing, for the nation's hoop is broken and scattered. There is no center any longer, and the sacred tree is dead.

Before he died, Black Elk called up a rain shower out of a blue sky in an effort to nourish the roots of the withered sacred tree. The Indian spirit was, and remains, hard to break.

Afterword:
Filming "The Last Stand"

by PAUL STEKLER

━━━━━━◆━━━━━━

Private Charles Windolph wrote that his first glimpse of Reno Hill was a sight he'd never forget. Soldiers staggered aimlessly, many wounded and bleeding, while terror-stricken stragglers fell through a disorganized skirmish line at the top of the ridge that looked down on the Little Bighorn River. The wounded lay screaming on the ground, many crying for water in the oppressive heat. Looking down into the valley, soldiers could see comrades who'd been left behind in the panic, surrounded by Sioux and Cheyenne warriors, being cut down and killed.

Just six years before, Windolph had fled his home in Bergen, Prussia, to avoid being drafted to fight in the Franco-Prussian War. Unable to find steady work in New York, he'd joined the army, saying it might be a good way to learn English. Now he found himself with the survivors of the 7th Cavalry at the Little Bighorn, wondering, as the battle continued around them, what had become of the five companies who'd ridden to the north earlier in the day with their commander, George Armstrong Custer.

From that direction, the soldiers could "hear the sound of distant firing echoing down through the hills and valleys." But Windolph and his companions had plenty to worry about where they were. As the late afternoon neared sunset, hundreds of Indians encircled their precarious position, putting the companies under siege. Snipers began picking off soldiers from the surrounding heights. Windolph later wrote:

Dan Hart and Roy Big Crane push Jon Else on a camera dolly as he films markers for the fallen members of the 7th Cavalry on the Little Bighorn Battlefield. *Maia Harris*

The three Crow ''scouts'' being filmed on a ridge next to Last Stand Hill. *Maia Harris*

The sun went down that night like a ball of fire. Pretty soon the quick Montana twilight settled down on us, and then came the chill of the high plains.... We felt terribly alone on that dangerous hilltop. We were a million miles from nowhere. And death was all around us.

One hundred and fifteen years later, in the summer of 1991, we returned to the same ground to make a documentary film, *Last Stand at Little Bighorn*. On the last day of shooting, a thunderstorm was approaching. Standing out exposed on top of the hill, our film crew was trying to recreate visually what Private Windolph and his fellow soldiers might have seen on the night of June 25, 1876. Flat on his stomach on an exposed skirmish line, Windolph lay next to the body of a friend who'd been killed by a sniper's bullet. He looked down into the valley of the Little Bighorn, toward the great Lakota Sioux and Cheyenne village, and later wrote of seeing "great fires and hear[ing] the steady rhythm of Indian tomtoms beating for their wild victory dances."

But there were other vantage points that night. Those wild "victory dances" that Windolph heard turned out to be Lakota and Cheyenne women singing mourning songs for their dead husbands and sons. Wooden Leg, a young Cheyenne who fought that day, was later quoted as remembering: "There was no dancing or celebrating in any of the camps that night. Too many people were in mourning. Too many Cheyenne and Sioux women had gashed their arms and legs to show their grief."

Our plan was to "recreate" these different perspectives, using the words of each man as we showed the contrast in what they saw: Wooden Leg's view looking up at the dark hill; Windolph's view looking down at the distant fires in the valley. The subsequent sequence would do more than merely present a narrative description of the aftermath of the battle. It would visually demonstrate how this "history" could be remembered in completely different ways depending on who—and where—you were.

All around us, we could see bursts of lightning, the clouds totally black and pressing in on three sides of us. It seemed like the only place it wasn't raining and thundering was right around us on the hill. Our cameraman, spooked by the warning of a park ranger, kept shouting at us to look out for the rattlesnakes that supposedly sought out the warmth of the paved road during storms. Far below us, Jim Welch was watching Gilbert Birdinground, the Crow owner of the property along the Little Bighorn River, pour enough diesel fuel on two slacks of firewood—our Indian bonfires—so that they'd stay lit, even if the coming rains caused a flash flood.

Over the walkie-talkie, Jim was signaled to "go," and he threw the first match onto the assembled piles. As the thunder grew louder and closer and the lightning more insistent, flames of the distant bonfires grew and stretched toward the twilight sky. Finally, the camera began to roll.

Suddenly I smelled smoke behind us. My first thought was that lightning had struck nearby, starting a grassfire. Looking around, I discovered our camera assistant, Roy Big Crane, a Salish filmmaker from the Flathead Reservation in Montana, crouched down with burning sweet grass in his hands. A big man with long braids, Roy was moving slowly, letting the smoke make a wide protective circle around us as he sang softly to himself. I stared at him for a few moments, dumbfounded and confused.

"Roy," I asked, "what are you doing?" He stopped, looked me in the eye, then looked up at the looming storm. He then turned back me and smiled. "Paul, what are *we* doing?"

We had come to the Little Bighorn to examine the battle from a variety of perspectives, white and Native American. To understand the controversy and debate that has surrounded its history for more than a century. Given the craziness of filming bonfires from a hilltop in the middle of a violent Montana thunderstorm, it somehow seemed appropriate that contrasting views of the world would pop up while we were making the film as well.

The Battle of the Little Bighorn, Custer's Last Stand, is the single most reproduced event in all of American history. It has inspired scores of Hollywood films, over a thousand documented paintings, and countless books, cartoons, and advertisements. Hundreds of thousands of people still trek to the battlefield in south-central Montana every summer, many of them busloads of tourists from throughout the world. Staged reenactments in nearby Hardin, Montana, featuring Crow Indians playing Sitting Bull and the Sioux—revisionist role-playing, as their ancestors were scouts for the 7th Cavalry that day—and a blond plumber from Michigan playing Custer, regularly sell out to large, appreciative crowds.

To generations of Americans, George Armstrong Custer is one of the most evocative characters in our country's historical narrative. The story of Little Bighorn is always cast with Custer at its center, a handsome young officer in buckskin with long blond hair. The drama builds to Custer's legendary Last Stand, as his small band of men is surrounded by an ever-narrowing circle of extremely angry Indians. The economic forces driving westward expansion, the evolution of the country's Indian policy, and other events that made Little Bighorn one of the final acts in the dispossession of the last free tribes on the northern plains are rarely part of the picture.

Nor does this picture change. Whether Custer is portrayed as a hero, as Errol Flynn did it in the World War II–era *They Died with Their Boots On*, or as a genocidal nut, as in the Vietnam-era *Little Big Man*, he is still the center of attention. The recent miniseries *Son of the Morning Star* depicted Custer as a naughty, hot-blooded, frat-boy type—but he is still the character that the cameras follow, the man whose death has always been the point of telling the story. No matter that in fact his famous hairline was beginning to recede, that his remaining hair was cut short, and that it was too hot to wear buckskin that summer day. Or that the Lakotas and the Cheyennes had no idea who had attacked them or which particular army commander they were fighting. More than a century after his death, Custer has the kind of name recognition that would make any aspirant for national political office jealous.

But if you switch the focus, the story becomes infinitely richer. Late on a cold November night, with the wind howling outside his trailer on the Pine Ridge Reservation, Johnson Holy Rock began talking to us about Crazy Horse. Nearly eighty, Johnson is a former tribal chairman whose father was a young boy in Crazy Horse's camp at the Little Bighorn. "Traditional history tells us that Crazy Horse could ride in front of a line of soldiers and they could all take a potshot at him and no bullet could touch him," Johnson said, moving his arms back and forth for emphasis. "He'd make three passes, and after the third pass, then his followers were encouraged to make the charge. 'See, I haven't been wounded. I'm not shot.' We would charge."

I was intrigued, not by Crazy Horse's ability to ward off bullets in the story, but by Holy Rock's use of the term "traditional history." Traditional history according to whom? Not the folks who wrote the history textbooks I read at Glen Rock Junior/Senior High School back in northern New Jersey. Amid George Washington, Abraham Lincoln, Franklin Roosevelt, and even George Custer, figures like Crazy Horse—and, in fact, centuries of Native Americans—rated barely a mention. Traditional history.

Jim and I saw our role, as scriptwriters, filmmakers, and amateur historians, as an opportunity to draw people into a story whose popularity guaranteed a big audience. Draw them in and then fool them. Not only would we give them the lives of Custer, Crazy Horse, and Sitting Bull, we would give voice to the "supporting" players in this drama. See the Indians for the people they were. Both the native people that Custer attacked and the native people who fought alongside him because they thought it was in their best interests. And listen to the hopes and the everyday observations of the ragged frontier soldiers and would-be settlers, who as often as not failed, who were not marquee names. Give voice to the people not usually heard in this long-playing epic. Change the focus of the events at Little Bighorn. Help change some of America's myths about the old west.

The west was never the constantly dramatic cowboys-and-Indians story that we grew up with in the movies. Despite the American advance across the plains that would eventually lead to a complete transformation in their lives, the native peoples in the west were largely concerned with life as it has always been. The pursuit of food. The buffalo. Kinship. Birth and death. It's instructive to note that in the winter-counts they drew, the visual records for the year 1876, almost no one included the victory at the Little Bighorn. The many bands who had been at the Little Bighorn chose to record the theft of a prized horse, the harshness of the winter's cold, the death of beloved relatives. Things they felt were more important to remember.

For the soldiers of the American frontier, life was at best dreary. Most of their time was spent building and maintaining isolated forts. Combat with Indians was rare. In its 1867–68 report to the Secretary of War, the 2nd Cavalry claimed to have patrolled five thousand miles looking for hostile Indians. In a year's time, they recorded wounding one Indian, burying three murdered settlers, and recovering a single stolen horse. During the same time period, 809 soldiers deserted and nearly as many were court-martialed. Evan Connell, in his *Son of the Morning Star,* wrote that "except for interludes of terror, life on the majestic plains alternated between tedium and ennui."

Rarely have these differing perspectives been merged in the telling of this history. In asking Jim to be part of the film production, it was my hope that he and I would mirror these differences, challenging each other's assumptions and giving fair voice to all participants, especially the native peoples whose story is rarely heard. That Jim's presence sent this message to the Indian people we met was clear. When Bill Tall Bull told Jim that he had read his books, his tone conveyed the importance of Jim's stories for him, conveyed that those stories really meant something to him. Throughout our travels, people approached Jim: a couple of Crow college students at a lunch counter near the battlefield; a Sioux or a Blackfeet we met on the road. Their faces would light up as they told Jim about the poems of his that they had read, the words that reminded them of their own lives. Late one night, in an old sparsely furnished cabin full of books up a dirt road near Wounded Knee, Mike Her Many Horses, a Pine Ridge tribal council member and Little Bighorn history buff, made coffee so strong you could walk across it and reminisced about listening to Jim read from an early novel a decade or more back. All of them believed that Jim, in some way, spoke of a life that was familiar to them, that represented their lives.

And Jim did not let them down. One afternoon, Dr. Beatrice Medicine, a retired Lakota anthropologist and one of Jim's former college professors, was showing us her family's ancestral land on the Standing Rock Reservation, Sitting Bull's homeland. By the banks of a small fast-flowing stream, she paused, looking at the birds flying above the treetops. Staring up at the sky, she said that an old man had once come to see her father. He'd told her father that on the dawn of the day of the battle an unusual number of birds had been seen above the Little Bighorn. People had taken note of the occurrence, wondering what it might mean. Later, in a dark editing room in Boston, Jim watched film we'd shot of birds flying in circles over the river fog of another dawn at the Little Bighorn. And then he wrote: "Among those in the Lakota and Cheyenne camps, it was said that flocks of birds over the Little Bighorn that dawn darkened the sky. Some thought it was a warning."

To research a historical story is to uncover the often forgotten stories of many people. There are times when you literally open a packet and find letters that someone, dead for a century, wrote to a loved one. You listen to stories late at night, feeling the presence of the storyteller's parents, grandparents, or even great-grandparents. You find a photograph, yellowed from age, in the bottom of a box.

We found sets of 7th Cavalry pension letters stored at the National Archives. Written to their families by the soldiers who had died at Little Bighorn, the letters were sent to the federal government as "proof" of family relationships, the only way wives or parents could receive the deceased's army pensions. Sitting in the quiet reference room, we would be handed these packets of letters, still tied together with aged red ribbon, would untie them carefully and read about the mundane and sad lives that most of the soldiers led. They came from rural towns and big cities back east. From Ireland, Germany, Italy, and Russia. Many wrote of their shame in not being able to send more money back home. They knew little of the mission they faced. On the eve of the 7th's departure from Fort Abraham Lincoln in 1876, Private William Criddle wrote to his father in Hardware, Virginia. "Father, we expect to leave here at any time, but I can't say where we are going. Some of the men seem to think that we are going to the Black Hills to protect miners and some say we are going to the Bighorn River to bring Sitting Bull in on the government reservation. That is if he ain't too many for us." He died at the Little Bighorn.

At the Museum of Natural History in New York, I was stunned to discover actual footage of Two Moons, a Cheyenne man we knew had fought beside Crazy Horse. I was watching a silent film commissioned in 1908 by the heir to a pharmaceutical fortune in Philadelphia, a man obsessed by both the Indians as a "vanishing race" and by the mysteries of Little Bighorn. The film's sequences were meant to preserve a record of the old ways. Demonstrations of smoke signals and sign language, reenactments of scouting parties. Unexpectedly, a title card announced: "Chief Two Moons, leader of the Cheyennes against Custer, tells the story of the Battle on the spot where Custer fell." And there he was, an old man standing next the marble grave markers on Last Stand Hill. "The whole valley was filled with smoke. We circled around them, swirling like water round a stone. It took about as long as it takes for a hungry man to eat his dinner."

In her Rapid City living room, Helen Wrede pulled out the diary kept by her grandfather, one of the many who rushed into the Black Hills after Custer to look for gold. A failure as a gold miner, he later helped found Rapid City. Still later, he was superintendent at Pine Ridge. Holding the diary gently, she read passages. "August 15th. A mail carrier from Fort Pierre was killed and scalped 8 miles south from Crook City on the road from Rapid to Deadwood. I do not remember his name. His home was in Indiana. Sunday, Rev. W. H. Smith was murdered on his way to preach the gospel. The Indians got away with his bible and his scalp."

One day, we walked along a ridge on the battlefield with Joseph Medicine Crow, away from the tourists taking photographs on Last Stand Hill. The bounce in his step belied his eighty years as he pointed out landmarks described to him by Custer's Crow scouts. Most had lived into the 1920s, and he had known them all, heard all their stories. One was his grandfather. Mr. Medicine Crow was wearing a big black cowboy hat and a buffalo bolo tie. Laughing, he looked out over the expense of plains and told us that when Sitting Bull heard the soldiers attack, he told all those around him that it was a good day to die. A good day to die.

A park ranger told us that he had heard that one of Charlie Windolph's daughters was still alive. Windolph had mentioned a daughter, Irene Fehliman, in the beginning of his memoir, *I Fought with Custer*. The former private had lived until 1950, still rocking on his front porch at the age of ninety-eight while battle buffs took snapshots of him. His daughter would now also be in her nineties. We began making calls to the towns in the Black Hills where she and her father had lived. Finally we found that she was still alive and living in Deadwood, South Dakota.

From a phone in the hallway of the only motel in Lodge Grass, Montana, we anxiously telephoned. Would she remember anything? Was she still able to talk? It was a spry, lively woman who answered the call, responding to the questions of my associate producer, Maia Harris, as I leaned toward the phone, trying to overhear. Maia asked Mrs. Fehliman if her father had ever talked about Custer. And very clearly, I heard: "My father told me that Custer didn't care at all about the men. He was mean." Within an hour, we were packed, in the car, and ready to drive the four hundred miles to Deadwood.

The geography of the northern plains and the artifacts people left behind spoke volumes to us as well. We stood where Sitting Bull stood, under the Deer Medicine Rocks, where he saw his Sun Dance vision of soldiers falling. Stood where Crazy Horse died. Looked up at the clouds over Fort Abraham Lincoln, up on a hill overlooking the Missouri River, clouds that people claimed to see a reflection of the 7th Cavalry in as it marched out on its way toward the Little Bighorn. Late one afternoon, near twilight, I climbed up alone to the top of Rattlesnake Butte on the Standing Rock Sioux Reservation and watched the sun set from a circle of rocks where Lakota men once caught eagles to collect their feathers. Saw the silhouettes of smaller hills to the west where young men once had visions, not far from the banks of the Grand River where Sitting Bull lived his last years.

We held the arrows that were found in circles around the bodies of Bill Thomas and his son, and the diary that lay on the ground next to him where he fell. And we saw an old photograph of Lakota Indians driving wagons piled high with buffalo bones. Once their lives had revolved around the endless herds, millions of buffalo. Now they were collecting all that was left, the endless bones, selling them at 6 cents a ton to buy food to keep from starving.

Near the end of our filming at the battlefield, Joseph Medicine

Crow asked if he might sing his grandfather's war song on camera. We hadn't anticipated this. Mr. Medicine Crow had already given us a wonderful interview, mostly on the stories that his grandfather, White Man Runs Him, and the other Crow scouts had told him about the battle. It was the end of a long, hundred-degree Montana afternoon. We walked with him down a long, sloping ridge off Last Stand Hill—the hills of the battlefield being deceptively steep, making one wonder what it was like to fight that day, or to be running for your life as all order fell apart. And as the thunder of yet another approaching storm grew louder, we decided to set up quickly to record the song.

We sat Mr. Medicine Crow on an equipment box. Two production assistants held a tarp above his head, out of the camera frame, to protect him from the drops of rain beginning to fall. He turned toward the camera and announced: "I would now like to sing my grandfather's war song. White Man Runs Him's war song." And then he began to sing, a deep raspy eighty-year-old man's voice—but strong, strong enough to resonate over the nearby hills. Out on the battlefield, with the ominous thunderclouds in the background, he was singing the same song that his grandfather had sung to Custer more than a century ago. He sang in Crow. The words translated: "Once you were a scout. Soon you will be a scout again." The song of a man who believed that he was about to die.

As he sang, Joseph Medicine Crow shut his eyes and raised his arm, pointing out toward a distant horizon. And then, as suddenly as he had begun, his song was over. He opened his eyes and looked off into the distance. The crew stood in stunned silence, with only the distant thunder and a few drops of rain heard.

It was an extraordinary moment, the kind that filmmakers can only hope for. The kind you never forget.

It was history.

Notes

CHAPTER ONE

[pp. 25–26] Account of Lewis's confrontation with Pikunis (Blackfeet) is taken from *The Journals of Lewis and Clark,* edited by Frank Bergon (New York: Penguin, 1989), pp. 452–57.

[pp. 27–29] Owl Child/Malcolm Clark incident is taken from John C. Ewers, *The Blackfeet: Raiders on the Northwestern Plains* (Norman: University of Oklahoma Press, 1958), pp. 246–47. Other accounts of this incident can be found in James Willard Schultz, *Blackfeet and Buffalo: Memories of Life Among the Indians* (Norman: University of Oklahoma Press, 1962); and in Ben Bennett, *Death, Too, for The-Heavy-Runner* (Missoula, Mont.: Mountain Press, 1982).

[p. 29] Sheridan actually said, "The only good Indian I ever saw was dead."

[p. 29] De Trobriand's quote is from Bennett, p. 65.

[p. 30] Sheridan's command to strike Mountain Chief's band is from Bennett, p. 101.

[p. 31] Kipp's recognition of the wrong band and Baker's response are taken from Schultz, pp. 303–4.

[p. 33] Amherst's assessment of the character of the Indians is from Angie Debo, *A History of the Indians of the United States* (Norman: University of Oklahoma Press, 1970), p. 81. His smallpox quote is from Alvin Josephy, *The Patriot Chiefs* (New York: Viking, 1961), p. 122.

[p. 34] Smallpox information is from Davis Thomas and Karin Ronnefeldt, eds., *People of the First Man* (New York: Promontory Press, 1982), p. 206.

[pp. 35–36] All of the quoted reactions to the Massacre on the Marias here are from Bennett, pp. 132–41.

[p. 39] Robert J. Ege, *Tell Baker to Strike Them Hard: Incident on the Marias,* introduction by Don Russell (Bellevue, Nebr.: Old Army Press, 1970).

[p. 44] The number of Blackfeet casualties in the Massacre on the Marias is from Ewers, p. 250. The number of 7th Cavalry troopers killed at Little Bighorn is from John S. Gray, *Centennial Campaign* (Bellevue, Nebr.: Old Army Press, 1976), p. 293.

[p. 46] The population figures of Indians of the Americas at the time of Columbus' arrival in 1492 are taken from Alvin Josephy, ed., *America in 1492*, (New York: Knopf, 1991), p. 6. The 1900 figure is taken from George L. Russell, *Quincentennial Map of American Indian History* (Phoenix: Thunderbird Enterprises, 1992).

[p. 47] Horace Greeley quote is from Frank Bergon and Zeese Papanikolas, eds., *Looking Far West* (New York: Mentor, 1978), p. 43.

[p. 47] As of the writing of this chapter, Dee Brown's *Bury My Heart at Wounded Knee* was not sold in the bookshop at the visitor center. However, I have recently heard that the Custer Battlefield Historical and Museum Association, which had the bookselling concession and therefore had to approve books to be sold, is no long associated with the battlefield or the Park Service in any capacity. I have also heard that this organization refused to change its name to Little Bighorn Battlefield Historical and Museum Association, which is out of line with the official name change of the monument. In other words, these are Custer buffs.

CHAPTER TWO

[p. 49] The Lakota name for the Sun Dance, *wiwanyag wachipi*, is from *The Sacred Pipe: Black Elk's Account of the Seven Rites of the Oglala Sioux*, recorded and edited by Joseph Epes Brown (Norman: University of Oklahoma Press, 1953), p. 67.

[pp. 50–51] There are many accounts of Sitting Bull's Sun Dance on the Rosebud. They vary slightly, depending upon the recollections of the participants and the accuracy of the interpretations, but all mention Sitting Bull's sacrifice and subsequent vision. Stanley Vestal, *Sitting Bull: Champion of the Sioux* (Norman: University of Oklahoma Press, 1957), offers a fairly detailed account on pp. 148–51. Black Elk, the Oglala holy man, in John G. Neihardt, *Black Elk Speaks* (Lincoln: University of Nebraska Press, 1961), gives a good account on pp. 95–99.

[p. 53] Chandler's communiqué is from Vestal, p. 139.

[pp. 54–57] Much of my account of Crook's Powder River expedition and subsequent attack on the camp of He Dog and Old Bear is taken from Gray, *Centennial Campaign*, pp. 47–58.

[pp. 56–57] Kate Bighead's account of the Washita attack is from Thomas B. Marquis, *Custer on the Little Bighorn* (Algonac, Mich.: Reference Publications, 1986), p. 80.

[p. 57] Custer's West Point career and Civil War exploits are chronicled by many historians. Stephen E. Ambrose, *Crazy Horse and Custer: The Parallel Lives of Two American Warriors* (New York: Meridian, 1986), puts a positive spin on Custer's impulsiveness at West Point: "What stands out, however, is not that he could not curb his impulsiveness and thus was always on the brink of dismissal, but rather that he *could* curb himself when it was necessary" (p. 100). On the same page, Ambrose points out that Custer "may have been last in his class, but he *did* graduate, and in any case emphasizing the fact that he was thirty-fourth in a class of thirty-four is entirely misleading. There were one hundred eight candidates for admission to his class, but only sixty-eight passed the entrance examination—Custer among them. Of the sixty-eight admitted, only half graduated—Custer among them...."

[pp. 57–58] Rosser incident is also from Ambrose, p. 203, as is Custer's presence at Lee's surrender, pp. 214–15.

[p. 58] Numbers of Indian casualties versus white casualties is from Ambrose, p. 288.

[pp. 62–64] Accounts of Custer's attack on the Southern Cheyenne camp of Black Kettle on the Washita River are rampant. I have used accounts in Connell (pp. 184–96) and in Peter John Powell, *People of the Sacred Mountain*, vol. 1 (New York: Harper & Row, 1981), which offers a very detailed account of the massacre from the Southern Cheyenne point of view (pp. 594–619). In *My Life on the Plains* (Norman: University of Oklahoma Press, 1962), General George Armstrong Custer gives his own account in laborious detail (pp. 230–62), with many lighthearted asides concerning his scout, California Joe, and remarks concerning the finery the dead, fleeing, or captured Indians left behind in camp, most of which was burned up.

[p. 65] Account of Custer's court-martial is taken from Evan S. Connell, *Son of the Morning Star* (New York: HarperCollins/Perennial Library, 1985), pp. 173–75. Also Ambrose, pp. 300–1.

[p. 65] Kate Bighead's account of the attack on the Northern Cheyenne village is taken from Marquis, pp. 82–83.

[p. 66] An abbreviated version of the proceedings that made Sitting Bull the head chief of all the Lakotas and Cheyennes is to be found in Vestal, p. 143. Robert Utley, *The Lance and the Shield* (New York: Henry Holt, 1993), argues that Sitting Bull, with the aid of his supporters, pretty much politicked his way into the leadership role seven years before the Battle of the Little Bighorn: "Most likely on the middle Rosebud Creek, probably in 1869, Sitting Bull's supporters contrived a ceremony to anoint him as supreme chief of the Sioux confederation [including the Cheyennes]. . . . A faction likely representing no more than minorities of varying sizes within each tribe lifted him to an office that had never existed and that was alien to Sioux thinking about political organization" (p. 87).

[pp. 67–70] The Treaty of 1868 is dealt with in several books I have used as sources, perhaps most thoroughly in James C. Olson, *Red Cloud and the Sioux Problem* (Lincoln: University of Nebraska Press, 1965). Edward Lazarus, *Black Hills/White Justice* (New York: HarperCollins, 1991), gives it a thorough going-over, as does Robert Utley in *The Lance and the Shield*.

[p. 67] The Sheridan quote is from Ian Frazier, *Great Plains* (New York: Penguin, 1990), p. 59.

[p. 67] The buffalo numbers are from Ambrose, p. 292. Likewise the figure of $150,000 a day is from Ambrose, p. 290.

[pp. 71–72] Sitting Bull's naming by his father is recounted in Vestal, p. 13.

[p. 73] Sitting Bull's message, "It is war," comes from Vestal, p. 141.

CHAPTER THREE

[p. 74] Conditions on the reservation are remarked on by many sources, including Olson, pp. 190–91.

[p. 74] Reference to Jack Red Cloud is from Ambrose, p. 411.

[p. 75] Gifts are discussed in Olson, pp. 109–11.

[p. 76] Utley, *The Lance and the Shield*, reports a small speech that Sitting Bull gave to some Assiniboins in his glory days of 1867 in which he announced his intent in dealing with the whites: "Look at me. See if I am poor, or my people either. The whites may get me at last, as you say, but I will have good times till then. You are fools to make yourselves slaves to a piece of fat bacon, some hardtack, and a little sugar and coffee" (p. 73.

[pp. 78–81] Most of the material relating to the American Indian Movement (AIM) comes from Lazarus, pp. 290–311, and from my article "Indian Summer at Wounded Knee," *Harper's Weekly*, August 23, 1976.

[p. 81] Sheridan's excuses for organizing the Black Hills expedition are discussed in Ambrose, pp. 374–75.

[pp. 81–82] Windolph material comes from Frazier and Robert Hunt, *I Fought with Custer: The Story of Sergeant Windolph, Last Survivor of the Battle of the Little Big Horn* (Lincoln: University of Nebraska Press, 1987), pp. 36–38. Also, Ambrose, p. 377, discusses Fred Dent Grant's drunkenness.

[p. 82] Johnson Holy Rock's quote of Red Cloud is from the film *Last Stand at Little Bighorn*, produced and directed by Paul Stekler.

[p. 84] Figures on number of miners in the first year are from Ambrose, p. 395.

[p. 84] According to James C. Olson, "The chiefs met briefly with the President—presumably after their meeting with Delano and Smith—and he told them personally of his desire that they give up the Black Hills and their hunting rights in Nebraska and move to Indian Territory." Olson, pp. 182–83.

[p. 85] Red Cloud's behavior and subsequent loss of standing among his own people are discussed in Olson, pp. 188–89.

[p. 85] The Sioux Commission's visit to the Great Sioux reservation is from Ambrose, pp. 392–94.

[p. 87] Red Cloud's list of demands is quoted from Olson, pp. 208–9.

[p. 89] The estimate of gold taken by the Homestake Mining Company is from Ambrose, p. 395. He further states that in 1975 it was the largest operating gold mine in the western hemisphere.

[p. 89] G. P. Beauvais's statement concerning presents is from Olson, p. 211.

[pp. 90–93] Much of the material concerning the Gilded Age is discussed in Richard Slotkin, *The Fatal Environment: The Myth of the Frontier in the Age of Industrialization, 1800–1890* (Middletown, Conn.: Wesleyan University Press, 1986).

[p. 90] Slotkin quote is from Slotkin, p. 6.

[p. 90] "Garden of the West" material is from Slotkin, p. 357.

[p. 91] Account of the skirmish between Crazy Horse and Sitting Bull and Custer is presented in more detail in Ambrose, pp. 362–65.

CHAPTER FOUR

[p. 101] "Look for worms" is from Gray, *Centennial Campaign*, p. 167.

[p. 101] Black Elk calls the Little Bighorn the Greasy Grass in Neihardt, p. 99.

[p. 102] The 1851 treaty which established the boundaries of Crow territory is mentioned in Dennis W. Harcey and Brian R. Croone, *White-Man-Runs-Him* (Evanston, Ill.: Evanston Publishing, 1993) p. 19.

[p. 108] The number of the people in the village has been wildly exaggerated by historians for over a century. The number has climbed to as high as fifteen thousand, with five thousand of them being warriors. John S. Gray, in *Centennial Campaign*, has done an incredibly complex study of the number of lodges of both the summer and winter "roamers," breaking the numbers down to how many lodges were in each band circle, how many people were in each lodge, how many warriors would likely be represented in such a gathering. His numbers are the most logical of any that I've seen: "This village of one thousand lodges would have contained 7,120 persons, including only 1,780 adult males. In response to an overwhelming threat to the women and children, older boys might have swelled the ranks of the defenders to as many as two thousand" (p. 357).

[p. 108] The "lone tipi" will be discussed later, as will all the references to the battle in this chapter.

CHAPTER FIVE

[pp. 111–12] The Santee uprising is discussed in Lazarus, pp. 27–28. Also, Vestal tells the account of the Battle of Killdeer Mountain, on July 28, 1864, shortly after Inkpaduta's Santees and Yanktonais came to the plains from Minnesota and the eastern Dakotas and camped with the Hunkpapas, Sitting Bull's band. The soldiers followed them, and the battle ensued. This was the first time the western Sioux, the Tetons, were involved in a major conflict with the United States Army. They were entirely innocent of any provocation against the whites. Vestal, pp. 50–57.

[p. 113] Gibbon's rank is confusing in that some historians give him the title "General," while most refer to him as "Colonel." Gray, *Centennial Campaign*, either clears up the confusion or adds to it by referring to him as "General John Gibbon, Colonel of the 7th Infantry" (p. 42).

[p. 113] Sheridan's letter to Sherman outlining the objectives of the three-pronged attack is quoted from Gray, *Centennial Campaign*, p. 94.

[pp. 114–15] For a more complete account of the Belknap scandal, see Gray, *Centennial Campaign*, pp. 59–71.

[p. 117] Stands in Timber's description of battle preparations is from John Stands in Timber and Margot Liberty *Cheyenne Memories* (Lincoln: University of Nebraska Press, 1972), pp. 184–85.

[p. 117] Crazy Horse's spotted calfskin cape, in keeping with the hailstone vision of his thunder dream, is mentioned in Mari Sandoz, *Crazy Horse: The Strange Man of the Oglalas* (Lincoln: University of Nebraska Press, 1961), p. 312.

[p. 118] Account of Grattan incident is taken from Connell, pp. 65–67. Sandoz also offers an account from the Indian point of view, pp. 24–30.

[pp. 119–20] Circumstances and account of Crazy Horse's dream and his father's reaction to it are described in Sandoz, pp. 104–5.

[p. 121] The number of warriors versus the number of soldiers and allies are taken from Gray, *Centennial Campaign*, p. 120. Gray breaks the figures down further: On Crook's side, "One thousand soldiers, 85 volunteer packers, teamsters, and miners, and 262 Indian allies [were] ready for action." On the Sioux and Cheyenne side, "The combined total of 500 lodges [at the time of the Battle of the Rosebud] could not muster a thousand warriors, and if no more than one-fourth stayed behind to defend the villages, the top limit on the attacking force becomes 750."

[p. 121] Jack Red Cloud incident comes partially from *Wooden Leg: A Warrior Who Fought Custer,* interpreted by Thomas B. Marquis (Lincoln: University of Nebraska Press, no date), pp. 199–200. Ambrose also mentions it, p. 422.

[p. 121] "Where the Girl Saved her Brother" incident is described in Stands in Timber and Liberty, pp. 188–89.

[p. 122] Fetterman Massacre of 1866 is described in detail in Ambrose, pp. 231–43.

[p. 122] The number of white and allied casualties is taken from Gray, *Centennial Campaign,* p. 123. Crazy Horse's figure is from Ambrose, p. 423.

[p. 123] Crazy Horse's strategy, in simple terms, can be found in Ambrose, p. 423.

[p. 124] Crook's seventy trout can be found in Connell, p. 92.

[p. 124] The notion that Custer was looking for a quick, decisive victory at Little Bighorn so that he could get back east, or at least have the news get back, in time for the Democratic Convention so that his name could be put up for the presidency of the United States has been widely, maybe wildly, circulated. Slotkin provides a more logical political fate for Custer: "Custer dined in New York with [August] Belmont and on his return to Washington with Senator Thomas Bayard, [who] was ... Belmont's hand-picked candidate for the Democratic nomination against War Democrat Samuel J. Tilden ... While a tie to Senator Bayard would have precluded Custer's own presidential candidacy, it ought certainly to have led to a place in the new administration for the Indian-fighting hero who had stood up to and exposed the corruption of the Republicans. . . . Custer's famous remark to his Arikara scouts—that after the expedition of 1876 he would be 'their Great Father in Washington'—has suggested to some his presidential ambitions. But the statement also suggests the possibility that Custer might have been appointed head of the Indian Bureau" (p. 426).

[p. 125] Crook's annual report concerning the Rosebud battle is quoted in Gray, *Centennial Campaign,* p. 124.

[pp. 125–26] Terry's orders to Custer are quoted in Gray, *Centennial Campaign,* pp. 147–48.

[pp. 126–27] Breakdown of Custer's command is from Gray, *Centennial Campaign,* p. 172.

[p. 127] Gray, *Centennial Campaign,* p. 98, mentions Custer's anonymous dispatches to the *Herald.*

[pp. 127–28] Custer quotes are from Ambrose, pp. 427 and 431.

CHAPTER SIX

[pp. 129–30] Custer's characterization of the American Indian is from his *My Life on the Plains,* pp. 13–14.

[pp. 130–31] Torture quote is from Custer, 161–62.

[pp. 136–40] Much of the horse material comes from John C. Ewers, *The Horse in Blackfoot Indian Culture* (Washington, D.C.: Smithsonian, 1980), pp. 1–19.

[p. 136] Advantages of horse over dog come from Ewers, *The Horse in Blackfoot Indian Culture,* pp. 304–9, as well as other sources.

[pp. 143–44] Chivington's attack on Black Kettle's village is described in Connell, pp. 176–79. Stands in Timber and Liberty also offers an account, pp. 168–70.

[p. 145] Quote from the Helena newspaper is from Bennett, p. 42.

[p. 145] Columbus quote is from Dee Brown, *Bury My Heart at Wounded Knee* (New York: Holt, Rinehart & Winston, 1970), p. 1.

[pp. 145–47] Historical material is from Dee Brown, pp. 1–9.

[p. 147] Population figures are from Dee Brown, p. 9, and Russell, *Quincentennial Map of American Indian History.*

CHAPTER SEVEN

[p. 150] The times of 12:15 P.M. and 2:15 P.M. are approximate, but within a very few minutes of the actual times, which are somewhat confusing and ambiguous. The time/motion studies in John S. Gray, *Custer's Last Campaign* (Lincoln: University of Nebraska Press, 1991), probably pin these times down a little more accurately, but there are enough variables in Gray's studies to question his exact times.

[p. 150] Custer "support" order is from Gray, *Centennial Campaign,* p. 174.

[p. 150] The "lone tipi" has become famous as the place where Custer made the important split in his command, separating his and Reno's forces.

[p. 152] Fatalistic comments by Crow and Arikara scouts are from Connell, pp. 272–74.

[pp. 152–53] The hardtack incident is mentioned in many sources, including David Humphreys Miller, *Custer's Fall: The Native American Side of the Story* (New York: Meridian, 1992), pp. 3–7. Also, Windolph, p. 75; Gray, *Centennial Campaign,* p. 170.

[p. 154] According to Miller, as the sounds of alarm spread through camp, Sitting Bull told his nephew, One Bull, to go out and meet with the soldiers: "Parley with them, if you can. If they are willing, tell them I'll talk peace with them" (p. 89). This seems to indicate that Sitting Bull thought there was a possibility of avoiding war. Then the shooting started.

[p. 154] Stanley Vestal writes about the lack of preparedness in the camp: "A Cheyenne prophet, Box Elder, sent a herald to announce that the people had better keep their horses tied up beside the lodges. . . . But nobody paid any attention to him. . . . Of course, everyone knew that soldiers were supposed to be looking for them, but they did not expect them so soon. Their scouts kept reporting that 'Three Stars' Crook was still going away, and that other soldiers [Custer's] were on the Rosebud [still a good distance away]. . . . But they danced no war dances, they sent no young men against the white men. Their preparations were purely defensive. As Sitting Bull said, 'Even a bird will defend its nest.'" Vestal, p. 155.

[p. 155] Gerard quote is from Miller, p. 81.

[p. 155] According to Ambrose, Crazy Horse knew where Custer was all the time, but did not see Reno's battalion break off in preparation for a charge down the valley directly at the camp. Thus, Reno's charge was the real surprise. Ambrose, p. 437.

[p. 155] Although many historians think that Custer's phrase "We've caught them napping" is apocryphal, it is almost universally quoted as part of the narrative of the battle. Gray is skeptical of such a positive reaction (*Centennial Campaign,* pp. 176–77). Ambrose reports it straight-on (p. 438).

[p. 156] Material on couriers Knipe and Martini is from Gray, *Centennial Campaign*, p. 177. Robert Utley also mentions Martini in *Custer Battlefield: A History and Guide to the Battle of the Little Bighorn* (Washington, D.C.: National Park Service, 1988), pp. 58–61. Martini's horse was shot in the rear, but the trumpeter made it through. Benteen disregarded the order, choosing instead to remain with Major Reno's besieged troops.

[p. 156] There are two versions of W.W. Cooke's desperate note to Benteen. One appears to be a later transcription of the almost unreadable original. I have used the transcription.

[pp. 156–57] Wooden Leg quote is from *Wooden Leg*, p. 218.

[p. 157] Utley has Sitting Bull engaging in the Reno valley fight, crossing the river to the bluffs where Reno retreated, then recrossing the river to restore order in the village and to protect the women and children. Sitting Bull did not engage in the Custer fight, according to all sources. Utley, *The Lance and the Shield*, pp. 151–55.

[p. 158] Wooden Leg quote is from *Wooden Leg*, p. 383.

[p. 158] The shot that killed Bloody Knife has been heralded many times as part of Custeriana. Walter Camp, in *Custer in '76* (Provo, Utah: Brigham Young University Press, 1976), is among the first to mention it. He quotes George Herendeen, a scout, as saying, "Bloody Knife was killed by a shot from east by Indians who had gone into brush from south—by Indians not more than 50 yds. away" (p. 223). Virtually all later accounts mention the fact that Bloody Knife's brains splattered Reno's face.

[p. 158] Manner of death of Isaiah Dorman, the Negro interpreter, has likewise been widely documented. I have used, among others, accounts in Miller, pp. 115–16, and in Connell, pp. 25–26.

[p. 159] "Lonesome" Charley Reynolds account is from Camp, p. 223.

[p. 159] Black Elk quote is from Neihardt, p. 114.

[pp. 159–60] Material on Herendeen, DeRudio, and others hiding out is from Camp, pp. 233–36.

[p. 161] Crazy Horse quote is from Ambrose, p. 440.

[p. 162] The best book by miles in the reconstruction of the Battle of the Little Bighorn is Gray, *Custer's Last Campaign*. Through his time/motion studies and graphs and charts and subsequent reconstructions of the movements of Reno, Benteen, and Custer, Gray allows the reader to put the whole battle into a single time frame. For instance: "Reno's men in the valley first spotted Custer's men on the bluff on the east bank of the river at about 3:05, only 4 minutes after Custer had left the North Fork. Then, while charging down the bottom, Reno's men again saw Custer's column on Reno Hill at about 3:13, 8 minutes later. This timing implies that Custer took the direct route along the rising ridge to Reno Hill, a distance of 1½ miles, in 12 minutes, at a lively pace of 7.5 mph" (p. 334). This is a book for serious students of the battle.

[p. 162] Boyer quote is from Miller, p. 122.

[pp. 162–64] Although Curley was scorned by most interviewers and historians, he did have his supporters. Thomas H. Leforge, a white man who was adopted into the Crow tribe, became a scout and interpreter for the U.S. Army, and was involved peripherally in the Little Bighorn Battle, says of Curley, "The persistent claim put forward for him by others, but as though it came direct from him, brought upon him from some of the Sioux the accusation, 'Curley is a liar; nobody with Custer escaped us.' But he was not a liar. All through his subsequent life he modestly avowed from time to time ... 'I did nothing wonderful; I was not in the fight.' I knew him from his early boyhood until his death in early old age. He was a good boy, an unassuming and quiet young man, a reliable scout, and at all times of his life he was held in high regard by his people." *Memoirs of a White Crow Indian* (Thomas H. Leforge) as told by Thomas B. Marquis (Lincoln: University of Nebraska Press, 1974), p. 251.

[p. 164] Utley's explanation of difficulty of Indian testimony is from his foreword to Gray, *Custer's Last Campaign*, p. x.

[p. 164] Mardell Hogan Plainfeather's "blanket" explanation is from "A Personal Look at Curley's Life after the Battle of the Little Bighorn," *Greasy Grass*, Vol. 4.

[p. 165] Miller is one who believes that Custer was killed at the ford (p. 128).

[p. 165] Gray quote is from *Custer's Last Campaign*, pp. 360–61.

[p. 166] The heroic four Cheyennes are mentioned in many sources, each a little differently in numbers and names. Wooden Leg offers one account in *Wooden Leg*, p. 229.

[p. 168] Since the time of this writing, Gregory F. Michno, in "Crazy Horse, Custer, and the Sweep to the North," *Montana, the Magazine of Western History*, summer 1993, has come up with pretty convincing evidence that Crazy Horse did not make the giant swing to the north of Custer's position that most historians have come to accept as gospel. Instead, after he left the Reno fight and rode through the camp, he crossed at Medicine Tail Coulee and rode up Deep Coulee to attack the southern end of Battle Ridge, at Calhoun Hill. According to Indian accounts, there were no warriors to the north of Custer's position. Michno's research took into account the eyewitness testimonies of Short Bull, Mrs. Spotted Horn Bull, Foolish Elk, Feather Earring, Lone Bear, Red Bird, Two Eagles, Julia Face, and many others. Michno concludes that Crazy Horse would have to have been "cruising at fifty-four miles per hour" in order to have completed the circle in time to participate in the Custer fight.

[p. 168] White Bull quote is from Camp, p. 211.

[p. 168] Kate Bighead's assessment of Indian tactics is from Marquis, *Custer on the Little Bighorn*, p. 87.

[pp. 169–70] All Richard Fox material comes from two books and a copy of his dissertation: Douglas D. Scott and Richard A. Fox, Jr., *Archaeological Insights into the Custer Battle: An Assessment of the 1984 Field Season* (Norman: University of Oklahoma Press, 1987); Richard Allan Fox, Jr., *Archaeology, History, and Custer's Last Battle* (Norman: University of Oklahoma Press, 1993); and Richard A. Fox, Jr., "Discerning History Through Archaeology: The Custer Battle," dissertation (University of Calgary, 1988).

[p. 170] Fox quote is from his dissertation, p. 81.

[p. 170] The idea that Custer's Last Stand was not the last of the fighting comes from Fox, *Archaeology, History, and Custer's Last Battle*, pp. 201–2.

[p. 171] Wooden Leg quote is from *Wooden Leg*, pp. 231–32.

[p. 171] Kate Bighead quote is from Marquis, *Custer on the Little Bighorn*, pp. 88–89.

[p. 172] For more information on "suicide boys," see Stands in Timber and Margot Liberty, pp. 194–95.

[p. 172] Bighead quote is from Marquis, *Custer on the Little Bighorn*, p. 96.

[p. 173] Bighead quote is from Marquis, *Custer on the Little Bighorn*, p. 82.

[p. 173] Custer's description of Me-o-tzi is from Custer, p. 282.

[p. 173] Gonorrhea rumor concerning George and Tom Custer is from Connell, p. 200.

[p. 174] Custer armament is from Miller, p. 128.

[p. 174] Facts about Comanche are from Connell, p. 298.

[pp. 174–75] Times of final fighting and Reno's charge are taken from Gray, *Centennial Campaign*.

[p. 175] Mrs. Spotted Horn Bull quote is from Thomas B. Marquis, *Keep the Last Bullet for Yourself* (Algonac, Mich: Reference Publications, 1985), p. 161.

[p. 175] Gray's times are from *Custer's Last Campaign*, pp. 368 and 391.

[p. 175] Godfrey quote is from W.A. Graham, *The Custer Myth: A Source Book of Custeriana* (Lincoln: University of Nebraska Press, 1986), p. 376.

[p. 177] Weir quote is from Graham, p. 376.

[p. 177] Rain-in-the-Face arrest is in Marquis, *Custer on the Little Bighorn*, pp. 60–65.

[p. 177] Description of Tom Custer's mutilated body is from Connell, pp. 287–88. Rain-in-the-Face's claim that he cut out Tom's heart is reported in Hunt, p. 171.

[p. 179] Joke about Brave Bear is from Marquis, *Custer on the Little Bighorn*, pp. 56–57.

[p. 179] White Bull account is from Vestal, pp. 170–71.

[p. 179] Medicine Bear's coup claim is taken from Hunt, p. 223.

[p. 180] Iron Hawk description of old women stripping soldier is from Neihardt, p. 128. Black Elk's description of fat *wasichu* is in Neihardt, p. 131.

[p. 180] Wooden Leg quote is from *Wooden Leg*, p. 263.

[p. 180] Stands in Timber quote is from Stands in Timber and Liberty, pp. 205–6.

[pp. 180–81] Black Elk quote is from Neihardt, p. 131.

[p. 181] Bloody Knife story is from Connell, pp. 14–17.

[pp. 181–82] Spoils of the battle are described in *Wooden Leg*, pp. 264–67.

[p. 182] Wooden Leg discusses the bottles of holy water in *Wooden Leg*, p. 246. Other Indians mention the whiskey.

[pp. 183–84] In *Archaeological Insights into the Custer Battle*, Fox writes: "Hedron (1973) has made an exhaustive study of [the soldiers'] cartridge-extraction problems at the Little Bighorn fight. He examined the available monument and private collections in 1972 and found that 3 cases out of 1,625 had had extraction problems" (p. 81).

[p. 184] Indian casualties are impossible to determine, because of conflicting testimony. Most estimates are between sixty and one hundred dead.

[p. 184] Godfrey account of Reno and Benteen conversation is from Graham, pp. 122–23.

[p. 186] Windolph quote is from Hunt, p. 106.

[p. 186] Reno quote is from Hunt, p. 168.

[p. 187] Godfrey quote is from Graham, p. 143.

[p. 187] Godfrey quote is from Graham, p. 146.

[pp. 187–88] A very detailed account of Curley's escape from Little Bighorn fight and subsequent oddessey is to be found in Gray, *Custer's Last Campaign*, pp. 373–80.

[p. 189] Details of Great Philadelphia Exposition can be found in Slotkin, pp. 4–5.

[pp. 189–92] I have quoted at length from a facsimile of the July 6, 1876, edition of the *Bismarck Tribune.*

[p. 193] According to Vestal, "The news of Long Hair's death sped to the agencies by moccasin telegraph and smoke signal. An Indian named Freighter rode day and night to carry the news to Standing Rock. Indians up and down the Missouri knew of the victory a week or ten days before white men heard of it" (p. 181). According to Miller, "In some mysterious way Crow and Shoshoni scouts serving General Crook in northern Wyoming—a full hundred miles south of the Little Bighorn—got wind of the tragedy the very afternoon it occurred.... Acting as spokesman, Plain Bull, a Crow, made the startling statement: 'Long Hair Custer, Son-of-the-Morning Star, all his soldiers, every one, were killed this morning on the Little Bighorn!' " (p. 196).

[p. 194] Black Elk quote is from Neihardt, p. 133.

[p. 196] Black Elk quote is from Neihardt, p. 135.

[p. 196] Manypenny account is from Lazarus, pp. 90–93.

CHAPTER EIGHT

[p. 203] For a more detailed but concise explanation of the Dawes Act, see Howard R. Lamar, ed., *The Reader's Encyclopedia of the American West* (New York: Crowell, 1977), pp. 290–91.

[p. 214] Gray quote is from *Custer's Last Campaign*, p. 412.

[p. 215] Body counts in Gray, *Custer's Last Campaign*, p. 410.

[p. 215] The Buford letter and Custer's other questionable financial dealings are discussed in Slotkin, pp. 421–24.

[pp. 219–20] For a more complete account of Thomas's journey, see Dave Walter, "Fatal Moves," *Montana Magazine*, September–October 1988.

CHAPTER NINE

[p. 228] Archilde quote is from D'Arcy McNickle, *The Surrounded* (Albuquerque: University of New Mexico Press, 1978), pp. 62–63.

[p. 231] Sitting Bull letter is quoted from Vestal, pp. 191–92.

[p. 232] Although most historians believe that Crazy Horse was involved in the Battle of Slim Buttes, at least two do not: Stanley Vestal and Robert Utley, both biographers of Sitting Bull. Vestal is adamant that Sitting Bull led the rescue forces, not Crazy Horse (p. 187). Utley asserts that Sitting Bull fought bravely at Slim Buttes. He does not mention Crazy Horse except to say that he was "in the neighborhood" (*The Lance and the Shield*, pp. 166–67).

[p. 235] Exchange between Bear Coat and Sitting Bull is from Vestal, p. 196.

[p. 236] Miles's assessment of Sitting Bull is from Vestal, pp. 199–200.

[pp. 237–39] There are several accounts of Mackenzie's attack on Dull Knife's village, including John Stands in Timber and Margot Liberty, pp. 214–19. Peter

John Powell, in *People of the Sacred Mountain,* writes in detail from the Cheyenne perspective (pp. 1056–71). From a white soldier's perspective see Sherry L. Smith, *Sagebrush Soldier* (Norman: University of Oklahoma Press, 1989), pp. 60–88. Ted Rising Sun's version of the battle is from an audiotape made in conjunction with the documentary movie *Last Stand at Little Bighorn.*

[pp. 238–39] Figures are from Gray, *Centennial Campaign,* p. 266.

[p. 240] Crazy Horse quote is from Neihardt, p. 140.

[p. 240] Miles's attack on Crazy Horse's village is from Neihardt, pp. 141–42.

[pp. 243–44] Both Sandoz (pp. 360–63) and Ambrose (pp. 461–63) describe Crazy Horse's surrender, including numbers of people, weapons, and horses involved.

[p. 245] Many sources discuss Crazy Horse's new wife. Some say she was a present from Red Cloud; others say White Hat Clark was instrumental in the nuptials.

[p. 246] Irwin quote is from Ambrose, p. 465.

[p. 247] McGillicuddy report is from Ambrose, p. 466.

[p. 247] Crook's plan (actually Phil Sheridan's) to send Crazy Horse to the Dry Tortugas is reported in Ian Frazier, *Great Plains,* p. 110.

[p. 247] Crazy Horse's statement concerning the Nez Perce and Grouard's mistranslation and the army officer's reactions to it are taken from Ambrose, p. 468.

[p. 249] Spotted Tail's speech is reported in Sandoz, p. 403.

[p. 251] Accounts of Crazy Horse's death are numerous. My sources, varied though they are, are Frazier, pp. 110–13; Sandoz, pp. 406–13; Ambrose, pp. 472–74; He Dog, a friend of Crazy Horse's, who was present at the killing; Red Feather; and White Calf, who was also present at the killing. He Dog, Red Feather, and White Calf were interviewed by Eleanor Hinman for "Oglala Sources on the Life of Crazy Horse," *Nebraska History,* Vol. 57, No. 1 (Spring 1976).

Chapter Ten

[p. 252] Sitting Bull's songs are recorded in Vestal, p. 208.

[p. 253] Sitting Bull did truly believe that he was safe in Canada. One reason was the presence there of a Major James M. Walsh, in charge of the Mounted Police at Fort Walsh. Walsh was a man of honor (in Sitting Bull's eyes) who would treat the Sioux with respect and allow them to live in Canada as long as they obeyed the law. Sitting Bull came to think of Walsh, whom the Sioux called "Long Lance," as a true friend, perhaps the only white man he had ever trusted. But Walsh and his superiors were already conniving with the U. S. government to have Sitting Bull's people sent back to the United States. Unfortunately for the Canadian officials, the U. S. government did not want Sitting Bull's people. It preferred that the Grandmother's country keep, house, and feed the Sioux.

[p. 253] Sitting Bull's response to Terry's terms is from Vestal, pp. 216–17.

[p. 254] The plight of the Nez Perce who made it to Canada deeply affected Sitting Bull and his people, although the Nez Perce, as allies of the Crows, were traditional enemies. Undoubtedly, the fact that they had fought the U. S. soldiers made them instant friends. But their arrival made the Sioux fear that Bear Coat Miles would follow them across the border and fight with them. Utley, *The Lance and the Shield,* pp. 193–94, and Vestal, pp. 214–15.

[p. 254] Accòrding to Utley, *The Lance and the Shield,* Sitting Bull's village consisted of eight hundred lodges, five thousand people (including Nez Perces) with fifteen hundred fighting men (p. 200).

[p. 255] Bear Coat did catch up with Sitting Bull once during this period. Sitting Bull and some of his people were hunting in the Milk River area south of the Canadian border and had just killed a good number of buffalo. While they were butchering, Bear Coat's troops appeared and a fight started. One Crow scout, a powerful warrior named Magpie, challenged Sitting Bull to a one-on-one fight. They rode toward each other, and Magpie raised his rifle and the weapon misfired. Sitting Bull blew his head off. But the encounter badly frightened the Sioux. Utley, *The Lance and the Shield,* p. 208.

[pp. 257–58] William Bowen's description of Sitting Bull as he led his people in to surrender at Fort Buford is from Vestal, p. 232.

[p. 258] Sitting Bull's celebrated appearance in Bismarck is described in Utley, *The Lance and the Shield,* pp. 236–37.

[pp. 259–62] Agent James McLaughlin's dealings with Sitting Bull are documented by many sources. McLaughlin himself wrote a book titled *My Friend, the Indian* (Boston and New York: Houghton Mifflin, 1910), in which he portrayed Sitting Bull as stubborn, untrustworthy, lying, cowardly, and lazy. It is quite clear that he feared Sitting Bull's presence on the reservation and went to great lengths to minimize the great chief's importance among his people.

[pp. 262–63] Sitting Bull's speech to the commissioners and Logan's response can be found in Vestal, pp. 240–47. Among other things, Sitting Bull told the commissioners, "You have conducted yourselves like men who have been drinking whiskey, and I came here to give you some advice." This did not sit well with the commissioners.

[p. 263] It is amazing that Sitting Bull did so much traveling as a member of Buffalo Bill's Wild West show. One must remember that Sitting Bull had spent most of his life avoiding white people out in the Dakotas, Montana, and Wyoming. To visit New York and Washington, among other cities, must have confounded the chief. But one must also remember that Sitting Bull was a household word in these great cities and that the whites were awestruck by his appearance. Interestingly enough, he was still considered a villain by many and his appearances were often greeted by boos and hisses.

[p. 263] The deliberate mistranslation of Sitting Bull's words is recorded in Vestal, p. 250.

[p. 265] A more complete explanation of the Dawes Severalty Act can be found in Lamar, pp. 290–91.

[p. 266] Red Cloud's objection to the Sioux Act of 1888 is commented on in Olson, p. 311.

[p. 266] McLaughlin records his own nefarious activities in *My Friend the Indian,* p. 285.

[p. 267] There are many, many accounts of the Ghost Dance religion that swept the Rosebud, Pine Ridge, and Standing Rock agencies. I am especially impressed by the concise account in Utley, *The Lance and the Shield,* pp. 281–89.

[p. 268] McLaughlin's paranoia is reported in Utley, *The Lance and the Shield,* p. 286.

[p. 269] The episode of Buffalo Bill's attempt to arrest his old friend Sitting Bull has to be one of the most bizzare events in frontier history. How Buffalo Bill got Bear Coat Miles to agree to this fiasco is beyond belief. And very sad. The episode is documented in Utley, *The Lance and the Shield,* Utley, pp. 293–95.

EPILOGUE

[p. 273] Windolph quote is from Hunt, pp. 101–2.

[p. 274] Vestal quote is from Vestal, p. 174.

[p. 277] Bradley quote is from Edgar I. Stewart, ed., *The March of the Montana Column: A Prelude to the Custer Disaster* (Norman: University of Oklahoma Press, 1961).

[p. 280] Walt Whitman's dealings with the *New York Tribune* are from Brian W. Dippie, *Custer's Last Stand: The Anatomy of an American Myth* (Missoula: University of Montana, 1976), p. 19.

[p. 280] "From Far Dakota's Canons" is from Walt Whitman, *Leaves of Grass*, edited by John Kouwenhoven (New York: Modern Library, 1950).

[p. 283] The presence of Queen Victoria and Edward, Prince of Wales (who would become King Edward VII), at Buffalo Bill's Wild West show is documented in Shirl Kasper, "Annie Oakley: The Magical Year in London," *Montana, the Magazine of Western History*, Spring 1992, pp. 23–37.

[p. 283] Elizabeth B. Custer, *"Boots and Saddles"; or, Life in Dakota with General Custer* (1885; new ed., Norman: University of Oklahoma Press, 1961).

[p. 283] Facts about Elizabeth Custer come from Shirley A. Leckie, "Custer's Luck Runs Out," *Montana, the Magazine of Western History*, Summer 1993, pp. 30–41.

[p. 286] Black Elk's moving reminiscence is from Neihardt, p. 276.

Index

Page numbers in *italics* refer to captions.